MOUNT McKINLEY,
THE HIGHEST MOUNTAIN IN NORTH AMERICA.   ALTITUDE, 20,300 FEET.
'W OF THE SOUTHERN APPROACH EXPLORED BY THE PARKER-BROWNE EXPEDITION OF 1

From a painting by Belmore Browne.

THE STORY OF THREE EXPED...
THE ALASKAN WILDERN...
McKINLEY, NORTH A...
HIGHEST AND MOST IN...
SIBLE MOUNTAIN

BY

...

APPEN... BY

HERSCHEL C. PARKER

...n 100 ILLUSTRATIONS FROM ... DRAWING ...
THE AUTHOR AND FROM ... ...
AND MAPS

NEW YORK AND LONDON
The Knickerbocker Press
1913

THE CONQUEST

OF

MOUNT McKINLEY

THE STORY OF THREE EXPEDITIONS THROUGH
THE ALASKAN WILDERNESS TO MOUNT
McKINLEY, NORTH AMERICA'S
HIGHEST AND MOST INACCES-
SIBLE MOUNTAIN

BY

BELMORE BROWNE

APPENDIX BY

HERSCHEL C. PARKER

WITH 100 ILLUSTRATIONS FROM ORIGINAL DRAWINGS BY
THE AUTHOR AND FROM PHOTOGRAPHS
AND MAPS

G. P. PUTNAM'S SONS
NEW YORK AND LONDON
The Knickerbocker Press
1913

FOREWORD

MORE than seven years have passed since I sat down in a smoking-car on the Canadian Pacific to enjoy a morning pipe. After several weary days we had left the monotonous prairies behind and were climbing upward through the beautiful foothills of the Canadian Rockies.

Sitting opposite to me was a man whose eyes never left the rugged mountainsides as they flew by the window. As I studied my companion I knew that his interest in the mountains came from a deeper feeling than the casual curiosity of a tourist, and while the train sped on we talked of mountains and mountain craft. From the Canadian Rockies our talk drifted back to other ranges we had known, and then I told of how, from high mountain camps in distant Alaska, I had looked longingly northward to where the great cloud-like dome of Mount McKinley—America's highest mountain—hung above the Alaskan wilderness.

And then I found that my companion was planning an attempt on Mount McKinley's summit the following year, and when I left the smoking-car I had cast my lot with his.

It is interesting, in looking backward, to see how small events can change the entire course of our lives. This book is the result of that chance meeting, and my companion in the smoking-car—Professor Herschel

v

Parker—has since been my "pardner" on many a rough wilderness trail.

To those of my readers who have never felt the lure of the mountains, I will give a few reasons for our undertaking so strange a task. The primal force at the base of all exploration is the call of the wild. Without this deep-seated love of adventure men would never be willing to meet the hardship that is waiting for them in the wilderness. But in addition to this there are many different sides of exploration, any one of which taken by itself is of sufficient interest to draw a man from civilisation. I know of no task more absorbing than the mapping of an unknown territory; there is nothing more stimulating to the imagination than watching the growth of rivers and mountain chains on a topographer's plane-table. Equally absorbing is the geological interest of "new country," which runs through the whole gamut of human emotions from the frenzy of the gold-mad prospector to the unselfish enthusiasm of the geologist.

Then come the daily study and companionship of the wild life, from the smallest bird that dares a flight of thousands of miles to rear its young during the short arctic summer, to the big game herds that roam the storm-swept mountainsides.

But always dominating man's endeavours is the struggle against the forces of nature—this is *Life*—and when all is said, this is the world-old magnet that draws alike scientist, explorer, prospector, mountaineer, and hunter. This was the force that brought the men who joined our ventures, and they came from every walk of life.

Without the love for the unknown they would never have undergone the hardships they bore so cheerfully, and the material reward they received was not sufficient to repay them for even one day of the weeks of toil and danger they endured. Without men of this kind nothing would be possible, and in looking back on those wild, free days in the open I realise that my happiest memories are of the sun-tanned faces of my old companions.

It is my hope to convey to the reader in the following pages a faithful impression of the wild lands we saw and the joys and sorrows that we experienced in our three struggles with North America's grandest mountain.

In compiling this book I am indebted to Alfred H. Brooks, of the U. S. Geological Survey, for valuable passages and notes taken from his report to the Department of the Interior; to the Outing Publishing Company, and the *World Today Magazine* for the use of photographs previously published by them.

B. B.

New York City,
January 18, 1913.

CONTENTS

ix

x   **Contents**

ILLUSTRATIONS

The Conquest of Mount McKinley

CHAPTER I

DESCRIPTION OF MOUNT McKINLEY

The difficulties of reaching the mountain—Polar condition of glacier travel—Comparison with pther mountain ranges—Geographical position—Early history of mountain—Russian accounts—Indian fables—Early explorations by American prospectors—W. A. Dickey's description of the mountain—Public interest—United States Government explorations—Brooks and Reaburn make their long journey—Judge Wickersham attempts the climb—Dr. Cook makes his first attempt to scale peak—Result of explorations.

MOUNT McKINLEY is the highest mountain in North America. There was a time not long past when this fact was disputed, but the increase in knowledge concerning Alaska and the fact that all of its large rivers have been explored proves conclusively that no unknown mountain approximating Mount McKinley in size can exist; for high mountains form extensive ice-fields, and these in turn necessitate large rivers to drain them.

This great peak, rising 20,300 feet above the sea, is formed by a gigantic mass of granite that was forced upward through the stratum of slate that overlaid it. On many of the lower peaks close to the mountain

1

this stratum of slate is still in position, giving them a strange, black-capped appearance.

The granite of which the mountain is composed is of a light tan colour, and at a distance its grim cliffs take on a pinkish hue which gives the mountain a delicate atmospheric appearance that differentiates it from all other mountains, and stamps it with a beauty and grandeur of its own.

One of the principal difficulties to be overcome by the mountaineer in climbing Mount McKinley is the low altitude from which it rises. It is safe to say that all of the known mountains in the world of the same height rise from plateaus of considerable elevation. This is particularly true of South America and Tibet where high mountains are plentiful. In both of these countries the mountaineer has reached an altitude of at least 10,000 feet before his climbing difficulties commence. On Mount McKinley the difficulties are exceptional. The only routes to the southern face lie over glaciers thirty miles in length,—there are no other possible routes.

If a party were to follow these glaciers in the winter time, dogs could be used to draw the provisions, but in the summer time it is necessary for the climbers to transport everything on their backs. After crossing the thirty miles of ice and snow, the only explored glacier broadens into a piedmont glacier 5000 feet in altitude, so that the climber is still confronted by 15,000 feet of ice and snow! On the northern face there are places where the mountain's icy flanks sweep down to 3000 feet leaving 17,000 feet of mountain to rise above the plain. While it is a difficult matter to judge the exact line of perpetual snow, on account of the yearly changes in the climate, and the local climatic changes on different sides of the range, one can measure accurately the point where the glacier ice ends, and an average of the glacier snouts would place this line at about 2500 feet. As the mountain ranges that separate the glaciers are too rugged to follow, the climber is forced to take to the ice at a low altitude, which necessitates polar equipment, and the transportation of large quantities of provisions. In the Andes, particularly, the conditions are incomparably easier, as any one will realise after reading Stuart Vine's account of his ascent of Aconcagua, 22,860 feet. During the climb his feet never touched snow, and his Swiss guide, having no use for his ice axe, left it on the summit as a memento for the next comer.

Herman L. Tucker, a member of our 1910 expedition to Mount McKinley, went to South America the following year with the Yale Peruvian Expedition. While in the Andes he joined in the ascent of a 20,000-foot mountain and in a letter to me he stated that they reached the summit of the peak with less exertion than we expended in reaching an altitude of only 4500 feet on Mount McKinley.

Geographically Mount McKinley seems to have been placed "in the most inaccessible position obtainable." It lies just north of "sixty-three" where "there is no law of God, nor man," and it is bisected by the 152d meridian, forming the apex and geographical centre of the great wilderness south of the Yukon and west of the Tanana rivers. Its glacier waters cool the Yukon on the north via the Kantishna and Tanana rivers and the Susitna on the south via the Tokositna and Chulitna rivers.

The nearest salt water, Cook Inlet, is 140 miles from the southern face as the crow is supposed to fly.

The Alaskan Range, of which Mount McKinley forms the crowning peak, is the most inaccessible and least known mountain range in Alaska. But for the insignificant break at Lake Illiamna which separates it from the mountains of the Alaska Peninsula, it would sweep in a grand arc from the Aleutian Islands to the headwaters of the Tanana River.

My first view of Mount McKinley was from the deck of a small steamer on Cook Inlet. The mountain rose like a dim cloud on the northern horizon, two hundred miles away. This view took me back in imagination to the days of the Russian explorers when the mountain and the great wilderness that guards it were wrapped in mystery. What thoughts the dim cloud-like shape suggested to Shillikoff and his wild companions we can only conjecture, but to this day in the Indian lodges many a weird tale is told of the mountain giant. If you can earn the confidence of the aged Indians they will tell you of days when the earth was covered with water, and how a god who was chasing his eloping sweetheart threw a rock with intent to kill, and how that rock rose above the falling water and stands to this day—the incomparable Doleika. And they tell of later days when Doleika belched flames and smoke, but unfortunately there is nothing to bear out this fable, for McKinley is not a volcano. "Doleika," or "the big mountain," the Susitnas call it, while the Aleutes speak of it as "Traleika." The Russians named it "Bulshaia," meaning "big."

Talkeetna Nicolae, chief of the Susitnas, told me a story that was handed down from the olden days, of a Russian adventurer who tried to reach Doleika and died miserably in the Kichatna swamps. The mountain has always been holy ground to the natives, and to this

MOUNT MCKINLEY FROM THE CHULITNA RIVER. ABOUT 43 MILES AWAY.

Photo by Meri La Voy.

day the surrounding country is supposed to be haunted
and the abode of devils.

In speaking of the Indian names for Mount McKinley,
Brooks writes as follows:

No one can know how many generations of natives have
wandered over this region, but it seems certain that the
indigenous population was greater at the first coming of the
white man than it is now. As the natives depended largely
on the chase for subsistence, they must have frequented
the slopes of the Alaskan Range, and the adjacent lowlands,
for this is one of the best game regions in the North-west.
Much of the range formed an almost impassable barrier
between the hunting-ground of the Cook Inlet natives and
that of the Kuskoquim Indians. It does not seem to have
been named, for the Alaskan Indian has no fixed geographic
nomenclature for the larger geographic features. A river
will have half a dozen names, depending on the direction
from which it is approached. The cartographers who cover
Alaskan maps with unpronounceable names, imagining
that these are based on local usage, are often misled.
Thus the Yukon Indians called White River the Yukokon,
the Tanana natives called it the Nasina, the Kluane
Indians called it the Nazenka, and the coastal tribe of
Chilkats had still another name for it. No one of these
can be said to have precedence over any other.

The immense height of Mount McKinley must have
impressed the Indian. It was used as a landmark in his
journeys. With its twin peak, Mount Foraker, it is
interwoven in the folklore of the tribes living within sight
of the two giant mountains. The tribes on the east side
of the range, who seldom, if ever, approached it, termed it
Traleyka, probably signifying big mountain. Those on
the north-west side, who hunted the caribou up to the very
base of the mountain, called it Tennally.

Captain James Cook, who discovered the great inlet

that now bears his name, did not catch a glimpse of the Alaskan Range as the mountains that rise so majestically above the water on a clear day were obscured by fog. The honour of the first mention of the range belongs to George Vancouver, one of Captain Cook's officers. He caught sight of the range from Knick arm at the head of Cook Inlet and in speaking of it says:

The shores we had passed were compact; two or three small streams of fresh water flowed into the branch between low, steep banks, above these the surface was nearly flat and formed a sort of plain on which there was no snow and but very few trees. This plain stretched to the foot of a connected body of mountains, which, excepting between the west and north-west, were not very remote; and even in that quarter the country might be considered moderately elevated, bounded by distant stupendous mountains covered with snow and apparently detached from each other; though possibly they might be connected by land of insufficient height to intercept our horizon.

In speaking of this description, Brooks says that:

Even Vancouver failed to mention specifically the two high peaks which tower above the range, though the description "distant stupendous mountains covered with snow, and apparently detached from each other" undoubtedly refers to Mount McKinley and Mount Foraker.

In 1834, a Russian mate by the name of Malakoff ascended the Susitna River, but it is improbable that he reached the forks as he made no mention of the Alaskan Range. Possibly the story handed down by the Susitna Indians concerning the Russian who died on the Yentna may have reference to one of Mala-

koff's men, for he was the only Russian who made an
attempt to explore the Mount McKinley region.

That the Russians knew of the Alaskan Range there
is no doubt, as Brooks says, "Grewingk, who summar-
ised the geography of Alaska in 1852, indicates on his
map the axis of such a range, to which he gave the
name of Tchigmit Mountains."

Dall named the Alaskan Range. He was one of
the engineers appointed to find a route for a telegraph
line; he did not come close to the range, but saw it
from a distance.

In speaking of the first mention of the big mountain
by Americans, Brooks tells us that:

In the fall of 1878, Harper and Mayo ascended the
Tanana a distance estimated at 250 to 300 miles, which
would bring them to the present town of Fairbanks. This
was the first exploration of the Tanana by white men.
They reported the finding of alluvial gold in the bars of
the river and also that there was a high snow-covered
mountain plainly visible to the south; this, of course, was
Mount McKinley.

Later on Brooks says:

In 1889, an Alaska pioneer, Frank Densmore, with several
others, crossed by one of the portages from the lower
Tanana to the Kuskoquim.

About the same time another prospector, Al. King, made
the same trip. Densmore must have had a glorious view
of Mount McKinley. Apparently it was his description of
it which led the Yukon pioneers to name it Densmore's
Mountain, and as such it was known on the Yukon long
before any one realised its altitude.

In 1885, Lieutenant (now Major) Henry T. Allen

crossed from Copper River to the Yukon, and in his story he says: "The range south of the middle part of the Tanana contains some very high snow-clad peaks."

Although the mountain was known among the pioneers along the Yukon, no news of it had as yet reached the outside world. W. A. Dickey, a young Princeton graduate, was destined to wake the mountain from its long sleep, and give it the prominence it deserved.

In 1896, with one companion, he "tracked" a boat up the Susitna River. He and Monks, his partner, were prospecting for gold, and in the course of time they reached a point where from some bare hills they got an open view of the Alaskan Range with Mount McKinley towering above it. With remarkable accuracy he estimated its height at 20,000 feet, and on his return to civilisation he wrote a newspaper article describing the location and grandeur of the great peak, which he called Mount McKinley.

A few years ago I asked Mr. Dickey why he named the mountain McKinley, and he answered that while they were in the wilderness he and his partner fell in with two prospectors who were rabid champions of free silver, and that after listening to their arguments for many weary days, he retaliated by naming the mountain after the champion of the gold standard.

After its rediscovery Mount McKinley again faded back into oblivion, for while it was known to a few prospectors who had pushed their way into the wilderness, no man had as yet reached its base.

In 1898, many additions were made to the knowledge concerning the Alaskan Range and Mount McKinley. Geo. H. Eldridge and Robert Muldrow led an expedition up the Susitna. Muldrow, the topographer, made

MOUNT McKINLEY. (VIEW FROM THE SOUTH-EAST.)

THE SOUTH-WESTERN RIDGE WHERE WE ATTAINED OUR HIGHEST ALTITUDE IS SHOWN ON THE LEFT.

Photo by H. C. Parker

a rough triangulation of the mountain that verified Dickey's estimate.

J. E. Spurr and W. S. Post of the Geological Survey ascended the Skwentna, a western fork of the Susitna, crossed the Alaskan Range, and eventually, after many adventures, reached Bering Sea.

The War Department despatched Captain (now Lieutenant-Colonel) F. W. Glenn to Cook Inlet to explore a route to the interior. His party reached the Tanana and retraced their steps via the Matanuska and Delta rivers.

In the same year a party led by W. J. Peters, to which Brooks was attached as geologist, was traversing the Tanana River on the north.

In summing up the year's work Brooks says:

These surveys of 1898 had circumscribed an area of about 50,000 square miles which was still unexplored. Within it lay Mount McKinley, the highest peak on the continent, as the general public, hitherto sceptical as to its reported altitude, was beginning to realise.

In looking backward over the history of the big mountain, it seems strange and unfortunate that the name of McKinley should have been attached to it. Any of the Indian names, or the Russian name of Bulshaia, would have been far more appropriate historically as well as sentimentally, while if any proper name was used it should have been named after Densmore, the old pioneer whose vivid word pictures of the mountain's grandeur made it known to the old-time prospectors along the Yukon.

And so five years went past before Brooks and Reaburn made their famous pack-train trip from salt water to the Yukon. Starting from Cook Inlet they broke through the Alaskan Range by a pass on the head-waters of the Kichatna River, and following the northern slope of the Alaskan Range they mapped the country as they advanced. Their route allowed them to take horses directly under the towering ice slopes on Mount McKinley's northern side and their triangulations placed the mountain's height at 20,300 feet.

The data collected by Brooks and Reaburn formed the first accurate report ever made of the Mount McKinley region, and as the mountain became better known men began to stir to the challenge of its virgin summit.

The first of these was Judge James Wickersham. Nothing to my knowledge has been written concerning his expedition. He started from the mining camp of Fairbanks on the Tanana River and used pack-horses to transport his supplies. The party was not prepared in any way for alpine work of so severe a nature, but an attempt was made to scale the mountain in the vicinity of the most westerly of the glaciers flowing north from Mount McKinley, which they named Hannah Glacier.

The second expedition to attempt the conquest of Mount McKinley was led by Dr. F. A. Cook, in 1903. Following the route blazed by Brooks and Reaburn, his party made an attempt on the peak in the vicinity of Hannah Glacier. The attempt ended in failure and the party retreated towards the Tanana and finally forced their way through a low pass, well to the eastward of the mountain. On reaching the southern side of the range they abandoned their horses, and by the aid of rafts eventually reached their starting-point on Cook Inlet.

While the men of this party accomplished a fine feat of wilderness travel, the results of their labours did not add materially to the knowledge of Mount McKinley, for the party was in no way prepared for the alpine side of their venture.

This was the history of the mountain and the attempts made upon it at the time that Professor Parker and I began to plan our first effort to climb it. As I will make clear later, the mountain was so difficult to reach at that time, that, in the light of later knowledge, the earlier attempts to climb it were relegated to the plane of reconnaissance trips, as no promising route to the summit had been discovered. At the time of our first expedition, therefore, the problem of *reaching* the mountain offered as many difficulties as *climbing* the mountain, and it was this perplexing problem that we determined to solve.

CHAPTER II

THE 1906 EXPEDITION

IT was on the 17th of May, 1906, that Professor Parker and I started on our first attempt to climb Mount McKinley.

Professor Parker had joined forces with Dr. F. A. Cook in New York City. Dr. Cook at that time was already well known from his trips to the Arctic and Antartic regions. As he had also made a trip to Mount McKinley we followed his advice in everything pertaining to our coming adventures and allowed him to choose the line of attack.

At this time the pack-horse was the only method of transportation that had been used in reaching the mountain, and we therefore secured a pack-train of twenty carefully chosen horses from the celebrated stock-ranges east of the Cascade Mountains in the State of Washington. The horses were all of the Western type, and they were all chosen for their strength and endur-

THE 1906 EXPEDITION SWIMMING THE PACK-TRAIN ACROSS THE YENTNA RIVER

From a drawing by Belmore Browne.

ance. In addition, however, we were equipped with a shoal-draft motor-boat for use on the glacier rivers. On our way to Alaska, the horses were housed in specially constructed stalls on the forward deck of the steamer, and the motor-boat was also placed on deck where we could finish some of the necessary carpentering details.

We were a party of seven men. Dr. Cook and Professor Parker were the organisers of the expedition. Dr. Cook had raised a good sum of money from a well-known Eastern sportsman, who was to join us in the autumn for a hunt for big game. Professor Parker advanced a substantial sum to defray the original expenses and at a later date he again advanced a substantial sum. The expedition therefore was really financed by Professor Parker and the Eastern sportsman, who, as it turned out later, was unable to join us.

As a "packer," or "Cargodor," we had Fred Printz, the veteran of Brooks's 1902, and Dr. Cook's 1903 expeditions. He was a small active man, as hard as nails, and probably as good a wilderness pack-train man as ever threw a diamond hitch. As a helper he had brought Edward Barrill, who was as tall as Printz was short, and who was also an excellent packer. Walter Miller was our photographer. He had been with Dr. Cook in 1903, and had had much experience in taking photographs in the open. All the topographical work was done by Russell W. Porter, who had been the topographer for the Baldwin-Zeigler Expedition. I joined the expedition as a freelance through Professor Parker's invitation. As our steamer ploughed northward we spent the days in doing the countless little things that are necessary in getting a large outfit into shape for entering the wilderness. As most of our work was on deck we could enjoy the magnificent mountain and glacier views through which we steamed and we looked forward eagerly to the day when our struggle with the wilderness would commence.

Finally after many days of steaming we reached Seldovia, a little village at the mouth of Katchimac Bay on Cook Inlet. Here we left the big steamer and boarded a smaller vessel. Our horses were reloaded and our launch was lowered into the water and towed up the Inlet.

A trip of about seventy miles brought us to Tyonik, a settlement of five or six houses, and the point where our labours were to commence.

The first difficulty was in getting our horses ashore. Their Indian blood made them difficult to handle, and as we had to lash them into slings and drop them overboard, we had an exciting time.

Once in the water the horses were left to look out for themselves, but at this point a totally unexpected interference occurred. A large pack of Indian dogs came down to the beach and attacked the horses as they landed. The dogs had never seen horses and thought evidently that they were a queer new species of moose or caribou. In the meantime we were all busy and when we eventually got all our duffel ashore and the tents pitched it was too late to round up our horses. The result was that some of them got so far away that we were unable to catch them all, as the large marshes covered here and there with dense brush made finding them a hopeless task.

Dr. Cook's plan was to divide the party into two units, a horse- and a launch-party. The horses were to go overland to the headwaters of the Yentna River, where they were to meet the launch-party, when an

advance in force would be made on that unexplored
portion of the Alaskan Range in the hope of finding a
pass that would lead us to the northern side of the
range.

In view of Dr. Cook's having already failed on the
northern approach of the mountain I am to this day
unable to understand why he was willing to risk the
finding of an unknown pass when there was a good pass
on the head of the Kichatna River on the line of
march that the pack-train were to follow. The result
of this plan placed the finding of a pass in a place of the
first importance, whereas the climbing of Mount
McKinley was our one reason for undertaking the
journey. Had the exploration side of finding a new
pass been worth the risk we would have improved our
chances greatly by sending the horses through the
Kichatna pass and attempting the new pass on foot,
for, as any one knows, a man can go where a pack-train
cannot, and in view of later knowledge I know that a
small party of strong packers could have crossed the
range at the head of the Yentna.

We, however, accepted the Doctor's plans without
question, and while the horses were being rounded-up
Russell Porter and I began the topographical work by
making a trip to Mount Susitna.

To reach the mountain we proceeded up the Susitna
River a distance of about ten miles to an old Indian
village called Alexander. The Susitna Valley is
broad and flat and the delta of the river runs through
a wilderness of marsh and mud flats in countless
channels and "slews." Mount Susitna is a granitic
boss rising about 4000 feet above the level valley and
its isolated position makes it one of the most important
landmarks of the region.

After putting us ashore at Alexander the launch returned to Tyonik to secure our outfit and start the pack-train on its long journey. The launch-party were to return to Alexander and pick us up in two days. As the launch turned downstream we waved good-bye and shouldering our packs began the ten-mile tramp to Mount Susitna. We found an old Indian trail that led us through beautiful deep woods broken now and then by beaver meadows. On one of the old beaver dams I found an otter trap that had been left *set* by some Indian—this is a common habit with them— and a little bird had stepped on the pan and had been caught between the steel jaws.

After a long tramp we came to the base of the mountain and pitched our camp in a beautiful little cañon below a waterfall. After a frugal meal I left Porter in camp and climbed up to the last scree slope below the crest of the mountain. After lighting my pipe I found a soft seat and gave myself over to the enjoyment of the beautiful view. It was my first climb of the year and with it came the wonderful feeling of exhilaration that sweeps over you when you stand alone on a mountainside after months spent in civilisation. The delta of the Susitna was spread out below me like a huge map and as I looked through the fast dimming light I thought that I could see a boat beyond the marshes on the waters of the Inlet.

It turned out later that it was our launch that had been caught on the tide flats, and when the tide came in again it was accompanied by a heavy sea and our companions had an unpleasant time of it before they won back to Tyonik. As we were to climb the mountain next day I did not go on, but returned to camp in the dusk and joined Porter in front of a cheery camp-fire.

The following day dawned dark and grey; Mount Susitna was hidden in a dense mass of mist and as we expected the launch we returned to Alexander. The launch had not returned and we spent our time wandering about the deserted village.

Our provisions were about gone and when we awoke to another day we began to bestir ourselves in the hunt for food. Three foodless Susitna natives glided past in their tiny birch-bark canoes on their way to a moose range on the headwaters of the Alexander River. We spent the day in drawing and Porter made some triangulations of Mount Susitna. Robins were singing everywhere and the air had a cool clean smell of mountains and evergreens. In almost all the northern rivers there is a small fish that runs at certain seasons on their way to the spawning beds. They are called hooligans by the Alaskans, and they average about six inches in length. The hooligan run was beginning at this time, but as we were separated from the main river by a back water we could not reach the main school of fish and had to satisfy ourselves with the fish that had died. We found that by splitting the stranded fish and eating only the upper side which had been cured by the sun and air, they tasted very good. We also found some oats in an Indian cabin and after roasting them we were able to extract a kind of brown water which Porter optimistically called coffee. In our hunt for fish we were joined by a starving Indian dog. He had been abandoned by his Indian owner and was pitifully weak from lack of food. In his suffering he reverted to the wild state; treating us with the greatest suspicion, and giving vent three times a day, morning, noon, and night, to the long wolf howl. Finally, after we too had reverted to wolves—in appetites at least—we heard the welcome exhaust of a motor and our launch shot into the river. There was quite a party aboard as in addition to Professor Parker, Dr. Cook, and Miller our expedition had been augmented by two new volunteers, Captain Armstrong, and Russell Ball, who were anxious to prospect on the headwaters of the Yentna.

Our plunge into the wild life had already resulted in some interesting adventures. The boat party had completed the work to be done at Tyonik, and I will set down tha account of what happened, in Dr. Cook's own words:

Porter desired to climb Mt. Susitna and Browne volunteered to join the venture. They desired to go light as the launch was expected back in two days, and therefore little food was taken with them when they left us at Alexander, a deserted Indian village. Since we had been much delayed we hastened downstream to catch the tide by the westerly channel. The boat now ran splendidly, but as we neared the tidewater through the delta we noticed that the tide was already going out fast, but kept on, our pilot saying it was all right. Passing out of the river and heading past an island upon which a barrel was placed we found the water rather deep, six to eight feet. With the brown water boiling behind us we went along in great glee, but soon after real dangers were at hand. The water shallowed, a heavy sea rolled under the bow, the engine stopped, the boat pounded lightly, we were aground, and the tide was fast going out. In less than half an hour there were fifty square miles of muddy flats about in place of the chocolate-coloured water. There was no shore-line within five miles of us, nor was there wood or water. We tried the surface water before it left us, and found it drinkable, though salty and thick with mud. We took the precaution to dip up a pail of this before it left us. We drank this water and ate some crackers, then threw out an anchor and without

SUSITNA INDIAN BOY IN SUSITNA BIRCH-BARK CANOE.

Photo by Belmore Browne.

blankets we spread life-preservers on the floor and tried to
sleep until such time when the tide might return and lift
us off.

The night proved dark and the clouds came out of
Turnagain Arm with a speed which indicated a blow. We
slept little but listened to the roar of the great waves as
they neared us. At about twelve o'clock midnight, the
boat was afloat, and soon after we put on power and headed
the swell and the wind. The seas rose and the winds
increased and whitecaps formed on every side. I suggested
to our pilot that we make for Fire Island, but Stephan
said, "I think all right, river good," from which we understood that he thought a course back into the river and
later for Tyonik was all right but that he preferred to return
to the river. We didn't like the idea of heading for ten
miles of mud-flats in the darkness, with a howling gale
behind us. So I said, "River no good—Tyonik good."
He replied with a grunt and some Indian mutterings which I
took to be swear words for the tone in which the utterances
came was not indicative of good humour. But for Tyonik
we headed. The seas now began to break over the bow,
and the wind carried the spray into Stephen's face with an
ugly force. With each rush of water the boy would grunt
and let drop an ugly Indian word. After about a half-hour
at the wheel Stephen said, "Me plenty sick," and Miller
and I might have said "Me too" but we did not confess.
We had been nursing the engine, for either the pump or the
carbureter was balking frequently. The boat had no
ballast and under the violent pitching of the sea we were
only able to crawl around in the dark, not daring to light
a lantern because we detected gasoline vapours. Miller
took the wheel to relieve Stephen and he too got soaked
from head to foot in the first few minutes.

By two o'clock there was a little burst of light in the east
and now we figured we were far enough away from the
dangerous shallows to set a course for Tyonik. The altered
course brought the seas to our fore quarter but we could

not use full power because the boat would hit the seas dangerously hard. Thus we took the seas as easily as possible while the tide carried us southward. By daybreak, about 3.30, we pushed behind the spit at Tyonik, dropped anchor, and blew our fog-horn for a boat to take us off. We were hungry, exhausted, and cold, but Prof. Parker had the cook prepare a meal for us before we got ashore, and food never tasted better.

The six horses which had stampeded were still at large, no trace having been found of them.

To make the search more thorough we decided to run the launch fifty or sixty miles south on the next tide and land wherever we could to trail the horses. Ball was sent in saddle along the sandy shore-line, while Printz and Barrill joined me on the launch. As the people of the town were starting their fires we were again on the rough waters. The weather was improving, but Turnagain Arm still had a steel-coloured lustre in its clouds, and vapour plunged into the Inlet, which did not promise good weather; but we were so eager to start the pack train on its long trail overland that we could not afford to wait. We passed in among the big boulders of Trading Bay and noted the dangers at low water. Here the beach is wide and the steep sandy bank, three hundred feet high, leads to a plain covered by spruce, birch, and cottonwood trees. In this bank in various places we saw thin strata of lignite, a coal in which the fibre and bark of trees are easily made out, but it seems to burn well and is said to be good steaming coal.

The first twenty-five miles of this beach had been searched as we hastened on to Redoubt Bay. Then far out in the mud-flats we saw some tracks but after a long search we decided that if the horses were to be found we must seek grassy lowlands near the point which separates the two bays. Here we met Ball, whose luck was like ours. He had secured no definite trace of the horses. We built a camp-fire and ate lunch, a lowed the tide to go out, leaving the launch on the tide-flats. Our camp-fire was spread by a sudden gale into a forest fire close to which we tried to keep warm, but the combination of smoke and wind drove us into the boat for shelter. After the wind subsided we began another search for the horses, but could find no further trace except the tracks which had been followed up to the outer tide-flats. Late that night as the tide was about half in we abandoned the horse chase and started for Tyonik. The wind came in gusts and the sea came up in dangerous hills. The night was not dark but the light was of such a quality that we could never be sure of our bearings. The launch laboured heavily in the tumbling seas and we were quickly exhausted, for we had been three days and three nights without proper rest or sleep, and food had been only taken as the conditions had permitted. Upper Cook Inlet has no harbours and seeing that the sea was too rough to make Tyonik and get ashore, we ran under a point of land below Tyonik, dropped anchor, and rode out the storm. The sea had broken over the boat so much that the floor and about everything on board was wet, but we spread the life-preservers out and on these we slumbered for about two hours. With the change of the tide the sea eased, the wind ceased, and a warm sun made the icy volcanoes glitter at 6 o'clock. On the morning of June 2d we tipped the anchor, headed the tide, and by eight o'clock we were again at Tyonik.

The programme for our campaign, as it had been formulated to the present, was to explore the headwaters of the Yentna River first, and from there we expected to get either by the westerly or an easterly route to the southwest arête of Mt. McKinley. From what we had seen of this area from Mt. Yenlo we had many reasons to suppose that there was an easy pass from the Yentna to the Tonzona. Our efforts were accordingly directed toward the big break in the Alaska Range forming the Yentna valley. The horses were to go with light packs cross-country to a point at the head of navigation, while the boat with most of our equipment was to go up the Yentna as far as possible.

We decided to spend the day in loading the launch for her second trip up the river and also to help the packers prepare the pack outfit for its great tramp through brush and forest, over marsh and glacial stream.

At about noon June 3d, Printz, Barrill, and Beecher mounted their horses and we turned the others loose. The train of fourteen horses bounded northward at a rapid pace, only a few of them carrying packs consisting of supplies for thirty days and a folding canvas boat for crossing streams. All the other things were to be carried by the launch to the headwaters of the Yentna. It was expected the two horses that had been chased northward would be found along this trail.

As the horses galloped up the beach toward the Beluga River the launch was started in the same direction. The sky was somewhat hazy, but the sea was as smooth as a glacial lake, with a glimmering silvery surface. The quiet town of Tyonik with its busy prospectors was soon left behind. The pack train moving at a good pace was seen for some time edging along the great high banks. The boat cut the water at an astonishing speed and in less than two hours we entered the mouth of the Susitna, a distance of thirty miles, and in another hour we were at Alexander anxiously looking for Porter and Browne who had been awaiting us with empty stomachs and eager eyes.

Our preparations were now complete. The pack-train with light packs had begun their overland journey, and our launch heavily loaded with supplies began to "buck" the swift waters of the Susitna. As soon as we reached the boat Porter and I went for the food lockers and after a good meal I hunted out a soft spot on the dunnage bags astern and fell asleep. I was awakened from my nap by a cold, wiggling, squirming sensation, and as I sprang to my feet I heard roars of laughter and found that I was covered with hooligans. While ploughing up the river the launch had run into a dense mass of these fish and all on board had begun to throw them into the boat with their hands. The fish were in such enormous numbers that we soon had several hundred. About thirty miles from the mouth of the Susitna we came to Susitna Station, and the bank was lined with prospectors and Indians as we came in front of the town. Our boat caused much interest as we had made the fastest trip on record between Tyonik and Susitna Station, and there was much talk as to whether we could buck the swift current of the upper river. We had sprung our propeller on a snag coming up the river and after two trips overboard I returned cold but successful and our new propeller gave us no more trouble.

There were many Indians about, and scaffolds lined the banks weighted down with long fringes of dried hooligans. The Susitna birch-bark canoes were everywhere, flitting light as leaves through the swift water. We saw quantities of prospectors heading for the great unknown interior, and dreaming of creeks with golden sands. Stories of gold filled their conversation—of men made rich in a day, but the gold was always "behind the ranges" on "some other river"; if they were there they would be satisfied.

CHAPTER III

THE JOURNEY UP THE YENTNA RIVER

Difficulties of navigation—Youngstown—The head of navigation—
Our reconnaissance party advances up the Yentna Valley—Dangers of
fording glacier streams—We reach the mountains—Discovery of what
appears to be a possible pass—Our food gives out—Hardships of our
return to base camp—Building trail for the pack-train—Porter's escape from a bear—The arrival of the horses—Loss of four horses in a
burning coal-vein.

ONE hundred yards above the Station you meet a
savage eddy where the combined waters of the
Susitna and Yentna foam around a high bluff.

As we started our engine the following morning the
Station's population gathered below the bluff to see
how our boat would behave in the white water. I kept
well inshore to get the benefit of the eddy but our
engine did not seem to drive us with its usual vigour,
and when we struck the white wall of water that roared
around the point the current threw us back and
we rounded up ignominiously at our old anchorage.
Something was wrong, and after a search we found that
the propeller tunnel was choked with snags. After
the engine was reversed everything was clear and we
ploughed strongly upstream past our dubious audience.
This time I eased her head very slowly and when we
hit the white water it came boiling over our bows,
but after the shock we moved steadily along and fol-

INDIAN CACHE AT SUSITNA STATION.
Photo by Belmore Browne.

OUR PACK-TRAIN CROSSING "TUNDRA" COUNTRY. WHILE IT LOOKS LIKE
GOOD TRAVELLING, IT IS IN REALITY A MASS OF BOGS AND THE PACK
HORSES BECAME VERY WEAK WHILE WE TRAVELLED
THROUGH IT.
Photo by Belmore Browne.

lowed by hearty cheers from the bank headed for the mouth of the Yentna.

As we pushed our way up the Yentna our difficulties and enjoyment increased. The great snow-fields of the Alaskan Range began to show to the westward. When one is travelling in the lowlands life in time becomes monotonous. The swamps and sluggish "slews" shut you in, fringes of ragged spruce form the horizon, and the low songs of rushing rivers serve only to accentuate the silence. These first glimpses of snow and ice called to us as a well-watered land would call to one who has travelled in a desert.

The Yentna is a typical Alaskan river—turbid, swift, snow-fed, and full of treacherous sand-bars that are formed by the accumulation of silt from the glaciers. The meaning of the word Susitna is "the river of sand" and in this respect the Yentna resembles it. The navigation was getting to be a problem due to the swiftness of the water and the numerous sand-bars. It was necessary to keep a man sounding with a pole, and even then we often struck submerged bars or snags. At night we camped on exposed islands as the mosquitoes were beginning to be troublesome. There was little sign of big game; we would see now and then where a moose or bear had wallowed through the soft mud, and at night we sometimes heard the soft bugle-calls of wild swans—but that was all.

On the lower Yentna we met a few prospectors "tracking" their river boats against the pitiless current and once a boatload of bronzed "sour-doughs" drifted past us headed for the "outside" and the delights of civilisation. These men will undergo any hardship to reach a country where gold is reported. Once let the whisper of yellow sands drift through the forest to their eager ears and everything is forgotten but the wild joy of "hitting the trail" and the frenzy of the stampede. "If there was any gold on McKinley," one of these prospectors said to me, "you 'd find a camp there damn quick!"

At Susitna Station we had heard reports of a mining camp called Youngstown away up on the South Fork of the Yentna and as we passed these occasional boat-loads of prospectors we always hailed them with the cry of "Where 's Youngstown?" and they would always answer, "Away up on the South Fork." At last when we were well up towards the forks we saw a lone prospector drifting downstream and as we hailed him with the familiar question he called back, "Youngstown is here in the boat with me—I 'm takin' the burg downstream!" He was the last man to leave the camp and having by himself formed its entire population he naturally thought that he represented the whole camp.

During all our twistings and turnings Porter had mapped the river from his lookout station on the stern deck. By this time we had passed the South Fork and we were now forging slowly up the North Fork. At last the day came when our little boat could go no farther. On a point near by was wood in plenty for "cache" and fire, so we made camp and called it "the head of navigation." During the last mile of travel we had great difficulty in making progress and we were driven to all sorts of strange expedients for ascending the swift water. In one particularly swift rapid, Miller and I carried an anchor upstream and stood on it in the ice-cold water while our companions helped the engine by hauling in on the capstan.

After making camp we busied ourselves in getting ready for our future work. Our launch, which we had

christened the *Bulshaia* after the Russian name for
Mount McKinley, was drawn in to the bank behind
a protecting sand-bar; caches were erected; Porter
measured a base line and took angles on Mount
Kliskon and Yenlo; and everything was done to make
the camp comfortable.

The pack-train was, in the meantime, working slowly
across the benches of the Alaskan Range and would
not arrive for many days. We could follow the valley
of the Yentna with our eyes as it wound away between
grim snow-covered mountains, and it was now our
duty to explore this valley for a possible pass to the
Kuskoquim, before the arrival of our cayuses.

After a council we decided to push on immediately.
The Doctor, Porter, Captain Armstrong, and I started
on this trip, leaving Professor Parker and Ball at our
base camp. On the first stage of the journey we
tracked our supplies in a canvas boat, but one day's
work in the swift water convinced us that our boat
could not stand the hard usage, so we camped and
again divided our party. We left Captain Armstrong
and Miller in this camp, and Dr. Cook, Porter, and
I shouldered our packs and pushed on into the unknown. We took food for three days in pemmican,
erbswurst, tea, beans, and bacon. Besides the food
and sleeping-bags we carried a tent, and Porter's topographical instruments I carried a 30:40 carbine.

Shortly after leaving our base camp we caught our
first glimpse of Mount McKinley—a great majestic
dome, rolling up cloud-like rom the Alaskan Range;
then the mountains shut us in and we settled down to
work.

Before us stretched a great glacier valley; four
miles broad; flat as a floor; and swept bare to rock and

sand by the fury of the spring overflows. At intervals great snake-like glaciers swept back among the rugged mountains. The rushing river was broken into dozens of snarling streams, that were always deep and swift enough to be troublesome. At times the rivers ran from one side of the valley to the other and we had either to climb the mountainsides or ford the swift water. The hillsides were covered with dense alder thickets, and with packs on our backs, we made slow headway. Once we chopped our way for three hours through the thickets, and at the end we had scarcely a mile to show for our toil. Usually we held to the middle of the valley and forded as best we could. When we found streams that were unfordable we had to follow them until a ford was found. The water was mostly glacial; at noon the streams rose swiftly from the melting of the snow and ice under the warm spring sun, and we were often forced to wait until midnight and ford when the water was less dangerous.

At that time of the year it was never dark and we travelled at all hours. After a day's travel we met two prospectors. On seeing the moving spots through the heat waves that danced above the level gravel bars I thought they were wild animals of some kind, and moved to intercept them. When I approached, I saw that the men were in a small shoal-draft river boat, headed downstream. The roar and rattle of a glacier river separated us, but I could hear them yell: "The glacier streams are runnin' on edge up above—yuh can't cross 'em." I yelled back that we had already forded the west branch, and that we were going on. They watched us dubiously as we started off, and did not answer the "So long" that we shouted across the water. These wilderness meetings stimulate the imagination, and the memory of them stays with you for years; for an instant two human beings meet; wondering at the unseen forces that have brought them together they converse intimately of their hopes and fears, and then without any reason they part, never to meet again. I have often thought of these two men, and of why they warned us to turn back.

When we travelled at night the mountains took on an added grandeur and solemnity. Through the heat waves of midday they hung like mirages in the sky and the glare of the sun on the snow- and water-washed rocks was blinding. Our camps scarcely deserved the dignity of the name: a small tent; a wisp of smoke from a brush fire surrounded by steaming, ragged clothes; some black pots, and three sun- and smoke-browned men hugging the fire—that was all. At a short distance we were nothing but an indistinct blur in the shadow of the mountains. A few chips and blunt axe marks on fallen trees is the only impression that we made on the valley of the Yentna.

Our real excitement came when the valley narrowed up. We found the rivers growing swifter day by day; the gravel was giving way to large boulders, and we were forced more often to the rugged mountainsides.

By this time we had all had narrow escapes while crossing the streams. A man with a heavy pack is helpless when he loses his footing in bad water and is "rolled." He is lucky if he reaches the bank with no worse hurt than torn and bleeding hands, and a bruised body. The Doctor and Porter used Alpine Rucksacks— a poor contrivance for wilderness packing. They do not hold enough, hang badly when full, are unsteady, and are dangerous in swift water as they can not be loosened quickly. I used a home-made adaptation

of the "Russian Aleute" strap, to my mind the easiest and safest strap in the world. We were wet to
the skin constantly, and dried our clothes at night,
sitting more or less naked about the fire during the
process. The wilderness too had set its brand on us;
we were as dark as Indians except where the mosquito
bites had blotched our faces with red, and our hands
were hard and swollen from contact with rocks and
devil's-club. We were a rough-looking crew. One day
I reached an island in the centre of a river that had
held us all night. The further channel looked unfordable, and as the Doctor and Porter were far away I
tried to get back. But I had waded downstream to the
island and found that I could not return against the
current. To make matters worse the hot sun was
striking the snow-fields and the roar of the water was
growing steadily louder. I then made a determined
effort to reach the bank but the water swept me from
my feet and I was rolled. My hands were cut open by
the rocks and my pack nearly choked me, but I could not
afford to let it go and held on until I reached my island
again. I then attracted the attention of the Doctor
and Porter with a rifle shot as we had enough rope to
get my pack ashore and I could then swim the channel.

As they were coming toward me I decided to try the
further channel, and after a most exciting ford I gained
the further bank. After my companions had joined
me we headed across the valley—we had had about all
the fording we could stand.

Luckily we had reached the point where we could
take to the hills for we were opposite a large glacier
that headed near Mount Dall and beyond we could see
our Mecca—the cañon of the Yentna. On it depended
all our hopes; if we could get horses through or around

FOLLOWING A WOUNDED BEAR INTO COVER.

From a painting by Belmore Browne.

it, our route to McKinley was assured. The indications
of a pass were favorable. The mountains seemed to
fall away to the westward and—best sign of all to a
mountaineer—a long, low line of clouds drifted steadily
southward through a gap in the range.

We were beginning to worry about our food. We were
now three days out from our base, and the first half
of our journey was still far ahead of us. We had only
taken three or four days' rations, as we thought that we
could get a glimpse of the pass from some high mountain.
The windings of the valley made this impossible, so
we took our belts in a hole or two and went on short
rations.

We climbed the mountains west of the cañon. As
the range was fairly smooth we travelled above brush
line, and followed on parallel to the course of the
valley. The scenery was of great grandeur and
beauty. Far below us spread the Yentna Valley with
its savage streams wandering like silver ribbons across
its brown floor.

Ahead the cañon ran like a jagged gash across a
cup-shaped basin, and we noticed with misgiving that
most of the water came from the cañon.

Beyond the valley a large glacier wound around a
grand delta-formed peak, and to the westward lay the
tangled mass of mountains that we wanted to cross.
They had a more cheerful atmosphere than the silent
valley. Hoary marmots whistled at us from their
sheltered homes in the rock slides. Bear sign was
fairly plentiful, and ptarmigan feathers lay among the
willows. We had hopes of finding sheep, but we did
not expect to find any until we reached the western
side of the Alaskan Range.

We progressed very slowly; the sun was hot, our

packs heavy, and the climbing was difficult. A shoulder of the mountain hid the view to the westward, and we panted on with the optimistic idea that once beyond the ridge we would see the Kuskoquim. Before long we encountered a deep gorge that barred our path, and we were forced to climb higher. Other obstructions came in their turn until we were no longer of the earth, but moving in that sphere where the valleys are a haze below you, and your only companions are the wind-swept rocks and snow-slides.

At last, at the foot of a cliff I found white mountain sheep hairs. It meant many things to me—the excitement of the chase, fresh meat, and the knowledge that we were within reach of the Kuskoquim. The snow-slides increased as we advanced, and on one of them, a wicked slope of snow that lay at a dizzy angle, the Doctor had an unpleasant experience.

Porter and I were above and crossed where the slope was not dangerous, but the Doctor was careless and crossed at a place where the soft snow sloped downward until it was lost in the valley haze. After starting he was afraid to turn back and we were unable to help him. By chance he was carrying a small axe and after a breathless period of step chopping he got across, a wiser and more experienced man. At the next shoulder we camped by a mossy pool below a snow-bank, and after climbing the hill above us we could see the rounded sheep mountains of the Kuskoquim! It was a wonderful feeling to stand there and look out over the unknown mass of mountains.

But even at that height the mosquitoes were troublesome, so with my rifle lashed to the plane-table tripod we pitched our little tent and rolled into our sleeping-bags.

Camps above timber-line are cold and cheerless. We had no fuel, and our food consisted of dry fruit and hardtack washed down with ice-cold water.

Early the next morning we were seated on a grassy shoulder where we could see the pass to better advantage. Porter did some topographical work and the Doctor and I made a moss fire, and studied the country below. As far as we could see the route looked possible for pack-train travel. Beyond us the cañon split. One fork flowed in a westerly direction toward the Tonzona River; the other fork headed between two large mountains, and offered a possible route for our horses. Between the forks stood a mountain of great beauty. It rose from dim mile-long sweeps of scree and sheep meadows, far below us, to a rugged pinnacled top that stood clear cut against the evening sky and scattered the clouds broadcast.

Since finding the sheep hairs I had been continuously on the lookout for moving white spots. When one realises that even to a well-fed man sheep meat is a delicacy, one can understand with what longing we searched the mountainsides.

By this time we had been on short rations for three days and all the food remaining consisted of a half-pound sausage of erbswurst, a handful of tea, and a quarter of a pound of bacon. Our fruit, bread, and sugar were gone, our work was still uncompleted, and we were four long days' travel from our base camp.

After talking things over we decided that we would climb down the mountainside and explore the cañon. There was no use in going farther but it was useless to go back without seeing whether or not the horses could follow the cañon bed. The descent to the cañon was the most difficult task that we encountered on the reconnaissance. We were weak from hunger, and the mountain fell off in numerous precipices, and was covered with dense jungles of twisted alders and devil's-club. We travelled mostly on our hands and knees, our packs catching in the brush and our hands and bodies swollen from bruises and devil's-club thorns.

We hoped to find good "going" in the bed of the cañon, but looking down from a great height is always deceiving. When we reached the bottom we found to our despair that the stream was dangerous and unfordable. So swift was the water that in a ford I attempted I could scarcely keep my feet in water that was only knee deep. We were famished and exhausted, so we built a fire of driftwood and cooked our precious erbswurst. The cañon was a dreary spot; the roaring of the water was deafening, and cold damp winds swept down from the snow-fields above. After our meal and rest we shouldered our packs, and the thought of our base camp, with food and companions, eased our climb from the gorge.

The retreat was a repetition of the first trip, but rendered more difficult by our lack of food. The lack of food did not seem to detract from our ability to travel but we were all more or less unsteady on our pins, and while we talked ceaselessly of food, I can say that I was less hungry on the last day than I was when our food first began to grow scarce. My greatest desire was to lie down in the sun and sleep. Our only disappointment was the lack of game, and over our fires at night we talked of the sheep steaks and "caribou butter" we would eat when we reached the Kuskoquim. One evening at dusk I jumped a bear, but the thick brush prevented a shot.

We reached our camp after eight days of travel and

ran the swift current to the head of navigation. Great
changes had taken place since our departure. A
strong cache was completed, a trail marked "Wall
Street" ran along the river, and over the main tent was
the sign "Parker House."

Now the question before us was meeting the pack-
train and getting the horses through the swamps and
timber to the open sand-bars. We first dropped the
Bulshaia downstream, to a sheltered "slew," and
then started our trail to timber line. It took us four
days to complete the trail, and then we settled down to
await the horses.

Trail chopping is always interesting, but it is hard
work. Ours wound ever towards the mountains;
now following an old moose trail, or the rut left in the
wet grass by a passing grizzly; now we would make a
detour to avoid destroying a song bird's nest, then
slash our way through twisted alder thickets toward
some big spruce, where the brush would be thinner.

As you rise you begin to catch glimpses of snow-fields
above, and the rivers far below you. When the trail
wound around a bald hill we would take a smoke,
looking out over the silent lowlands, and say, as we
wiped the sweat from our faces, "Three hours more and
we 'll be above the mosquitoes." But this was rank
optimism for we never were. We finally camped on
top of a snow-capped mountain, and the mosquitoes
swarmed about us.

After the trail was finished Porter and I camped
above timber line while he continued his topographical
work, and in this lonely camp he had his first adventure
with an Alaskan brown bear.

We had had a wet day's trail chopping through the
willows when we pitched our tent on a mountainside

above a deep valley. As I came out of the tent the next morning I saw a brown bear and a cub in the amphitheatre below me. Hastily pulling on my wet socks and drawers, I warned Porter and started down the mountainside.   On reaching the bottom of the valley I could no longer see the bear, and after a careful stalk I heard a hail from Porter.

On reaching camp he told me that the bear had either winded or heard me and that she had run uphill through a little draw and had blundered into our camp.   This second meeting with mankind had frightened her badly and Porter added that the cub seemed pretty tired by the time it reached the mountain top.   After breakfast Porter climbed the mountain to take some angles, and I stayed in camp and dried out our wet duffel.   After a while I heard a noise below me, and to my surprise Porter appeared climbing slowly uphill. He was tired out, scratched and torn from contact with brush and rocks, and as soon as he regained his wind he told me his story.   On reaching the mountain top he had followed a narrow arête that joined the mountain to the main range.   On this narrow ridge he had been charged by the bear, and it was probably due to the fact that he rushed instantly down the steep mountain that he did not lose his life.   I picked up my gun and climbed at my best speed to the mountain top.   On reaching the narrow arête I found the tracks in the snow where the bear had pursued Porter, and after leaving him she had returned to her cub and continued along the arête towards the upper snow-fields.   Before I had gone far a terrific storm swept across the Susitna Valley. The lowlands turned as black as night, and the wind shrieked and moaned among the cliffs. Great flashes of lightning followed

ED. BARRILL FORDING THE EAST BRANCH OF THE KAHILTNA RIVER.
Photo by Belmore Browne.

WHEN THE HORSES BEGAN TO WEAKEN
Photo by Belmore Browne.

by earth-shaking crashes of thunder shook the mountains and the air was full of the noise of falling rocks and avalanches. At times I had to cower among the rocks so strong was the wind and lashing rain. After a miserable night we returned to base camp, and the next day the pack-train arrived. Only eleven out of the fourteen animals had survived the hardships of the journey, and ill-luck had dogged their footsteps from the start. At the first camp out of Tyonik the horses had been turned out to graze; now the coast line at that point is seamed with veins of coal, one of which had in some mysterious way caught on fire, and into this hidden oven some of the horses blundered.

Printz told me later that strangely enough the horses made no effort to extricate themselves when they felt the burning embers, but crouched down, trembling. They were all rescued eventually, but only two out of the six animals that were burned were able to travel. The rest were relieved of their suffering along the trail.

CHAPTER IV

THE ATTEMPT TO CROSS THE ALASKAN RANGE _fails_

The advance up the Yentna Valley—Dangers of swimming loaded
horses across the glacial rivers—Professor Parker's narrow escape—We
reach the cañon of the Yentna. Exploration of the cañon—Dangers
in the cañon—I kill a bear—Barrill and I see the Kuskoquim Sheep
Mountains—Our retreat through the cañon—Our horses give out—
Barrill spends a night in the cañon—Retreat to base camp.

WE lost no time in pushing forward. Captain
Armstrong and Ball returned down the Yentna
in the canvas boat, and we moved up the valley with
our entire outfit.

The work of swimming loaded pack-horses across
glacier rivers is the most dangerous form of exercise
that I have ever indulged in. The horses served as
pack-animals and ferry-boats. We were forced to
swim the animals with their packs on, and we either
sat behind the packs, or held on to the ropes while we
were in the water.

Several times members of our party were in imminent
danger of drowning. In some of the fords the horses
swam eighty to one hundred yards, and this distance,
in swift ice-water, is trying to man and beast, but the
short fords in savage swimming water are more nerve
trying, and the legs of the horses suffer from stumbling
about among the sharp rocks. At times the river banks

were steep and after a hard swim the horses would be unable to climb out, then, unless we "kept cool"—not an
easy thing to do in glacier water—trouble would result.
Professor Parker probably had the narrowest escape.
He was crossing a swift chute of water above a rapid
that lashed the base of a high bluff. The Doctor,
Printz, and I had crossed safely, and the Professor was
half-way across when his horse turned around and lost
his footing. Luckily the current swept Professor
Parker past a point and Barrill helped him ashore,
but the horse disappeared from view in the rapids.
We thought the animal was dead and as soon as we
had pitched camp, Printz, Barrill, and I returned down
stream to find the horse and recover the pack. We
rode on horseback and to our great surprise we found
the horse alive about a mile below our camp. His
pack was intact, and my rifle which I had pushed under
the cinch ropes was in working order. I was riding a
powerful roan that Dr. Cook used in fording and as our
lost horse was on an island I forced the roan into a
rapid well above. This was a different thing from
riding a heavily loaded horse, and the great roan took
me down through the white water as if I weighed
nothing—it was a thrilling ride. After landing on the
island I put the pack on the roan and brought both
horses to the mainland, and we returned joyfully to
camp.

Our camps were picturesque in the extreme. They
were usually situated on a bar of the glacial rivers.
The camp-fires were built in the great piles of driftwood
that the river brought down during the spring freshets.
The men moved half naked, like savages, in the crimson
glow, while above the haze of the valley the Alaskan
Range stood clear cut against the evening sky.

After several days of hard, wet travel we reached the cañon that was the deciding factor in our crossing the range. We had overcome all the difficulties of summer exploration: swift water, trail chopping in heavy rains, camps without horse-feed, quicksands, swamps, and mosquitoes. We made camp near the mouth of the cañon and prepared for a mounted reconnaissance.

The following morning the Doctor, Printz, Barrill, and I mounted four of the strongest horses, and entered the cañon. We and the horses were stripped down for the struggle with the water. We rode mountain pack-saddles, as they are good to hold on to in rapids.

At the first ford in the cañon we realised the danger and difficulty of the undertaking. The water was swift and white and our horses shrank in fear from it. Our misgivings proved to be well founded, for not one of us was able to return to camp by way of the gorge.

Barrill led and after we had made six desperate swimming fords, the cañon split. The Doctor and Printz took the smaller or right-hand fork and Barrill and I followed the left. The right-hand stream swung to the east and carried "fresh water," showing that there was no glacier at the headwaters. Our stream carried the original dirty glacier torrent, which grew swifter as we advanced until it required all our courage to make us drive the horses into it. At the last of six cruel crossings we came to a glacier that completely dammed the cañon. It was of a deep bluish green colour and the river spouted upward from a great cavern in the face of the ice. Scattered about us were tons of granite that had fallen from the cliffs above, and now and then a crash heard above the thunder of the water would tell us of a new arrival.

We had realised long before that it would be impossible to take a pack-train through the gorge, but the interest of our explorations, added to a man's natural dislike for turning back, led us on. Barrill unlashed an axe from his saddle, and I carried my rifle. We left the horses securely tied, and chopped steps across the glacier. We found that the stream tunnelled under the ice, and above the cañon grew narrower and we were forced to climb the walls.

About two hundred yards above the bed of the gorge we found sheep sign, while ahead of us, as we climbed, we could see miles of sheep pasture, everlasting scree slopes, and a great ridge that shut off the view of the pass.

As we advanced we found more sheep sign than I have ever seen before or since, and the promise of game put strength into our tired, water-soaked legs.

Finally we reached a high knoll that overlooked the valley and we sat down to take in our wild surroundings. Suddenly as my eyes were roving over the valley I saw a large brown bear cross an opening in a thicket below us. Barrill was unarmed, but in the excitement of the moment he followed me downward. The bear was travelling steadily along the mountainside, and I waited for him on a steep slope. When he came into view his great, dark hulk stood out in strong relief against the blue haze of the valley. At the first shot he rose on his hind legs and a second shoulder shot sent him crashing down the mountainside. Below us was a little knoll which commanded the whole hillside. From this point of vantage I could see that bruin had rolled into a dense jungle of alders that grew in the wildest confusion among the great boulders of an old moraine.

I saw that when I reached the thickets I would not be able to see about me, so I asked Barrill to direct me from the hillside. The bear's trail showed plainly until I reached the masses of brush and rock, where it disappeared. Glacial erratics weighing many tons lay scattered all about, making it impossible either to move rapidly or see any distance; the grim wildness of the spot made it a fit background for a bear killing. At last I found arterial blood and following it through the dense brush came again to fault in the shadow of an upright shaft of granite. Not a sound broke the stillness, and knowing that the bear was hard hit, and close at hand, I decided that he was dead. I therefore called to Barrill and asked him if I was on the right track, and he answered that the bear ought to be close to the spot where I was lying. The brush made moving in an upright position an impossibility. I had just raised my rifle to crawl farther when I heard a slight noise, and turning quickly I saw a great brown head rising slowly through the brush about ten feet away. The bear did not utter a sound, and his small eyes gazed steadily into mine as I pushed my gun through the branches and fired. He rolled down the mountainside and when I reached him he was dead. Since then I have understood why so many accidents happen while tracking wounded bears, for while I was close enough to touch him with a fishing-rod, I was unable to see him among the tangle of rocks and branches.

Barrill soon joined me and while we were preparing to skin our prize we made an interesting discovery; the bear's chest and belly were a patchwork of ugly wounds. Some of the cuts had festered and despite our hunger we could not bring ourselves to eat the meat. As the beast was thin and weighed close to 700 pounds, the bear that inflicted the wounds must have been a powerful adversary.

"FERRYBOAT."

THIS HORSE CARRIED FRED PRINTZ AND THE
AUTHOR IN ADDITION TO HIS PACK OVER MOST
OF THE BAD FORDS OF THE YENTNA RIVER.
THIS PHOTO WAS TAKEN AT A TIME
WHEN MANY OF OUR HORSES WERE
EXHAUSTED AND UNABLE TO
CARRY ANYTHING.

Photo by Belmore Browne.

WHAT STARVATION AND THE ALASKAN MOSQUITO CAN DO.

Photo by Belmore Browne.

After leaving the bear we climbed about one thousand feet and on reaching a high shoulder we could look down onto two passes that led to the Kuskoquim. Our cañon split again and between the forks rose a high rounded mountain. We lay for a few minutes looking sadly and yearningly towards that promised land, our "happy hunting ground," and then we slowly turned towards the back trail, for while we were through the worst part of the range, we knew that horses could not follow us. This is the only time as far as I know that men have crossed through the Alaskan Range between Mount McKinley and the passes at the head of the Kichatna.

We were filled with anxiety on nearing the cañon, for the sun had been melting the snow, and the deep, sullen roar from below told us that the stream was more dangerous than it had been in the morning. Our fears were realised when we reached the gorge. The stream below the glacier was now a seething ice-laden torrent, and it looked impassable.

We would have waited for the water to subside, but night was approaching, our poor horses had weakened perceptibly since morning, and we ourselves were tired and our food was gone—we had to go on. Barrill, who had undergone the strain of leading in the morning, asked me to lead now, and I did so gladly. Our poor horses were terrified, but it was pathetic to see the eagerness and bravery with which they undertook the cruel task. There was no wild scramble or panic with them—they knew the danger of the water, and they made the most savage fords slowly and cautiously.

My horse, "Ferry-boat," had carried Fred Printz and me across every ford that we made on the Yentna and I have never seen a horse who knew water better than he. He lacked strength, however, and it was a lesson to me when I saw the intelligence of the faithful old animal in these moments of danger.

In each ford a misstep would have cost us our lives, but the noble animals braced themselves against the ice and current with splendid courage and intelligence. On the gravel bars between the fords our horses left a trail of blood, but on they went never hesitating. I did not touch Ferryboat's head during the entire trip, but his pointed ears were always turning towards me as I cheered him on.

We expected an easier time when we reached the main cañon, but to our horror it was a raging flood. Horses and men alike were weak and numb from cold, but in we went. As I was searching the further bank there was a splash behind me; Barrill's horse had fallen and he and his mount swept past me in a smother of foam. At times I could see nothing but the swirling water. Once I saw Barrill's hat on the crest of a roller, and then instantly his horse's hoofs appeared lashing the white water, and then down I went into the choking, freezing flood. At last after feeling blows and hearing the sound of rushing water in my ears I felt the convulsive heaving of Ferry-boat's body and I found myself on the rocks. I lay there some time and then raising my head I saw Barrill below me. There is something terrifying about savage glacier water, and it was getting dark, as well, and a freezing wind was sucking through the cañon. I remember that my pockets were full of ice dust from the river. The cold seemed to sap the life from us; our energy and courage were gone, and we urged our horses into the next ford in a kind of stupor.

We made three more fords, and then Barrill's horse

pulled him from the water on the very edge of the black cliffs, and mine staggered ashore just above.

Our next attempt was the last; Barrill's horse collapsed after going into the river and wallowed ashore on the same bank, and I by leaving Ferry-boat's back and swimming landed safely on the opposite bank. Ferry-boat was done for and I started to lash him as he lay, but I could n't do it, and eased him by taking off his saddle.

Barrill, wisely, refused to make another attempt. We could not talk as the thunder of the water drowned our voices, but as I knew that he had matches and firewood I waved good-bye to him and began to climb the cañon walls. As I climbed, Ferry-boat tried to follow me, and as I gained the crest I could see him standing by the river watching me wistfully. Barrill stayed in the cañon all night. The next morning the river was unusually low and Printz brought Barrill to camp without having to swim the current, and our horses followed.

On reaching camp I found that the Doctor and Printz had also had a dangerous experience in the cañon, and after having their horses rolled in the rapids, had returned to camp over the cañon walls. The stream they had followed ended in a box-cañon and they reported that there was no possibility of breaking through the range in that direction. This strenuous day ended our attempt to cross the Alaskan Range. The only chance left to us was to return to our base camp and from there strike out along the southern foothills of the range towards Mount McKinley. Our retreat was enlivened by quicksands, high water, and trail chopping.

On the last day we forded all of the united streams of the West Fork.

The quicksands were our principal difficulty, and

some of the horses sank so deep that only their heads were visible above the water.   Even the land some distance from the river was soft, and in pack-train parlance would "bog a snipe."

CHAPTER V

THE START TOWARDS THE SOUTHERN SIDE OF MOUNT McKINLEY

We cross the Yentna Valley and climb Mount Kliskon—We find prospector's and gold-bearing streams—Our horses begin to weaken—We are joined by an Indian—We reach the Tokositna glacier—A night on a mountain peak—An adventure with a bear—Exploration of the McKinley glaciers—We give up hopes of climbing Mount McKinley—The retreat—Arrival at Youngstown—The boat and pack-train are reunited.

WE lost no time at base camp, and after chopping at rail across the valley to the East Fork, we started for Mount McKinley. We crossed the East Fork, swimming our horses, at the site of Youngstown, and after two days of heavy rain we drove our horses across Mount Kliskon, a rounded hill about 3000 feet in height. The country was soft, the mosquitoes lay in black clouds, and our horses were exhausted.

While the horses rested for a day we climbed the highest part of Mount Kliskon, and were repaid by a magnificent view of the Alaskan Range. From Mount McKinley on the north-east to the volcanoes Redoubt and Iliamna in the south-west stretched an unbroken chain of jagged peaks and glistening snow-fields. Then we dipped into a low country splashed with black lines of spruce, and cut by rushing streams. We found grayling, trout, and salmon, no end, and added

47

them to our simple bill of fare. Deep in the moss we found the antlers of two giant moose that had locked their horns while fighting and died miserably. Our horses struggled bravely through the swamps but they were growing pitifully weak.

I remember one day in particular when we travelled all day and made only two or three miles. Sometimes we would have several horses "bogged down" at one time, and while we were unpacking, pulling out, and repacking these animals, others were becoming bogged in the swamps. Work of this kind, when the northern sun is hot and the mosquitoes hang in dense clouds, is hard on all hands, but it is the sight of the horses that you are fond of growing weaker day by day that makes you hate the lowlands and the cruelty of lowland travel. At "Sunflower Creek," a gold-bearing stream, we found a new settlement of a few miners. We also picked up an Indian, "Susitna Pete" by name, who said that he could guide us to the big mountain. As a piece of local colour he was a great success, but as a guide his services were of no value. While fording a beautiful stream called Lake Creek by the miners Susitna Pete told us an interesting story. He said that in the lake at the head of the stream there lived an enormous fish. The fish was so large that it could eat caribou. A friend of his once followed four caribou so relentlessly that they were forced to swim the lake to escape, and while the hunter stood on the mountainside sadly watching his escaping quarry the huge fish rose to the surface with a hissing sound and—swallowed the caribou. I asked him why some Indian did n't kill it, and he answered, "Indian no ketchum—too big— some day white man he sit down long time—maybe ketchum." At the great glacier that heads the Ka-

OUR "MOUNTAIN BASE CAMP" BY THE SIDE OF THE BIG BOULDER ON THE
TOKOSITNA GLACIER.

Photo by Belmore Browne.

THE VIEW OF THE "BIG GLACIER" AS IT LOOKED FROM OUR CLOSEST CAMP
TO MOUNT McKINLEY IN 1906. THE GLACIER CAN BE SEEN COMING
THROUGH THE "GREAT GORGE" ON THE LEFT. THE "AMPHITHEATRE
GLACIER," OR GLACIER NO. 2 AS WE CALLED IT IN 1910, CAN BE
SEEN ON THE RIGHT. IT WAS ON THIS GLACIER THAT DR.
COOK TOOK THE FAKE PHOTOGRAPHS OF MOUNT McKINLEY.

Photo by Belmore Browne.

hiltna River we had some cold, dangerous fords, as we forded just below the ice tongue.

We then climbed to timber line and swung towards Mount McKinley. The country changed to high, rolling caribou hills, minus the caribou, and one sunny morning a brown bear ambled amiably into camp while we were eating breakfast.

At the head of the Tokositna (the river that comes from the land where there are no trees) we found two glaciers. Susitna Pete said that the smaller glacier was called Kahnicula by the Susitnas. It headed in a nest of rugged mountains. The other glacier was large and extended far into the range towards Mount Mc-Kinley.

We were now close to Mount McKinley and as the country was too rough for pack-train transportation, we turned our horses loose by the side of the Tokositna glacier, and prepared for the real struggle. First the Doctor, Professor Parker, and I climbed a high mountain west of the Tokositna glacier that gave us an un-obstructed view of the southern and western faces of Mount McKinley.

At the first glance we all saw that the scaling of the peak was a hopeless undertaking. We knew only too well the weak condition of our commissary, and between us and the mountain was a tangled, chaotic mass of rugged mountains and glaciers. The night air was already beginning to have the tang that presaged the coming of frost, and we knew that with the coming of the frost our horses would die.

From the point where our camp was, the climbing of Mount McKinley would be a summer's task—if it were climbable. We could see the southeastern, south-ern, southwestern and a part of the western faces of

4

the great peak, above an altitude of about 9000 feet. Below that the walls were hidden by the rugged peaks of the main range.

There was a steady drift of clouds moving across the great ice slopes, and with hopes of a better view the Doctor and I decided to remain on the peak all night. After Professor Parker had left us we pitched our mountain tent with the entrance facing the mountain, and after a cup of tea we rolled ourselves in our sleeping-bags and prepared for our long vigil. It was a wonderfully impressive experience. Lying on top of the sharp peak we looked straight out through space to the icy walls of this wilderness giant. The night air had a chill clean tang, and as the cold crept downward the sound of falling water ceased until the whole world seemed steeped in frigid silence. The mountain stood out clear cut against the northern sky and as the hours passed the clouds settled slowly in the cold air until we saw the whole sweep of the mighty mountain. As we watched we talked in whispers, and we agreed that even a summer's campaign might be too short a time to allow of a complete traverse of the southern base.

As the cold increased an occasional, deep, thunderous roar would sweep, echoing back and forth, across the range and we would know that an avalanche had fallen from the grim ice walls. From our aerie we could see a grand unnamed peak that rose to a height of about 15,000 feet on Mount McKinley's south-eastern side, and for want of a better name we spoke of it as "Little McKinley." From our point of view, south-east, the mountain looked absolutely unclimbable. Our only possible chance was to work farther north and east across the Tokositna glacier and attempt to reach the Eastern Arête, but the country we had to cross was gashed by great parallel glaciers; it was a discouraging outlook.

In my original magazine article I place our position too far to the east. Porter had not yet completed his map of this region and I made my observations largely by guesswork. I spoke of the Eastern Arête as the Northeastern Arête, as we did not know at that time that there were three great ridges falling from the North-eastern face of the mountain. In this book I will speak of this ridge as the Southern North-east ridge.

We started across the Tokositna glacier after two days' delay on account of rain. We carried heavy packs and the travel was difficult as the glacier was about two miles wide and covered with crushed granite, which ranged in size from coarse sand to blocks the size of a house. The glacier rises in the vicinity of "Little McKinley" and it is the main feeder of the Tokositna River. Bounding the glacier on the north and east was a high mountain ridge, which we climbed. From the top of the ridge we secured a good view of McKinley.

North of our ridge was another huge glacier that seemed to come from Mount McKinley, and after talking it over we decided to use this glacier as a reconnaissance route.

On our first trip to the high dividing ridge we advanced in force. Professor Parker, Dr. Cook, and I were to make a reconnaissance, while Porter with a helper was to carry on the topographical work. Printz and Barrill packed loads to the summit of the ridge and then returned to camp to guard the horses.

As we were climbing the ridge I had an amusing adventure. A brown bear and I divided the leading part between us, and we were ably supported by a large company that made up for their lack of training by their remarkable enthusiasm and lung power. The scene was set on the grassy mountainside aforementioned, and the jagged peaks of the Tokosha Mountains formed the background. The comedy opened with the discovery of a brown bear by the main party. They had no arms but their ice-axes, which on the whole are not suited to bear-hunting. They at once began shouting to attract my attention, as I was about four hundred yards ahead of them and had in my possession a high-power pistol. This weapon of ill omen was a patent arm covered with complicated safety stops, and filled with ingenious machinery. It was guaranteed to shoot a whole broadside in three seconds, and was sighted up to a mile—if it had been sighted on a ten-foot range it would have served my purpose better. I was carrying it for Professor Parker and had not practised with it.

When I heard the shouts of the main party I accepted the leading rôle, and starting towards them, soon discovered the bear. I was on a grassy hillside, and the bear, unconscious of the excitement he was causing, was digging at a squirrel burrow in a little ravine between me and my comrades. Just above him was a granite boulder, and selecting this rock for a stalking mark, I began the approach. I could see my companions—six in number—sitting in an interested line, and a thrill of pride swept over me as I thought of the large audience that would witness my triumph.

Everything went splendidly at first; I reached the rock without alarming bruin, and on looking over it I saw him busily at work, not more than fifteen feet away. Without losing a minute I aimed my infernal machine at his shoulder, and pulled the trigger. Nothing happened! From this point on to the curtain of the farce, the bear held the centre—and all four corners—of the stage. I was so close to him that I was afraid to move away for fear that he would charge me, so I sat down back of the rock and tried a rapid-repair-act on my pistol. The bear in the meanwhile had discovered my companions, who, realising that something had gone wrong, began to execute a "song and dance" with the idea of distracting the bear's attention. Their plan succeeded for he left his digging and stalked past me and sitting down about ten feet away began to study my companions, turning his head from side to side. He was now directly between me and my companions. Luckily for them I had removed the magazine during my repairing operations, or I might have added homicide to my other sins. At last the bear turned around and saw me, and as long as I live I never expect to receive such a disgusted look as that bear gave me. I sat in as apologetic an attitude as I could, with the pistol in one hand and the magazine in the other. After giving me a thorough looking-over, he turned slowly, the hair on his back standing in a stiff ridge, and stalked away.

As soon as I was sure that he was leaving, I returned to my repairing, and succeeded in driving the loosened magazine home. The gun went off like a bunch of fire-crackers, and the bear, wild with terror at the noise, dashed downward towards my companions. They began to take immediate notice, and for a few minutes there was a sound of shouting and a dizzy blend of figures on the mountainside, and then silence once more settled among the hills. Whether they were afraid of my pistol or the bear I will never know, for I wisely decided to let the matter rest—I had had enough excitement already.

That night we camped on the summit of the ridge, and weathered a savage wind and rain storm. We had anchored our tent with boulders and ice-axes. The view from the mountain was beautiful; two thousand feet below us on either side were giant glaciers, and over them the black storm clouds tore themselves to shreds against the cliffs. We had a wild night and our tent rattled like a sail in a storm.

On studying the big glacier we saw that to reach it we would have to cross either an ice wall or a swift glacier river. We tried the river first but the water was too strong for us. We followed the stream until it plunged into a great cavern in the ice wall.

Below the cavern the wall continued around the base of the Tokosha Mountains. The ice wall was formed of solid green ice covered with great granite slabs, and as we could see from the ridge as far as our food supply would allow us to travel, it would have been a foolish risk to attempt the wall. We skirted the wall as far as the Tokosha Mountains without finding a break, and then returned to our camp. The Tokosha Mountains are a magnificent mass of sharp knife-blade peaks that form the dividing wedge between the lower ends of the two great glaciers. We named them Tokosha after the Tokositna River which encircled the base of the range.

The weather was cold and rainy, our enthusiasm was gone, and as Dr. Cook was expected at Tyonik to meet the Eastern sportsman who had partly financed the expedition, we turned our faces towards the base camp. Porter in the meanwhile was hard at work on his map-making, and he joined us a day later at the base camp.

A "COUNCIL OF WAR" STUDYING THE STREAMS OF THE KAHILTNA GLACIER FOR THE BEST FORDING POINT.

Photo by Belmore Browne.

THE LOCKED SKULLS OF TWO GIANT MOOSE THAT FOUGHT AND DIED.

Photo by Belmore Browne.

During all our wanderings Susitna Pete had been consumed with curiosity about our reasons for entering this country. To our answers that we wanted to climb Doleika he shrugged his shoulders with an air of amused tolerance. White men always wanted gold, and Pete decided that the search for gold must be our mission. He therefore told us of creeks where we might find the precious metal, and retired in outraged dignity when we showed no enthusiasm. Porter's topographical instruments mystified him greatly and he finally decided that in some way those mysterious instruments were connected with the thing we sought. One day Porter set up his theodolite by the side of the glacier and took some angles. On leaving the theodolite for a minute we were amused to see Susitna Pete eagerly place his eye to the telescope. In an instant his body stiffened with excitement—he had seen a bear; the theodolite must therefore be a new and marvellous instrument for the finding of big game! Porter at once rose in Susitna Pete's estimation, and we were no longer bothered with questions.

Our retreat was carried out in the "devil may care" spirit that comes over men whose chief purpose in life has been removed.

We no longer had to exert all our energy of mind and body towards the overwhelming mania of speed, regardless of cost. We drifted, rather, as a band of gypsies would, as free and irresponsible as children. Laughter and rough jokes rippled back and forth along the pack-train, and we learned to play wild, shrill marching tunes on the turned edge of a red willow leaf.

The horses, as a whole, had improved slightly in condition, but it was due more to the light loads they were carrying than to a return to strength. Horses furnish the chief topic of conversation among pack-train men, and the argument as to which type and colour of horse shows the most stamina is a world-old bone of contention. For example Brooks in his most interesting account of his long pack-train drive from Cook Inlet to the Yukon says:

"Experience proved that the buckskins, bays, and sorrels had more endurance than the black, or, especially, the white animals.

"The white horses suffered most from mosquitoes and were the first to give out."

After many hard trips with pack-horses in different parts of the West my experience has brought me to an almost totally different conclusion. For instance I never remember having packed a sorrel that was worth his salt. On our trip to Mount McKinley the two weakest horses we had were sorrels. As far as buck-skins and bays are concerned I heartily concur with Brooks but I would also place roan horses at the head of the list. But strangest of all in view of Brooks's statement is my experience with white horses, for on every trip where I have driven a horse that proved to be a particularly strong and faithful animal, it has been a white horse. As an example I will take our beloved "Ferry-boat." This faithful old animal did double duty throughout our long trip. Fred Printz and I worked together in choosing the many fords along our trail and when we forded we both used "Ferry-boat"— hence his name. We usually took turns in the fords, one of us holding to the pack-rope while the other rode behind the pack. Even with this handicap he was one of the best swimmers and weight carriers that we had.

Ferry-boat went through the strain of the cañon

swimming without any apparent ill effect, while the sorrels were spared this arduous experience.

These contradictory experiences lead me to believe that the *kind* of a horse is more important than the *colour* of a horse. In our pack-train there were times when individual horses were practically incapacitated by the mosquito hordes, and yet Ferry-boat at no time seemed unduly distressed, and stood the ordeal as well as the best.

These reminiscences take me back to an amusing feature of pack-train driving. At the beginning of every pack-train journey each man chooses a particular animal as his personal charge. In very rough country he leads the horse, if necessary, and when a river is encountered he fords on his own favourite. To "jump" another man's horse at a ford would be a deadly insult. As time goes on each man's fondness for his favourite horse grows stronger. He saves every little delicacy, such as a small piece of bacon-rind, or a mouldy biscuit, for his own animal, and sees to his comfort in every way. It is not strange then, under the circumstances, that a man's opinions become slightly biassed, and in my loyalty to white horses I know that I am strongly influenced by my affection for Ferry-boat.

Susitna Pete had left for parts unknown while we were exploring the glaciers near Mount McKinley. We did not see him again until we had returned across the glacier streams of the Kahiltna glacier and were camped on the plateau that lies west of the river. He joined us in the evening and he was wet and tired from his struggle with swift streams. He told us that after we had crossed, the glacier had broken, and that the streams were almost unfordable. By "broken" he meant that the glacier had flooded. There are many of these "flood glaciers" in the north, and they are a source of great danger. The glaciers are so formed that they block or dam certain valleys or cañons. In these natural reservoirs the water begins to gather, until in some cases large lakes are formed. All goes well until the movement of the glacier changes the location of the ice dam, by the formation of a crevasse, or a crevasse moving in front of the reservoir. A mighty flood ensues. It comes without the slightest warning and the effects are often felt in the lowlands far below. After the flood has occurred the valley or reservoir remains dry until it is once more dammed by the moving ice, and the water rises once more until another break in the ice wall allows the flood to escape.

After Pete had joined us we pushed forward over our back trail. We reached Sunflower Creek the following day.

We were joined at this time by Mrs. Susitna Pete—a typical Susitna Indian woman, and she was the innocent cause of one of the most amusing incidents that occurred during our travels. As we reached a stream on the first day that she joined us, one of the men gallantly lifted her onto one of the horses. It was a new and unexpected pleasure to her and thereafter she always expected a lift whenever we reached a stream. Instead of being gratified at his wife's comfort, Susitna Pete was envious. He told us that he too wanted to ride. Now all our fording horses were in use. We had with us, however, a small bay mare. She was as wild as a hawk, and although almost every man in our party had tried to ride her, every attempt had ended in failure. We at once became certain that providence had been saving the bay mare for Pete, so we ran to help him. One man held the mare's head, while two men grasped Pete. At a given word Pete was hoisted onto her back and the head man turned her loose.

Before she really began to buck Pete was in the water, and he came out of the ford with his Indian stoicism rudely shaken. To his questions as to what had caused the trouble the men told him that the mare's impoliteness was undoubtedly due to the fact that his red sweater had frightened her. On reaching the next ford Pete without a word removed his red sweater. With ill-disguised attempts to hide our amusement Pete was again hoisted onto the mare's back. · On this occasion there was a high bank above the water and as the mare cleared the bank she arched her back and gave a mighty buck. Pete went so high that we thought he would never come down and when he finally hit the water he did so in a cloud of foam. As the laughter ran back and forth along the pack-train we heard a shrill cackle from the head of the line —it was Mrs. Susitna Pete in a paroxysm of mirth over her husband's downfall. To our amusement she little realised that there was a difference between horses, and she was firm in her conviction that Pete's ill-luck was due alone to his lack of horsemanship.

After an uneventful trip we once more gathered at the site of Youngstown.

At this point we were confronted by several difficulties. In the first place Dr. Cook wanted the horses driven down the river to the Kichatna, as he wanted to use them on a hunt when he was joined by his sportsman friend. As a second attempt on Mount McKinley that season was out of the question, Professor Parker decided to return at once to New York.

Dr. Cook urged me to stay with him and help to

make the hunting trip a success, and I agreed to do so. Porter and a prospector hired for the occasion remained in the Lake Creek country to finish the map of that portion of the Alaskan Range.

There was an old camp site some miles below us on the main river, and thither the main party drove the pack-train. Dr. Cook, Miller, and I started across the valley of the Yentna to get the launch and take it downstream where we were to rejoin our party.

We had a hard trip as we had to cross on foot the many streams that cut the valley, and in one or two instances we had to swim. The water was bitterly cold. Miller could not swim, and we got him across the largest channel by felling trees from each bank and helping him across. We finally got so chilled that we had to build a fire in a swamp. We placed the fire on a platform of sticks and stood in the water while our bodies became warmed by the cheerful flames.

On reaching the boat we had a huge meal and turned energetically to putting the *Bulshaia* in commission. After a day's work we had everything in order and started downstream.

The channel was so narrow and the water so swift that I would have done better by taking the boat down backwards, but I attempted to gain time, and paid for it by hitting a "sweeper" below a sharp turn in a rapid. "Sweepers" are the curse of Alaskan river navigation, and they are feared by every one who has engaged in this form of travel. A "sweeper" is any tree that has had its roots undermined by the current until it has leaned far out over the stream. They are usually spruce trees, and they are found, as a rule, over-hanging the swiftest and most dangerous reaches of the northern rivers. Many a prospector or trapper,

THE ICE WALL ON THE WESTERN SIDE OF THE "BIG GLACIER"
WHICH WE FOLLOWED TO MOUNT McKINLEY IN 1910. THE
TORRENT IN THE FOREGROUND PLUNGES UNDER
THE ICE AND DISAPPEARS.

Photo by Belmore Browne.

rafting to the sea, has had his raft overturned by one of these treacherous obstructions and has lost his life or his outfit. When we struck the sweeper it bent the iron stanchions that formed the cabin, and Miller, who was standing on the stern deck, was nearly swept into the river.

In our desire to reach our companions we travelled too late, for in the dusk it was hard to choose the right channel, and I ran the boat aground. We waded ashore and spent a miserable night, lying on the rocks, without blankets, by the coals of a driftwood fire.

On the morning after our accident we began the discouraging task of hauling the *Bulshaia* off the sand-bar. We worked as follows. One man would carry an anchor well astern and sit or stand on it while the others would haul on the capstan. We would make about one foot in a half-hour, but in the end patience won and we were soon at the old camp-ground where we rejoined our companions. We left Barrill behind at this camp. He was to await our return and take care of the horses until we ascended the Kichatna on our hunt for big game.

On the way down the river we carried away our rudder on a snag, and I fitted two large steering chocks on the stern and from then on we steered the *Bulshaia* with large sweeps.

CHAPTER VI

THE RETURN TO THE COAST

WE reached Susitna Station on August 1st. Coming down the river we had heard rumours of a boat accident that happened in the Kahiltna cañon, and, on reaching Susitna Station, we met some of the men who had gone through the terrible experience.

Five miners were coming down the Kahiltna River in a boat. One of them was an experienced riverman, the others knew little or nothing about small boat navigation. Before reaching the Kahiltna cañon the experienced riverman tried to coach his companions in the safest method of running the cañon, but they laughed at his suggestion of running the boat through stern first, and he finally gave way to their optimistic viewpoint. All went well until the boat was nearly through the cañon walls, when a large partly submerged boulder appeared ahead. As they were rowing with the current the boat was moving with terrific speed and the steersman being in the upstream end of the boat had little or no control over the craft.

They struck the rock with great force, and the boat was broken to pieces. The men managed to cling to the rock and eventually they succeeded in drawing themselves out of the rapids.

There was, however, only a very small portion of the rock exposed above water, and on this tiny surface one man at a time could partly dry his chilled legs; the rest were forced to stand in the icy water.

One of the men decided that death by drowning was preferable to a living hell. Almost naked he took to the water and by the aid of a portion of the boat which had stuck on the rock, he succeeded in reaching the shore. Before him was a long journey through the most rugged part of the Alaskan wilderness, and yet he finally reached a miner's cache or cabin and found food. The other men faced their fate amid the roaring waters of the cañon. I believe that four days went by before the impossible happened. What those dark chilling nights must have meant to the men, no one but they will ever know. One day when hope was gone and death had marked them for his own, a boat shot downward through the white water. For an instant the bronzed miners that manned her looked in horror and surprise at the huddled group on the submerged boulder, and then the current swept them on.

But they returned and with the aid of a tracking line eventually rescued the men from the rock. They were brought down in easy stages to Susitna Station, where we found them on their return. They were in a pitiable condition, and their legs were black and swollen from the long immersion in glacier water, but I believe that they all recovered. The North holds hidden thousands of these tales that will never be written. But the more you see of the Alaskan prospector, the more you admire his breed, for these men pay a thousand-fold more in toil and suffering than the treasures that they win are worth.

From Susitna Station we ran quickly to the delta on our way to Tyonik. As we entered Cook Inlet we encountered a good-sized sea. I was familiar with the dangers of navigation on this part of the Inlet, for, besides hearing many tales of the terrific winds that sweep down from the great fiord known as Turnagain Arm, I had on more than one occasion sailed on different parts of the north coast in small boats.

Turnagain Arm is known locally as "the Cook Inlet compressed-air plant," and the greatest danger results from the savage winds beating directly on the Susitna flats, which extend across the head of the Inlet for many miles. Any heavy wind blowing on these shallows builds up mountainous seas. After leaving the delta the wind began to blow with great force. The sky above Turnagain Arm had a sinister look and knowing that we were in for trouble I called the Doctor out and advised him to turn back while there was yet time.

Printz and I were steering the *Bulshaia* from the stern deck with sweeps. The body of the boat was covered with canvas which was stretched lightly over iron stanchions. After a look around the Doctor said that we might as well keep on, for in case we got into trouble we could run into the Beluga River. Now the Beluga River was a small river that ran into the Inlet in the centre of a great expanse of level marshes. At low tide the mud flats extended for miles into the Inlet, and I felt certain that it would be an impossibility for any man to follow the tortuous channel through the heavy sea. Printz however said that he knew the channel, but later on I found that his knowledge of the

river was gained by having swum pack-horses across
it on two occasions! I however agreed and once more
eased the *Bulshaia's* head towards Tyonik. The seas
rose rapidly and Printz and I had to be lashed to ring-
bolts in the deck or we would have been swept overboard. We had a small canvas canoe inverted over the
canvas house and lashed in place with small ropes.
Suddenly a savage puff of wind caught the canoe,
broke the lash ropes, and carried it off to leeward where
it filled partly with water.

After this exhibition of what the wind could do I
realised that we could not make the delta or Fire
Island, our only two possible shelters, as our canvas
house would not stand the strain of driving into a head
sea.

The storm increased steadily. Do what we would
we could not keep all the seas from breaking over our
frail canvas house, and on two occasions solid green
combers rolled over us.

If the canvas had broken or a stanchion given way
we would have filled. Printz had had no experience
with boats, and told me between the waves that were
striking us that he preferred the "hurricane deck of a
cayuse."

Opposite the Beluga River we ran in to take a
look and the sight we saw was what I expected—a
great white line of foam-crested breakers were thundering onto the shoals a mile out from shore—there was
not a break to be seen.

As we swung the *Bulshaia* back on the Tyonik course,
the engine gave a dry cough and stopped. We were
on a dangerous lee shore, our engine was red hot, and
our ground-tackle consisted of one thirty-pound anchor.
It was an unpleasant predicament. The only thing

Printz and I could do was to keep the boat's head up wind, and as we were standing in the open we could see that the sea and wind were driving us rapidly towards the line of breakers.

The engine trouble was due to the glacial silt in the river filling our pumps and stopping the water circulation.

Our engine was an expensive and powerful auto-marine engine but it was built for clear water and fair-weather boating; it was in no way fitted for the rough conditions found on the Alaskan seacoast.

Through the canvas door we could see the men working at the engine. The pumps had to be removed and cleaned out and the engine cooled off before we could start again. Some of the men were seasick, and the boat was pitching heavily.

By this time we were only about one hundred yards from the outer breakers and I was figuring on what would make the best buoy in case our engine balked, for in that case it would have been "every man for himself and the devil take the hindmost." At last they began to crank the engine, and after several trials the exhaust grew regular and we began to wallow through the seas and leave the white breakers behind. With thankful hearts we squared away, but I soon realised that we would be helpless at Tyonik. It was an unprotected anchorage and we would be unable to land. I therefore called to the Doctor and advised him to take the launch across the Inlet, where we could anchor in the lee of the bluffs. He answered that there was a small creek near Tyonik and that we might run into it. I advised against it as I knew the entrance and it was difficult to enter in good weather, but the Doctor insisted, so Printz and I pulled on our sweeps and we

THE TOKOSHA MOUNTAINS, NAMED AND PUT ON THE MAP BY THE 1906 EXPEDITION. THE BIG GLACIER CAN BE SEEN ON THE LEFT.

Photo by Belmore Browne.

MOUNT McKINLEY AS IT LOOKED FROM OUR NEAREST CAMP IN 1906.

Photo by Belmore Browne.

headed for the river. To get a view of the river
entrance we had to run into the surf, and in an
instant a huge comber caught us and swept us with
terrific force towards the bar. As we were shooting
along the *Bulshaia's* head began to pay off. I pulled
on my sweep with all my strength, and yelled at
Printz to do likewise, but we could not hold her.
Our sweeps were dragging bottom as the big wave
passed us. The next roller caught us in a smother
of foam but the *Bulshaia* shook herself free and we began to creep offshore, meeting wave after wave until
we passed the line of surf. The water at times had
swept us from our feet and if we had not been lashed
to the deck we would have been washed overboard.
The Doctor was a little chastened after this experience,
and we took the bit in our teeth and headed for the
south side of the Inlet. Night was already upon us and
I had no liking for a lee shore in the darkness. As we
plunged along through the dusk I began to be aware
that the waves were losing their force. In a short
time I was sure of it—the great Cook Inlet tide was
cutting down the swell, so we once more turned the
Bulshaia's head towards Tyonik.

We arrived opposite Tyonik in inky darkness. A
heavy swell was breaking on the beach, and there was no
sign of life to be seen. As I knew the lay of the land
by the loom of the bluffs against the sky, I got into
the little 12-foot canvas canoe and Printz lay between
my feet for ballast.

I backed in slowly until I caught a big wave that
shot us in to the beach. I had warned Printz to jump
the minute we struck, but as the roller that had carried
us broke into foam a number of dark forms loomed out
of the darkness and we were carried boat and all

above the reach of the surf. A keen-eyed Aleute
hunter had seen the *Bulshaia* against the black sea,
and had told Durrell Finch, who ran the A. C. Co. trading post. He in turn had called out all the population,
which was composed mostly of Aleutes, and they had
stood by to aid us as we ran the surf. Finch then
gathered a crew of expert Aleute boatmen and they
succeeded in getting through the surf in a dory and taking off our companions. In the meantime Printz and
I had been taken in hand by Red Jack, a well-known
Cook Inlet character. We had been wet to the skin
for hours and were numb from the cold. Following
Jack to his cabin we got out of our wet things while
our host prepared generous glasses of hot whisky, and
the next thing I remember was that it was morning,
and that we were all glad to be on land. The storm
was one of the worst in years, and we were lucky to get
through as easily as we did. A dory, containing three
men, that we met and spoke on entering the Inlet was
never heard of again.

The western coast line of Alaska is always treacherous on account of the big tides and tremendous glacier-
bred winds, and after one or two experiences of this
kind a man learns that discretion is the better part of
valour.

Professor Parker now returned to New York and Dr.
Cook accompanied him to Seldovia to meet his friend.
He returned alone from his journey stating that the
Eastern sportsman could not join us, and we therefore
began to make new plans. Dr. Cook was anxious to
secure some specimens of big game for an Eastern
museum and as he had a large party he decided to
split it up into small units and send it in search of game.
Printz and Miller were to take some horses and go up

the Kichatna. I had remained in Tyonik from a desire
to see more of the Alaskan Range. Had the hunting
trip been carried out as we expected we would have all
crossed the Kichatna Pass and I would have then seen
the Kuskoquim country.

Dr. Cook however decided to take Barrill and a
new hired man and prospect the upper Susitna River to
see if reaching Mount McKinley by that route was
feasible. He asked me if I would go up the Matanuska
River on the northern slopes of the Chugach Mountains
and collect some zoölogical specimens for him. I
told him that if he contemplated exploring the southern
foothills of Mount McKinley I would prefer going with
him. He answered that he would do no exploring outside of seeing whether or not the water route was prac-
ticable and he again urged me to aid him with his game
collection. I agreed to help him, and went aboard a
small steamer that was lying at Tyonik on her way to
the mouth of the Matanuska.

The details that follow are hard to understand and
harder yet to write about. But for the sake of truth
and in order that posterity may be able to judge
correctly the events that followed, I feel it my duty to
put down every detail of what followed my departure.

Before leaving Tyonik I invited Dr. Cook aboard to
take luncheon with me, and while he was on board or
while the boat was at Seldovia he sent the following
telegram to a well-known business man of New York
City:

"Am preparing for a last, desperate attack on
Mount McKinley."

I proceeded up the Matanuska and the Knik rivers
and returned after a short and successful hunt to
Seldovia.

Printz and Miller were the first to join me. On the head of the Kichatna River they had found miles of tangled brush and morasses. The poor horses grew too weak to travel and the report of a rifle echoing through the silent spruce forests was their only requiem.

The death of the horses left Printz and Miller without means of transportation, until they reached the Kichatna River and built a raft. They finally reached Susitna Station after a narrow escape from death by drowning, and proceeded by boat to Seldovia.

At this time we heard the rumour that Dr. Cook and Barrill had reached the top of Mount McKinley. We knew the character of country that guarded the southern face of the big mountain, we had travelled in that country, and we knew the time that Dr. Cook had been absent was too short to allow of his even reaching the mountain. We therefore denied the rumour. At last the Doctor and Barrill joined us and to my surprise Dr. Cook confirmed the rumour. After a word with Dr. Cook I called Barrill aside, and we walked up the Seldovia beach. Barrill and I had been through some hard times together. I liked Barrill and I knew that he was fond of me for we were tied by the strong bond of having suffered together. As soon as we were alone I turned to him and asked him what he knew about Mount McKinley, and after a moment's hesitation he answered: "I can tell you all about the big peaks just south of the mountain, but if you want to know about Mount McKinley go and ask Cook." I had felt all along that Barrill would tell me the truth, and after his statement I kept the knowledge to myself.

Dr. Cook was detained at Seward by a lawsuit over a pack-train, and he kept Barrill with him. The rest of the party returned to civilisation.

I now found myself in an embarrassing position. I knew that Dr. Cook had not climbed Mount McKinley. Barrill had told me so and in addition I knew it in the same way that any New Yorker would know that no man could walk from the Brooklyn Bridge to Grant's tomb in ten minutes.

This knowledge, however, did not constitute proof, and I knew that before I could make the public believe the truth I should have to collect some facts. I wrote immediately on my return to Professor Parker telling him my opinions and knowledge concerning the climb, and I received a reply from him saying that he believed me implicitly and that the climb, under the existing conditions, was impossible.

I returned to New York as soon as possible and both Professor Parker and I stated our convictions to members of the American Geographical Society and the Explorers' Club.

Many of these men were warm friends of Doctor Cook. We, however, knew the question was above partisanship, and were willing to give Doctor Cook every chance to clear himself. Nothing official had as yet been written by Dr. Cook, and before we could make any formal accusation against him it was necessary for us to wait until his account of the climb was published. Before his book was published, however, Dr. Cook sailed *secretly* to the North. Both Professor Parker and myself were present at the gathering of the Explorers' Club when his farewell telegram was read. It was rather significant in view of the fact that he had many good friends in the club that no applause or signs of enthusiasm followed the reading of his message.

After the appearance of Dr. Cook's book Professor Parker and I found ourselves in possession of irrefutable proof that Dr. Cook had made countless misstatements in his description of the route he followed to the mountain, and the equipment he used. Many of the misstatements we knew to be downright falsehoods. We were influenced, however, by our own ideas of fair play as well as the suggestions of our friends, and we refrained from publishing anything derogatory to the Doctor's character while he was absent, and unable to defend himself. During his absence in the North Professor Parker and I were planning another attempt to climb Mount McKinley.

The reader will remember the excitement of Dr. Cook's return and the Polar controversy that followed, and I will skip all the public details of this period of Dr. Cook's notoriety.

In looking back on that remarkable controversy I am still filled with astonishment at the incredible amount of vindictive and personal spite that was shown by the partisans of Doctor Cook. Men who had never seen an ice-axe or a sled-dog wrote us reams of warped exploring details and accused us of untold crimes because we had dared to question Cook's honesty.

I was visiting Professor Parker at that time and scarcely a day went by when we did not receive abusive anonymous letters. In the face of this blind public partisanship, we realised that we would need more than documentary and circumstantial evidence to convict Doctor Cook irrevocably. The Polar controversy had put an entirely new light on our claims against Cook. Originally our claims against him were really more or less private and personal. While Mount McKinley was a splendid mountaineering prize, our attempt to climb it had been in the nature of a sporting proposition. We did it for the love of ad-

"GOING STRONG."

OUR PACK-TRAIN CROSSING THE KAHILTNA-TOKOSITNA DIVIDE.

Photo by Belmore Browne

venture and our attack on Cook was simply a question
of mountaineering ethics. But the North Pole was an
international prize, that had claimed the heroic efforts,
and lives, of the explorers of many nationalities for
many years. There was no sport here—it was a question of international importance.

We did have a chance to convict Dr. Cook of fraud
before a committee chosen by the Explorers' Club.
Both Professor Parker and I were called as witnesses
and Doctor Cook appeared. A well-known man opened
the meeting by telling Dr. Cook that he was not to
consider himself in the light of a guilty man being tried
to prove his innocence, but rather as an honest man
who was being given a chance by his friends to clear
himself from suspicion.

I can truthfully say that the majority of the men
who formed the committee were men whose sympathies
were, at that time, with Dr. Cook. But Dr. Cook
refused to testify before the committee. He said that
his hardships in the long Polar night had affected his
memory and that he could not answer any questions
without consulting his diary.

He asked for two weeks' time, and before the expira-
tion of that time he had disappeared. At this time we
were busy on our plans for our second attempt to
scale Mount McKinley, and the last chapter of the
Polar controversy will be found in the following account of our 1910 expedition.

THE 1910 EXPEDITION

WHEN Professor Parker and I decided to make a second attempt on the southern face of Mount McKinley we were influenced by three distinct desires. In the first place we had actually underestimated the difficulties of travel on the southern glaciers, and, knowing that the water route was the easiest way of reaching the big mountain, we thought that if we failed on the southern face (which from our knowledge of the mountain seemed probable) we would still be able to swing the Southern North-East Ridge and attack the mountain from that new and untried quarter. This north-eastern approach we knew to be the most promising line of attack, but it was at this point that our other plans entered and forced us to choose the southern.

Our principal reasons for attacking the southern side consisted first, in duplicating Dr. Cook's photographs and settling once and for all time his Polar claim, and secondly the mapping of the impressive mass of peaks and glaciers that guard the great mountain's southern flanks. The northern side had already been mapped

ALASKAN BROWN BEAR AND CUBS.
THESE LARGE ANIMALS ARE FOUND AMONG THE RUGGED PEAKS AND
GLACIERS OF THE ALASKAN RANGE.
From a painting by Belmore Browne.

by Brooks and we, therefore, looked forward eagerly
to adding this chaos of mountains and glaciers to the
map of Alaska. The northern also was more inaccessible
than the southern side. We knew that we could reach
the southern approach in the summer time in time to
benefit by the good weather. In the late summer the
snow-fields throw off such an immense amount of moisture that the big mountain is continually wrapped in
clouds which would double the difficulties of an attack,
or, possibly, render a successful ascent impossible.
Our starting point for the northern approach would
have to be Fairbanks, which is the largest town on the
Tanana River, and 160 miles north-east of the big
mountain. Now it is extremely easy to reach Mount
McKinley from Fairbanks, if you go in the winter time
and use dog teams. But neither Professor Parker nor
I were able to make a winter trip at that time. In
the summer, the Fairbanks approach is practically
out of the question, for in using horses one would be
forced to wait until the snow had gone, the ice broken
in the streams, and the grass abundant enough to
insure feed for the stock. These complications would
delay the final climb and the early summer months
would be wasted.

The suffering of our pack-train in 1906 had made us
resolve to do without horses on our next venture, and I,
therefore, turned all my energy toward the designing
of a boat that could carry heavy loads through the
rushing rapids of the northern glacier rivers. Knowing
that the head of navigation would be at least thirty
miles from the mountain, we also enlisted a party of
exceptionally strong packers, as all our provisions
would have to be carried on our backs across the
glaciers. It was a boat and back-packing proposition.

Professor Parker, Professor Cuntz, and the writer were fellows of the American Geographical Society and we had the official sanction of that society, and reported to them on our return. We also represented the Explorers' Club, as members. On this trip as on our other two, Professor Parker and I jointly led the expedition. For while Professor Parker advanced most of the expedition expenses, I outfitted the party and led the expedition in the field.

The outfitting of a large party in the North is a laborious affair that necessitates an intimate knowledge of wilderness conditions. Our river outfit differed in no way from the usual Alaskan outfits. But our mountain equipment, with the exception of somewhat lighter clothing and sleeping-bags, was the same as that used in Polar work.

Our party consisted of eight men: Professor Parker; Professor J. H. Cuntz, of Stevens Institute, who was our topographer; Valdemar Grassi, of Columbia University; Herman L. Tucker, of the United States Forestry Service; Merl La Voy, of Seattle; J. W. Thompson, who handled the boat engine; Arthur Aten, of Valdez, Alaska; and the writer. Our party was the best equipped expedition from a mountaineering point of view that had ever been organised in America. We left Seattle on the 5th of May. Our boat, which we had named the *Explorer*, after the Explorers' Club of New York, was run down under her own power from Tregoning's shipyard, near Seattle, to the steamer, and hoisted on to the upper deck.

After a busy but uneventful trip we once more found ourselves in the familiar harbour of Seldovia.

At this point we left the steamer and transferred all our belongings to a smaller boat called the *Tyonik*, for our voyage up Cook Inlet, and the *Explorer* made her maiden plunge into the cold northern waters. We tried out the engine in Seldovia harbour and although it had not yet "found itself" we got some splendid bursts of speed out of her, that gave us confidence in our ability to conquer the rapids of the glacier rivers. The engine had a powerful exhaust and during her trial spin the *Explorer* made so much noise that we were much amused on returning to the ship to find that she had been nicknamed the *Exploder!*

Seldovia is the principal port on Cook Inlet. A few warehouses flanked by the grass-thatched Russian Aleute cabins face the beach. The harbour is wonderfully protected and the coast line being of rock formation many little rock islands rise above the beach, like miniature fortifications. To the east the rocks rise in lines of cliffs that tower above the sea, and here in the summer time the northern sea-birds nest in thousands. Close to the town, groves of Alaskan spruce insure firewood to the inhabitants, but as the hills roll upward, these give place to the almost impenetrable jungles of Alaskan alder, which in turn disappear below the perpetual snow-fields of the surrounding mountains.

Below the town you come to the burial-ground where three-armed Greek crosses speak mutely of the early Russian days. Bidarkas—three-hatched kyaks —and dories line the beaches as the Seldovian travels by water and seldom penetrates the alder thickets of the back country.

At the head of the bay a salmon river furnishes the native population with food, for the Aleute takes life easily and gives hardly a thought to the morrow.

As hunters they are of little use, although with

careful handling they make fair packers and camp fol-
lowers. But in their long sealskin bidarkas they are
at home, and they brave the most savage seas in these
light boats that a man can raise above his head with
his two hands.

On landing from the steamer, I asked for two young
Aleutes with whom I had hunted the Kenai Mountains
in days gone by. "They went to sea in a bidarka"—
my aged informant answered—"and they fastened to
a white whale, but the harpoon line caught on the
bidarka's prow and when the whale sounded they went
to Heaven."

To save time, the *Tyonik* towed the *Explorer*, and
our trip down the Inlet proved to be an eventful one.
Off Anchor Point at the edge of Katchimac Bay the
wind began to blow, and before long there was a heavy
sea running. As the *Explorer* was shoal draft and as
light as a feather the least tug on the towing line would
make her shoot forward and overrun the cable.

It finally grew so rough that communication was
cut off between the two vessels, and Herman Tucker
and I found ourselves marooned. Luckily there was
a gasoline blow-lamp and a crate of eggs aboard or we
would have had a hungry time. Tucker manufactured
a sort of basin out of an oil tin and after filling it with
eggs he would hold it over the blow-lamp and we would
have a meal in short order. The navigation was most
difficult, and on several occasions I thought that the
Explorer was doomed. She would overrun her cable
so far at times that the bight would be far astern, and as
she lost headway and the *Tyonik* took up the slack,
the cable would come taut with tremendous force.
I managed to save the bitts from being torn out by
running her off at an angle as we shot forward, and

then when the rope tautened with a jerk some of the
force was expended on pulling the *Explorer's* head
around. It was touch and go for a long time and the
night seemed to last for ever, but we reached Beluga
safely. Durrell Finch and the A. C. Co.'s store had
left Tyonik, the scene of our landing after the storm in
1906, and had taken up a new stand on the Beluga
River, which was the same river that we tried unsuccessfully to enter during the 1906 storm. On this day, however, the sea was as smooth as glass and we moved slowly
up to the new wharf and after a hearty greeting from
Finch and Red Jack we began to unload our equipment.

Finch told us that the ice had not yet come out of
the Susitna, or any of the rivers, and he showed us
from where we stood the white cakes massed in the
Beluga River above the wharf.

As we had to wait for the ice to break we gladly took
possession of an empty log cabin and began to keep
house.

Cook Inlet is such an imposing sheet of water that
I find it difficult to dismiss it with a few words. It is
the largest estuary in Alaska and its lonely beaches
and the towering snow-covered mountain chains that
encircle it give it an atmosphere of wildness and
grim desolation that is even more impressive than the
more picturesque fiords farther south. The Kenai
Peninsula forms the Inlet's southern boundary, and
as the mountains break down towards the sea they
flatten out into the rolling timber-covered country
that enjoys the distinction of being the world's best
moose ground. In fact the Kenai Peninsula is a wonderful big game range, for in addition to the moose
that range the lowlands, the mountain meadows are
dotted with bands of the white mountain sheep.

The northern side of the Inlet follows the base of the Alaskan Range for a distance of seventy miles. While these mountains that tower above the sea are extremely impressive they seem dwarfed by the two great volcanoes, Iliamna and Redoubt, that raise their snowy steam-crowned summits far above the main range.

There is scarcely one good harbour on the northern side of the Inlet and the erosion of the mountains has built up great flats of mud and sand that complicate navigation.

As you approach the head of the Inlet, the mountains break away and the water blends almost imperceptibly into the marshes and flats of the great Susitna delta. On account of the extreme tides this part of the Inlet is particularly dangerous, and many men have lost their lives by being caught in small boats among the savage seas that break miles from shore on the shallow mud-flats.

Near the north-eastern end of the marshes a narrow opening allows the sea to rush into two arms that are called Turnagain and Knik Arm. Turnagain Arm received its name from the old navigator Captain Cook, who after repeated efforts to ascend it in his search for the mythical north-west passage, gave up in despair and turned back to the Pacific.

This fiord and its sister Knik Arm are still true to their old reputation and the savage glacier-bred winds still lash the seas to froth, and the tide bores can still be heard miles away as they come roaring in between the narrowing mountainsides. It was one of these savage glacier gales that threatened us with destruction in 1906, and on account of its propensity for breeding dirty weather Turnagain Arm has earned

MOUNT DAN. BEARD, MOUNT McKINLEY'S MAIN SOUTHERN BUTTRESS

Photo by Belmore Browne.

the descriptive title of "The Cook Inlet Compressed
Air Plant."

The Beluga River is named after the Beluga or
white whale and as the tide comes in, their glistening
bodies can be seen shining in the sunlight as they come
to the surface to breathe. Their oil is highly esteemed
by the natives of Alaska, who use it for cooking purposes and the preservation of fruits or berries. I have
eaten it at times while living with the natives but the
oil has a strong rancid taste that does not appeal to a
white man's palate.

The Beluga River has its source in a rugged portion
of the Alaskan Range and it enters the Inlet through
the north-western portion of the Susitna marshes.
Small amounts of gold have been found along the river
but never as yet in paying quantities. It is a "salmon-
river," however, and during the run of fish its banks are
the home of the great Alaskan brown bear. Where it
enters the sea it passes through the great marsh that
is famous for its mosquitoes and wild fowl. I have
seen marshes many miles in extent literally covered
with geese, brant, ducks, and snipe, and during our
stay at Beluga the wild fowl made a welcomed addition
to our simple bill of fare.

Reorganising was an easy matter, for each man saw
to his personal duffel, and I had packed all the expedition food in marked packages, in the order in which
they would be wanted. After the *Tyonik* left, the
Explorer was made fast at Finch's dock and I slept on
her at night in case the ice came down without warning.

Shortly after we were settled the river-steamer
Alice arrived. It was her first year on the Inlet, and
she had been sent up by the A. C. Co. to carry freight
and passengers to a new trading post at the upper forks

6

of the Susitna. This trading post was called Talkeetna Station after the Talkeetna River which joins the Susitna at that point. On this steamer was a rival Mount McKinley expedition which had been sent out by the Mazama Mountaineering Club of Oregon. The expedition consisted of four men: C. E. Rusk, the leader; Cool, a guide; Rogec, a photographer; and Ridley, an ex-forest ranger. They were to proceed to Talkeetna Station on the *Alice* and then ascend the Chulitna River in a poling boat, until they reached the nearest approach to Mount McKinley's southern side. They were a pleasant party of men, and the friendly competition that existed between the two expeditions added greatly to the amusement and interest of our adventures.

A few nights after the departure of the *Alice*, I was awakened by Finch, who told me that the Beluga had broken and that the ice was coming. We turned out all hands instantly and armed with long pike poles began an exciting battle with the ice. The stream of small bergs was ceaseless and at times they came with such force and in such numbers that the wharf was threatened and we feared for the *Explorer*.

The beautiful long northern twilights had begun, and across the marshes a great silver moon hung in the sky while behind us the east was rosy from the scarcely hidden sun. The "break-up" on a northern river is a sight worth travelling far to see. And yet I doubt if there have been any more beautiful from an artistic standpoint than the breaking of this small river. The clear floes came sweeping down in a stately procession and as the moonlight or the warmer reflection of the rising sun struck them they gleamed and flashed like precious gems. The ice, weakened by the spring heat and torn from its hold on the river-beds by the fury of the water, moved as majestically as an army, that, beaten and retreating, still keeps its dignity and courage. Phalanx after phalanx, winter's beaten cohorts swept to the sea, and as we fought the floes the harsh clanging calls of wild geese told us that they too knew that winter was gone and that the water-lanes were open.

For two nights we fought the ice, snatching a few hours' rest when the flood tide backed the water up, and then saying good-by to our friends at Beluga we headed for the Susitna.

The Inlet was comparatively free of ice but the instant we entered the Susitna we began to meet floating masses of broken bergs and all the way to the Station we had to dodge swift-moving floes. In 1906 we had followed the northern channel but we were told at Beluga that almost all the water was coming down the southern channel, so we did not pass Alexander, where Porter and I had dined on dead hooligans in bygone days. I brought the *Explorer* from the delta to Susitna Station, a distance of about thirty miles, without touching bottom once, a feat which I never accomplished in the *Bulshaia*. The difficulties of navigation were increased by the ice-floes and made the ascent of the swifter portions rather serious work.

At the Station we met a lot of old friends. The camp had changed to quite a little village. The A. C. Co. had erected a large store and warehouses, but the Indian cabins were still in evidence. We found the stern-wheel steamer *Alice* moored at the river-front, and I imagine that the scene resembled some of the river-scenes on the Mississippi in the old days of the fur traders. We left a recording barograph with Mr. Wood of the A. C. Co., and he was to wind it at regular

intervals and replace the marked sheets. Professor
Parker and I enjoyed a civilised dinner, which boasted
a chicken as the *pièce de résistance,* at the home of
Doctor Kevig. The Doctor and I were old friends as
we had run 150 miles of the Stikine River in an Indian
canoe several years before.

The *Alice* had had a narrow escape coming up the
river; an ice jam had broken and they were just able
to escape destruction by running downstream and
darting into a small tributary called Willow Creek.
The ice was still running in large quantities and we
decided that we would lose no time by waiting over
a day as we could then make better speed.

It was interesting to watch the river. Dirty masses
of bar ice were sweeping and grinding towards the
sea; here and there brilliant glittering phalanxes of
clean ice showed where some distant mountain tributary had broken free and sent its clear covering to the
main river, while great tree trunks and fields of drift
spoke mutely of the overwhelming power of the spring
thaw. As you looked you knew that every stream in
every distant wilderness valley of the interior had risen
at the call of summer and burst its winter bonds.
But as you looked you thought too of the miles of
river that stretched before you, and of the hard knocks
your boat and engine would receive before the flood
was beaten.

CHAPTER VIII

THE ASCENT OF THE SUSITNA AND CHULITNA RIVERS

Difficulties of northern motor-boating—The *Alice* passes us—We arrive at Talkeetna Station—We pass the Mazama expedition—Difficulties of navigation—Accidents—We reach the Tokositna River.

OF all the problems in northern motor-boating, the choosing of an engine proved to be the most serious. If you take a cupful of glacier water and let it stand until it has settled you will find that about one fifth of the fluid is composed of the finest kind of pulverised silt. This silt is the natural tailings of nature's stamp-mill and is composed of glacier- and water-crushed rock. In the water-cooling systems used in gasoline engines, this silt clogs the cylinder water-jackets, and as your engine heats you have a very perfect but undesirable imitation of a brick-kiln on your hands. This was what occurred during the storm of 1906, and since then I have taken a frenzied interest in the different water-cooling systems. The continuous rain and humidity of the Alaskan Range likewise affected our electric batteries. Another difficulty that we encountered was the lack of gasoline in the Cook Inlet ports, and as the steamers that carry gasoline only run at long intervals, the fuel question was a constant annoyance.

With all these harrowing details in view we turned our eyes in 1910 toward kerosene engines, and finally selected an 18 h. p., two-cylinder engine that developed 26 h. p. when tested.

It was the uncertainty concerning the power and reliability of this engine that made me dread the struggle with the swift water.

As the *Alice* was going directly to Talkeetna, eighty miles up the river, Professor Parker took passage on her and we agreed to meet him later.

We left Susitna Station on May 26th and once again I found myself steering a boat along the crowded river bank towards the eddy that roars around the bluff. But this time the deep steady exhaust promised us power to spare and when we struck the white eddy wall the *Explorer* took the lashing foam over her bow and kept steadily on. Many of the "old timers" were sceptical about our ability to "buck" the Chulitna, but I had had more experience with engines in swift water than they and I knew that if we could get water enough and the engine did its work, we would win our fight with the river.

Now the navigation of swift water is fairly safe as long as you are careful and do not hurry. In bad water all men will, of course, use caution and do their utmost to keep away from danger, but in ordinary water this is not the case; time is of value, and a good river-man, by using his knowledge of currents and eddies, and by the skilful handling of his boat, will cover many more miles in a day than an overcautious man who holds to the main current.

On the first morning out the *Alice* passed us; we were having some slight engine trouble at the time and Captain Malmquist, who had taken a lot of interest in the *Explorer*, gave us a derisive whistle as he forged ahead.

THE "EXPLORER" LEAVING SUSITNA STATION ON THE WAY TO
TALKEETNA STATION.

Photo by H. C. Parker.

THE "EXPLORER" AT "WRECK ISLAND" AFTER THE ACCIDENT ON THE
CHULITNA RIVER.

Photo by Belmore Browne.

Our greatest joy was in the return to wilderness camps and the exhilaration of our struggle with the river. The long spring days were a great help and during the three days that we spent in reaching Talkeetna, I stood at the wheel for fourteen, fourteen and a half, and fifteen hours respectively. As we advanced the beautiful peaks of the Talkeetna Mountains seemed to follow us on the south-eastern horizon, while Mounts McKinley, Foraker, and Roosevelt (as Mount Hunter is known among the prospectors) stood up grandly against the northern sky. As you watched the great cloud-like shapes hanging above the blue foothills, it was hard to realise that they were in reality stupendous masses of rock and ice.

We arrived at Talkeetna Station only five hours behind the *Alice*. Professor Parker was overjoyed as the river-men prognosticated that we would not show up for two days, but the *Explorer* was running like clockwork and we beat the small boat record by twelve hours. On the way up the river the *Alice* had rescued a prospector whose boat had been crushed by the ice while he was descending the river. He was sighted early in the morning, sitting on a log-jam in the river, a few hundred yards from the main channel. He appeared to be so weak that he could scarcely sit up, and he took no apparent interest in the approach of the steamer. In speaking of the rescue, Mr. Rusk, of the Mazama party, says:

The *Alice* was quickly landed a short distance above, on a little sandy island. Pilot Gordon and mate Blair jumped into a dory and went to the man's aid. He was brought aboard, put to bed, and given some light food. He proved to be one John Schmidt, and had been on the jam for six days and nights in such a cramped position that he could not keep entirely out of the water. Having started from Talkeetna in a small boat just after the ice went out, he overtook the jam at this point. Just as he reached it, it broke and swamped his boat. He managed to get onto the logs, where he remained until saved by the timely arrival of the *Alice*. This same man and a companion were wrecked at this identical spot in the spring of 1909 and remained on a jam for several days, until they were rescued. In fact the boat which they had on the first mishap was still lying on the island and it was now taken aboard the steamer. Twenty-four hours longer on the logs, and Schmidt would undoubtedly have been beyond help; but, as it was, he soon recovered from his trying experience.

On our arrival at Talkeetna, we saw Schmidt sitting on a stump by the river, and we could see by his distended appearance he had been making up for lost time in the food question.

The Rusk party had left a few hours before, so not to be behindhand we waved good-by to our new friends and headed for the mouth of the Chulitna.

Many river-men who had heard of the Chulitna cañon questioned our ability to run it in the *Explorer*.

The Rusk party were using a poling boat, a slow but sure way of reaching the Tokositna, and we were overjoyed, therefore, on entering the Chulitna to see the smoke of their camp-fire a short way above us on another branch of the river. After supper Professor Parker and I walked across the valley to where we could see their camp but several rushing streams kept us from paying them a visit.

The following morning things began to happen at the very start. Usually an accident on a northern

river comes like a thunderclap out of a clear sky, and
almost invariably the cause of the trouble is some
minor accident that, taken by itself, *under ordinary
conditions*, would be of no consequence. In the delta
of the Chulitna the river is cut up into so many small
channels that the water is extremely swift and shallow.
After breaking camp we were trying to force our way
up one of these narrow chutes where there was no room
for manœuvring. At last I sent four men ashore
with a tracking line, and with the extra pull that they
exerted we began to make headway. Everything was
going finely, when suddenly the tiller line broke. In
an instant the trackers were pulled off their feet, and
the current swept us over a submerged bar, and crushed
the *Explorer* against the bank.

Making the boat fast we gave her a thorough exami-
nation and found that the propeller was broken, the
tunnel badly scarred, and the shaft worn. Nothing
but a complete overhauling would fit us for our fight
with the Chulitna cañon. Our first duty was to haul
the stern out of water, and as the *Explorer* was lying
with her bow upstream, we had to turn her around.
As the current was exceedingly swift, we were afraid
to let the current take her bow around, so we made a
line fast to the bitts with the idea of easing her. After
anchoring the stern firmly we cast off the bow, but a
battleship's hawser would not have held against that
current, and when we finally succeeded in pointing her
stern upstream, we had broken our hawser, torn the
bitts out by the roots, and nearly hurt a man who got
tangled in the line.

Before turning her, we had unloaded all our duffle—
a good-sized job in itself. Then, after hauling the
Explorer's stern out of water with the help of a dead-

man sunken in the frozen gravel, and a block and tackle, we recorked the tunnel, and sheathed it with tin from kerosene cans. We then put in a new steel shaft and propeller, melting our babbit in a frying-pan over a fire made from native coal that we picked up on the river bar.

At this point I realised the difficulties that confronted us and decided to sacrifice everything aboard that we could possibly do without. This extra duffle we placed in a cache against our return. Twelve hours later, with a new tiller-line insuring our steering-gear, we were flying up the Chulitna with everything in better working order than before the accident.

During the afternoon we were prospecting a bad rapid for a route, when Thompson shut off the engine and yelled: "Throw out an anchor!" We were about fifty yards above bad water so we dropped two anchors which we always carried on the forward deck ready for instant use. The current ran with such force, however, that we dragged our anchors, and came up with a thud on a bar at the head of the rapid. In a case of this kind it is "Every man overboard!" and into the water we went. The water under her bow where we had to work to push her off was about three and a half feet deep, and so swift that we could scarcely stand against it without holding on to the *Explorer*. When we began to push, we had to stoop and the rushing glacier water ran over our shoulders. Working over a boat under these conditions is about as unpleasant a task as I know of, and when the day is cold and raw, with downpours of rain drenching your back, the roar of the rapids is not loud enough to drown the explosions of "language" from the workers. When we finally got the *Explorer* into deep water, we found that in some mysterious way the tail shaft had become loose and would have slipped out into the river had not Arthur Aten grasped it with his bare hands—he was a truthful man who said, "It is the unexpected that always happens."

Our third camp was made where the distant spruce-crowned walls of the Chulitna Valley began to come together.

Besides forcing most of the water into one channel, the narrowing walls told us that we were approaching the cañon of which we had heard so many wild tales. On the following morning therefore we made an early start. Little by little the bluffs increased in height and drew together until the whole river was rushing and boiling along in one channel. At last we came to a rock point and beyond we could see the river sweeping around other straight rock walls, and we knew that we were at the foot of the cañon. I ran the *Explorer* into a large eddy below the bluff and we gave her a thorough overhauling.

When everything was shipshape the exhaust began to thunder and we were off. I cut straight through the big eddy and a great spout of spray flew up when we hit the swift water, but the *Explorer* ploughed along, and I drove her diagonally across the current to an eddy on the farther bank. Here we picked up headway again and once more we drove in clouds of spray across the river and caught an eddy above the big bluff.

In this way, using every eddy and backwater, we shot back and forth, slowly climbing the current as a salmon climbs a fish-ladder. It was thrilling work and a large part of the pleasure came from the magnificent way in which the *Explorer* behaved.

With my hands on the wheel I could feel every

vibration of the staunch little craft, and there was a splendid exhilaration in feeling the steady force of the propeller as the white water drove against us. As commands would have been drowned in the roar of the rapids, I had installed bells, and Jack Thompson stood with every nerve on edge for the first clang of a signal.

In this work in swift water I have often noticed a strange fact for which I am unable to give an explanation. In very swift water it sometimes happens that the boat will come to a standstill. For a minute maybe you will not gain an inch, and then, just as you are beginning to give up hope and are searching the river for a new point of attack the boat will begin to climb. Very slowly at first, inch by inch, she will force her way along until, with the help of her momentum, she ploughs steadily upward past the dark bluffs. I know that there is some simple explanation for the boat's seeming increase in power, but we used to say that the *Explorer* had playful moods and would not exert all her strength until she had to.

At the head of the Chulitna you get your first smell of the snows, and as we came out of the cañon's walls the grey clouds lifted and we could see the great blue foothills of the Alaskan Range, running up to the everlasting snow-fields.

Above the cañon the river was difficult to navigate. Cañon water is swift but it is usually deep, and as a rule you have more difficulty in the swift shallow rapids. The valley of any Alaskan river the size of the Chulitna is usually several miles broad and as flat as a table. Through this level waste of water and gravel the river forces itself in countless channels that change from day to day, and the helmsman must be skilful indeed who unerringly chooses the right course.

"MOUNT HUBBARD."

Photo by Belmore Browne

You may be speeding up a fine stretch, in a broad channel, when suddenly the river will split. One branch will follow a dense fringe of timber that marks the edge of the valley, while the other may lead across the broad valley, where you know there are scores of channels crisscrossing back and forth. If the streams are of equal size you must put all your experience to work in choosing the right course. The masses of driftwood and snags that rise above the water can be seen a long way off, and they usually indicate the location of the largest channels.

"Cut" or straight banks usually indicate deep water, and the points of forest land that run far out on the gravel bars will give you an idea of the location of the main channel.

The best-looking channels, however, are often "blind" at either the upper or lower end; for instance many small streams may overflow from a main channel and join each other one by one until a mile below they form a stream that appears to be as large and navigable as the true channel. A man coming upstream may easily choose the "blind" channel, and, being unable to see far ahead on account of the flatness of the valley, he will continue until the water gives out and he is forced to go back. As he has not room to turn his boat around he has to drift slowly backward, and when he finally reaches the main river again an hour has been wasted.

Sometimes we found places where the river was divided into three or four main branches of the same size, and we would patiently try them in turn. Occasionally they would all seem equally hopeless. The first step in a case of this kind is to find the branch with the shortest shoal. Two of the crew should then stand beside you—one to port and one to starboard, and take

constant soundings with slender poles. The rest of
the party should move forward at the command of
the captain to counteract the sag of the boat's stern
when she runs into exceptionally shallow water.

We passed a miserable spot of this kind above the
Chulitna cañon. I could not get deep soundings
anywhere and was forced finally to choose the most
promising channel and ring "full speed ahead." As
the water began to shoal I called the men forward,
until finally I had Professor Cuntz sitting on the bow
like a figurehead with his legs dangling alongside the
cutwater. La Voy and Grassi were taking soundings,
and for what seemed an hour to me they kept calling,
"Two feet!" "Two feet!" To relieve the monotony
they would occasionally call, "Two feet—who 'll make
it three?" And then, sadly, as the shoal continued,
"Two feet—no takers."

In this rapid our propeller was touching bottom for
long periods, and there is no sound more harrowing
than the grating of a grounding propeller; it comes up
through your feet from the quivering hull and rings a
danger signal in your brain far louder than the roar of
the exhaust, the cries of the sounders, or the snarling
of the rapids.

Glacier water is an opaque, milky-looking fluid, that
hides every inequality of the bottom, and you must
depend on your eyes to find the signs that denote a
deep channel. These signs consist of minute differences
in the formation of the surface waves, and they can
only be learned by experience. When you see the
surface "boiling," you know that you have at least
three feet, and as the boils increase in size you know
that the water is deepening.

When you see rough water sliding into large, oily

eddies you know that the water is running over a shoal
into a deep channel.   The signs are many and the
differences are often so minute as to make a description
misleading.   The best training for river-work is "tracking," as then you are forced to look for shallow water
to wade in, and when a bath in ice-water is the result
of a mistake, a man is inclined to study the current
with fervid interest.   Eventually you will be able to
approximate closely the condition of the bottom by
"the look o' the water."

Shoal water is always dangerous, while cañon navigation, provided you have a fast boat, is fun in comparison.
The terrific force of the water, however, makes careful
steering imperative.   There were times in the Chulitna
cañon, while we were taking the big swells, that the
water swept across our forward deck, but these struggles
with white water between grim cañon walls are the
pleasantest part of northern motor-boating, and the
memories of the breathless moments when you hung
poised in the suck of the rollers will remain with you for
years.

There is another side of river navigation that embod-
ies all the excitement and danger without the dramatic
setting of the cañon work.   On all the northern rivers
you will encounter long straight chutes of the current
that rush past "cut banks" covered with dense timber.
The current in these places is often almost irresistible
and the only method of making appreciable progress
is by hugging the banks.   As all the soil in the bottom
lands is composed of fine silt, these banks are continually caving in, and as the banks melt away the forest
trees come thundering down, throwing up great spouts
of spray as they strike the rushing water.   On the day
that we left Talkeetna, a large cottonwood tree fell as

the banks caved in and just missed the *Explorer's* stern.

Equally dangerous are the submerged snags, which, luckily, can be traced by the waves and whirlpools that mark their hiding-places.

Navigating swift water among the snags and "sweepers" requires the greatest mental concentration, and your course is a constant series of problems in distances, pressures, and speeds. You may be barely holding your own in the racing stream with a half-submerged snag bellowing six feet astern of your propeller, a sweeper hanging over you, whose lower branches had to be chopped off to make a passageway for the boat, and a log jam ahead around whose jagged edges the current is torn to foam. At these times the helmsman cannot take his eyes, even for a fraction of a second, from the current ahead, as a failure to "meet" an over-boil of the current would mean disaster. He must depend on his crew for intelligence concerning the progress of the boat. Standing with your eyes glued on the water while your companions cry, "She's holding her own! She's holding her own! She's going back a little! Now, she's going ahead!" is exciting enough to make your hair turn grey.

We passed a point on the Chulitna where the water shot between two points with terrific speed. I tried twice, by dropping astern and then hitting the current full speed, to climb the swift water. On my second failure I saw that the water above some big snags had overflowed among a grove of small cottonwood trees, and on the third attempt I drove the *Explorer* through the cottonwoods on the edge of the swift water. Our propeller was beating an insane tattoo on the saplings, and left a trail of match-wood behind, but we got through.

In another rapid our progress was arrested by a large spruce sweeper. Just above the sweeper was an eddy that was the key to the successful navigation of the rapid. By forcing our boat to full speed we could just beat the current, and La Voy threw the bight of a line around the tree trunk. With our engine still going to take some of the pressure from the straining line we hung to our precarious anchorage while La Voy chopped through our evergreen obstruction. When the tree fell it was sucked under instantly by the rushing water and we had a clear road to our coveted eddy.

As the reader will understand, this kind of work is a great strain on the best of boats or engines, and where chances such as these are taken accidents are sure to result. It was for this reason that I took so many extra engine parts and propellers, and we made good use of them before we said good-by to the rushing waters of the Chulitna.

After we had crossed the large flats above the Chulitna cañon, we kept to the left of the valley and watched for the mouth of the Tokositna. As we advanced the great spires of the Tokosha Mountains broke through the clouds, and my thoughts flew back to the day in 1906 when we crouched in our mountain tent above the Tokositna glacier and gave the range its name. The river that we were now looking for—the Tokositna—was the river after which we had named the range.

The Chulitna River now swung to the north-east, following the foothills of the Alaskan Range, and at the bend we caught our first glimpse of the great glacier that drains Mount McKinley's southern ramparts, and then a streak of white water showed where the

Tokositna came rushing into the Chulitna. With a feeling of exultation we headed the *Explorer* up "the river that comes from the land where there are no trees," and an hour later we had come to the end of our long water journey.

There were old choppings on the bank where we landed and on going ashore to prospect for a camping place we found a well-constructed but tiny cabin. In all probability it was built by Dokkin, the prospector, who accompanied Dr. Cook and Ed. Barrill to this point and remained after their departure to trap and prospect for gold. It was a good camp-site, for a dry bar just above a cut bank gave us both deep and shoal water for docking or hauling out the *Explorer*, and a grove of spruce trees furnished us with firewood and boughs.

The excitement of our journey up the Chulitna had driven all thought of the Mazama expedition from our minds. But as the navigation became easier, I studied the banks carefully for "tracking" signs, and as I was experienced in this form of travel the results told me that no one had ascended the river before us. With the knowledge that we had passed our rivals we were filled with delight, but there was no personal feeling in our happiness; it was merely the gratification of having won a race, although our success following the prognostications to the contrary from the river-men gave me a certain satisfaction. The race, however, was only begun for the Mazamas were also headed towards the ice-crowned summit of McKinley, and our friendly rivalry was not yet over, although we had won the first heat. Had it not been for this fact, I would have gladly run the *Explorer* downstream and given Mr. Rusk and his men a helping hand.

OUR "PACK TRAIN" LEAVING "CAMP 2." FROM LEFT TO RIGHT: ATEN,
TUCKER, PARKER, CUNTZ, LA VOY, AND GRASSI.

Photo by Belmore Browne.

THE TERMINAL MORAINE OF THE "BIG GLACIER." TOKOSHA MOUNTAINS IN
DISTANCE.

Photo by Belmore Browne.

CHAPTER IX

THE ADVANCE UP THE BIG GLACIER

Parkersburgh—Reconnaissance trips—Trail chopping—Packing—
Ascending the glacier—We travel at night—We send back for more
food—Gas poisoning.

A S the little cabin that Dokkin had built on the
banks of the Tokositna River was to be our home
during the summer, a description of its position in
relation to Mount McKinley will not be amiss. Our
camp was situated thirty-seven and a half miles from
Mount McKinley. The country between it and the
mountains was a piedmont gravel bed that extended
along the base of the Alaskan Range. This strip of
lowland was covered with typical Alaskan forest
growth except where the treacherous muskegs lay,
and at frequent intervals glacier- and snow-water
streams rushed down to the Tokositna. A few miles
away in an air line rose the terminal moraine of the
great glacier that was to be our roadway to the big
mountain. The moraine was covered with rock and
soil for a long distance back from the glacier's tongue
and on this precarious foothold groves of spruce and
tangled jungles of alders grew. The ice in reality
continued much farther than one would suppose as the
carpet of forest growth hid the dividing line. On one
of my reconnaissance trips I was forcing my way

through the masses of undergrowth and moraine débris well down toward the valley floor, when, to my surprise, I came upon a wall of solid ice one hundred feet high that had forced its way upward through the earth.

From the tongue of the glacier rushed a quantity of glacier-streams, and as the weather grew warmer the overflow of water from the huge masses of ice filled the streams until they were well-nigh impassable. The great glacier itself was shrouded in mystery. Dr. Cook had named it the Ruth glacier but the name had not "taken" and to this day the great ice-river stands nameless on the Government maps. There is a lot of sentimental foolishness connected with the naming of geographical features, and it is strange to note how little taste or forethought is shown by the average man when it comes to naming national monuments. These great mountains, rivers, and glaciers are firstly the property of all the people, and secondly, as they form important geographical monuments or dividing lines, they should when possible be given historical or descriptive names. The Board of Geographical Names in Washington was organised with this point in view. In the use of proper names lies the principal source of trouble, for a large number of the names found on the map are the names of people who are of little interest to the general public. In the use of proper names those of famous or illustrious men or women only should be used, and wherever possible a name that carries an historical significance. An excellent illustration of a geographical monument, bearing an illustrious and at the same time an historical name, is the Malaspena glacier. On hearing the name for the first time the traveller will inquire into its origin. And in the ensuing description he not only hears for the first time of the exploring feats of this early navigator, but obtains, as well, a glimpse into the early history of this portion of the Alaskan coast. This name, therefore, serves two purposes: it is a monument to a brave man, and it reminds us of the early history of that bleak coast. The name of the Susitna River will serve as an example of a descriptive name that is historical as well; Susitna means in the language of the Susitna Indians, "the river of sand" or "the sandy river." No name could be chosen that better describes the natural peculiarities of this great stream, and at the same time it will perpetuate through centuries to come, not only the name of one of the Alaskan tribes, but a sentence from their language as well. No one can belittle the importance of geographical names after giving the matter due thought, for America is filled with "horrible examples" of this thoughtless manner of conferring names; the highest and most beautiful snow-clad mountain in the United States is known by the misspelled name of an Englishman who never saw the peak and whose only important historical connection with our country was as an enemy.

With this human weakness in view Professor Parker and I strove to refrain from complicating an already complicated state of affairs by abstaining as far as possible from conferring personal names that might or might not remain, and in our explorations in the Mount McKinley region we spoke of the natural landmarks by such titles as their forms suggested, or by numbers in the order in which they occurred. The large glacier which we followed to Mount McKinley we spoke of as the "big glacier," and in view of the fact that the United States Government has conferred no name upon it, I will still speak of it as the "big glacier" for purposes of identification.

Our first duty on the completion of our water journey was to dry-dock the *Explorer*, so that Thompson, who was to remain at the base camp, could make such slight repairs as were necessary. This feat was easily accomplished with the aid of rollers and a block and tackle.

With the *Explorer* in a safe place we could turn our thoughts towards the important work, which was the location and construction of a good trail to the top of the big glacier. This duty necessitated a thorough knowledge of the country and I therefore divided our party into three units of two men to explore separate routes to the ice.

This reconnaissance constituted our first real wilderness day, and as an example of the importance of physical training it is worthy of a few remarks.

The day's work consisted in travelling through brush, soft snow, swamps, and glacier streams for about ten hours. With the exception of one or two men who put a biscuit in their pockets we took no food with us. The day's work was in no way difficult, for we carried no loads; our condition from *the civilised standpoint* was splendid; we were well-fed, sun-browned, and fairly hard—and yet we all came into camp *thoroughly tired out*. Two months later, after our adventures on Mount McKinley's icy flanks, we came down through the same stretch of country. The snow however had melted, leaving dense thickets through which we had to chop our way; the mosquitoes hung in clouds; and four of us, Grassi, La Voy, Tucker, and I, were carrying packs running from 95 to 120 pounds. From the civilised standpoint *we were not well-fed* and we did not

look well—our eyes and cheeks were sunken and our
bodies were worn down to bone and sinew; and yet we
came into camp as fresh and happy as children, and
after a bite to eat and a smoke we could have gone
on cheerfully.

On the following day we followed out our best reconnaissance line and chopped out a good trail to timber
line. This brought us out on the bare morainal hills
that lie on the northern side of the big glacier, and as we
turned campward we could see an easy approach to the
back of the great ice-river. We had reached our
base camp, which we had named Parkersburgh, in
Professor Parker's honour, on the 31st of May, and on
June 5th everything was in working order and we had
advanced 625 pounds of mountain duffle to camp 2.
The distance separating our camps as we moved forward always depended on the character of the country.
We usually counted on advancing two loads per man
per day; one in the morning and one in the afternoon.

We increased the weight of our packs as our bodies
grew accustomed to the toil, and on June 6th we
carried seventy-pound loads comfortably. In packing
we worked systematically and each man of the packing
squad knew just about what his share amounted to.
Grassi, La Voy, Tucker, and I carried the bulk of our
equipment, although both Professor Parker and Professor Cuntz gave us much appreciated aid.

Packing, when a man carries all he can stagger under,
is one of the most exhausting occupations in the world.
Only men of sound build and physical courage ever
succeed in becoming expert weight-carriers. You can
never tell from a man's looks how much he can shoulder,
although short, compactly built men are usually the
strongest. Men of over six feet in height are seldom

able to carry heavy loads, and the best packers usually stand between five feet five inches and five feet ten inches.

Our packing squad was particularly well fitted for this arduous toil. Valdemar Grassi had held the strength test of Columbia University to within a short time prior to his joining our expedition. He was the tallest man in our party, standing close to six feet, and he weighed, in condition, about 176 pounds. He was used to the active forms of outdoor sport, but he had not as yet had any experience in the gruelling labours of a wilderness life. He learned quickly and carried heavy loads.

Herman L. Tucker was inured to the hardships of a life in the open. He was stockily built, standing about five feet ten inches in his shoe-packs. The muscular development of his lower limbs was unusual, and he carried heavy weights with ease and rapidity.

Merl La Voy had spent his whole life in the open, and with one or two exceptions he was the best packer that I have ever travelled with. He stood about five feet ten inches and strangely enough his body showed only normal physical development, although he was capable of far more physical hardship than the average frontiersman.

I was the smallest member of the packing squad, standing five feet six inches and weighing about 145 pounds when in training.

The task that confronted us was a journey of thirty-seven and a half miles in an air line over glacial ice and snow. But as we travelled the distance was much farther. Our outfit at the beginning of our journey weighed about 1200 pounds.

In carrying our loads we used an adaptation of the

Russian-Aleute pack-strap of my own make. It was composed of padded canvas, and when it was adjusted over the shoulders, the principal weight came on the chest strap. There was no possibility of chafing, and the harness was light and easily adjusted. Whenever heavy loads are carried the "tump-line" or forehead strap is a necessity, as a heavy weight can be borne on the head and neck.

There are many pack-bags or sacks on the market but they are only useful for ordinary camping trips. In really serious packing the loads carried are so heavy and of such bulk that a pack-bag of a restricted shape is useless. Our personal belongings were stowed in waterproof bags and in addition each man carried a waterproof pack cover.

The bulk of our weight was in pemmican and alcohol, and the cans were packed in wooden boxes. Until our backs got hardened to the toil, they were raw from the constant contact with the hard wood. But bearing pain with stoicism must be one of a packer's attributes, and for this reason good packers are made—not born. Our alcohol was denatured and undrinkable, and on one occasion one of our party was heard to say that he wished it was "good-natured." Our pemmican was the usual kind, consisting of pulverised raw meat mixed with sugar, raisins, currants, and tallow.

We drank nothing but tea while we were on the ice. Coffee is rarely used in the wilderness.

Our work progressed steadily until on the 6th of June we had our first accident. On the way home from camp 2 I slipped on a rotten log and sprained my ankle so badly that La Voy, Grassi, and Tucker carried me to camp. I kept my ankle in glacier water and although the swelling did not disappear for six months I was soon able to travel and carry loads of eighty pounds. By the 9th of June we had advanced all our equipment to camp 3, and a part of it to camp 4, which was situated on the edge of the big glacier.

Since leaving Beluga we had been keeping pace with the vanishing snow; but in the shadow of the Alaskan Range it was still winter and we were forced to use our long Susitna snowshoes between camps 3 and 4. Back-packing in soft snow is hard work, but the snow below timber line was really an advantage, for it covered the dense thickets of alder and willow.

On June 11th we had our last wood-fire. We had packed 1200 pounds of mountain duffel to the back of the glacier and from there on we were to travel through Arctic surroundings. The conditions were the same as those that prevail in the lowlands in the early spring when travelling is attempted only in extreme cases. During the day the snow turned to wet slush that clung to our snowshoes until they dragged like leaden weights. Our packs averaged seventy pounds at this time but we carried more as our muscles hardened.

The glacier was rough and cut up into innumerable hollows, lakes, and sharp ridges, and under either the blazing sun or the weird blue light of the northern night the contours blended into flat masses. We all began to suffer from snow-blindness, and finding a good trail under such conditions was largely a matter of chance. We were comforted somewhat, however, by the knowledge that the going would be better when we reached the hard-packed mountain snow, and a glimpse now and then of Mount McKinley, as it shook off its mantle of clouds, and towered clean cut against the northern sky, would encourage us to greater efforts. After one experience with packs under the hot sun we rested

FORDING THE LAST STREAM BEFORE TAKING TO THE ICE.
Photo by H. C. Parker.

TUCKER AND THE AUTHOR PACKING AT "GLACIER POINT," SHOWING OUR
METHOD OF CARRYING LOADS.
Photo by H. C. Parker.

The benefits [handwritten annotation]

during the heat of the day and travelled at night. The
change benefited us in two ways; it saved our eyes,
and the snow grew firm from the frost.

Camp 5 was situated on the northern edge of the
glacier. A high range of mountains formed the glacier's
northern wall, while directly opposite rose the beautiful
Tokosha Mountains that ended in the great ridge on
which Professor Parker and I had camped in 1906. I
climbed the mountain behind our camp and in addition
to a good view of the glacier found a large brown bear
who objected to my society and left me to the enjoyment
of the magnificent scene. As the travelling conditions
seemed to be growing worse our thoughts turned to an
old sled that we had found beside the cabin at Parkersburgh and in the hope that it would aid us in advancing
our supplies, Professor Cuntz and Aten returned for it.

Even under the weight of a heavy pack the night
travel had a great fascination for me. We would move
slowly along across the great sombre snow-fields. The
silence was absolute and the slow, rhythmic crunching
of our snowshoes seemed but to accentuate the quiet.
I do not remember ever having seen skies of greater
beauty; they were green, or claret, or golden, and under
this light the grey snows seem to spring into life, and
change to every shade of blue and purple. After we
had dropped our precious loads we would trot back to
camp with the long rolling snowshoe gait, and trudge
slowly away under a second heavy load. The work was
monotonous but we never knew monotony for always
the great saw-tooth ranges that guarded McKinley
beckoned us on.

Professor Cuntz and Aten rejoined us at camp 6
with the sled. But to our disgust the temperature
refused to drop as night came on and we were unable

to use it as the snow was too soft. They also brought
us the news that the Mazama expedition had reached
the Tokositna.

On the night of June 15th it rained, and after breaking a long trail to the top of a *serac* or ice fall, we were
forced to give up and lie shivering in our damp bags,
for the trail did not freeze and we could not pull the sled
over it. When daylight came we arose and by a combination of back-packing and sled-work we advanced
our camp to the face of the serac. The snow was wet
and our exertions terrific. At 2 A.M., we crawled
exhausted into our bags and slept until morning. The
scenes through which we were moving were of Arctic
desolation; great green blocks of ice rose high above
our camp and stupendous ice-covered mountains
surrounded us. In addition to Mount McKinley we
could see Mount Foraker—17,000 feet, which is called
Mrs. McKinley by the Indians; and Mount Hunter,
14,960 feet.

Mount Hunter, as it is called on the United States
Geological map, is the same mountain that Dr. Cook
and I saw and spoke of as little McKinley when we
spent the night on the peak west of the Tokositna
glacier in 1906. The name Mount Hunter is unknown
to the Alaskans and in 1910 it was called Mount
Roosevelt by the prospectors of the Susitna watershed.
We were now about opposite our last ridge camp of
1906, and strangely enough the views of the glacier
that I had obtained at that time were a benefit now,
although four years had passed, for the seracs ahead of
us cut off all view of our route. The weather too
combined with the glacier to hold us back, and before
we reached our eighth camp, we had been held by
several severe snow and wind storms.

I had been studying the food question from day to day, and despite our original 1200-pound outfit, I began to realise that if we intended to climb Mount McKinley we would have to conserve our food. We were averaging about a mile a day in advancing our camps, as we had to make so many relays. Something radical had to be done, so we sent back Grassi, Aten, and La Voy, with instructions to get more food. We would in this way be using less mountain food, and would eliminate the useless drain on our commissary due to the constant delays in our reconnaissance work.

Camp 8 was at the top of the first system of seracs and from this point we could get a good view of the glacier ahead. On account of a heavy snow-storm we only advanced a half march from this camp and Professors Parker and Cuntz, after carrying forward their own belongings, decided to spend the night, so we pitched a tent for them before returning and called the new camp "camp 8B." The following morning dawned beautifully clear, and we started early with heavy packs for camp 8B. There had been a snow-storm during the night and even our fresh trail was smoothly covered by the white mantle. It was with the greatest surprise, therefore, that as I approached the tent, I saw a fresh deep-ploughed trail leading from the tent to the distant mountains. But my surprise was even greater as I drew near and noticed that the fresh trail did not lead from the tent. Turning off to examine it, I found the explanation. The trail had been made by a great brown bear!

Professors Parker and Cuntz were still sleeping and as I wished them good-morning, I laughingly asked them if they knew that they had had a visitor during the night, and Professor Parker answered: "Why, yes; I heard one of the boys moving about, and asked him to come in and get warm, but he went away without answering me." When he and Professor Cuntz saw the kind of visitor they had invited into the tent they were glad indeed that their invitation had not been accepted!

It was at this camp that we divided the party and sent the men to base camp for more food. In many letters that I have received from sympathisers with Dr. Cook, I have been told by these gentlemen (that have never back-packed on a glacier) that there was no reason why Dr. Cook could not have climbed Mount McKinley and returned to the Tokositna River with a forty-pound pack. If the reader will compare with the map the numbers of days that we and the Mazama party spent in following the big glacier, they will understand, I am sure, that no rules of travel can be applied to ice work. One little serac, not indicated on any map, may block the advance of the most determined party; one small crevasse may detain a party for hours; or one mountain storm hold the travellers storm-bound for days. On the first night after the division of our party we encountered a large crevasse that was filled with running water. At last Herman Tucker found a point where a huge glacial erratic had bridged the chasm and we were able to cross in ease and safety. Fearing that more streams would intervene and cause us trouble, we headed once more for the edge of the glacier, and pitched our ninth camp on the snow-covered moraine. At camp 9 we underwent one of the most unusual and unpleasant experiences that it has been my ill fortune to be subjected to. On the night of June 18th it began to sleet and blow. Cold followed, the temperature dropped below freezing,

and the storm increased to a blizzard. We lay helpless in our sleeping-bags, listening to the lashing of the
wind and snow on our tent. On the next day the storm
continued. On several occasions we had difficulty in
lighting our alcohol stoves, but we reasoned that the
frozen tent was air tight and after enlarging the aperture in the door the stove burnt well. We all felt
badly during the afternoon, but we attributed our
troubles to lack of exercise. The glaciers and mountains
presented a desolate sight through the wind-driven
clouds of snow and mist. About 8 P.M. I began to feel
so weak that I determined to go outside, storm or no
storm. I had been conscious for a long time of an
unpleasant feeling of depression. Later my mind was
filled with queer illusions. Finally I staggered to my
feet and went outdoors. As the cold air filled my lungs
a feeling of relief came over me and then my mind was
stunned as if some one had struck me on the head with
a club. I remember sinking to my knees although I
fought to stand upright. I saw, as in a dream, Professor Parker come out of the tent, stand for an instant,
and then fall headlong in the snow, and lie there motionless. Without surprise I heard my own voice, a long
way off, calling to Tucker and then—nothing. How
long the unconscious spell lasted I do not know but I
was brought to by hearing Professor Cuntz calling my
name. I tried to answer but at first no sound came,
although eventually I succeeded in making myself
heard.

He could not find me at first as I had slid down the
moraine and under a great granite boulder, but when
he came to me he brought a steaming cup of hot tea.
After the welcome drink I crawled to the top of the
moraine, and saw both Professor Parker and Tucker

lying in the snow. But with the help of Professor Cuntz's tea they too soon revived and we gathered in a miserable group beside the granite boulder. We were attacked by nausea and vomiting, and later by violent spasms of shivering. Later we returned to the tent and drank more tea, and after a good sleep we seemed none the worse for our adventure. The cause of our unpleasant experience was the use of alcohol stoves in a small tent where the oxygen had already been exhausted by our breathing; carbon monoxide gas resulted and we were lucky to recover as easily as we did. We attribute Professor Cuntz's immunity to the fact that he was sitting upright, working on his topographical notes, during the greater part of the day and as his head was above the small aperture in the door he received some fresh air. We profited by the experience and thereafter when we were storm-bound we thoroughly ventilated the tent at frequent intervals.

CHAPTER X

THE END OF THE POLAR CONTROVERSY

*We arrive at Glacier Point—We duplicate Dr. Cook's pictures—
We find the peak shown in his "summit picture"—We explore Glacier
No. 2—We find the fake peak.*

FROM the summit of the moraine where camp 9 was
situated, we were able for the first time to see the
head of the lower portion of the big glacier. The first
tributary glacier entered from the south-west side.
This was the glacier that I had chosen as the *probable*
site of Dr. Cook's Mount McKinley photographs, and
had indicated as such in a sketch which was copied
and published by the *Metropolitan Magazine.* But
on closer scrutiny the mountains did not resemble
Dr. Cook's photographs as they were covered with
what appeared to be perpetual fields of deep snow.
The second tributary glacier joined the big glacier
from the north, and here we saw at once a striking
resemblance to the type of mountains shown in Dr.
Cook's photographs, reproductions of which I carried
with me. We were also influenced to some degree by
the map of this glacier shown in Edward Barrill's af-
fidavit, in which he shows that Dr. Cook's photographs
were taken on this glacier which we called "glacier 2."

But we realised that Barrill's testimony could not be
believed by many people as he had confessed to having

made misrepresentations concerning his Mount Mc-
Kinley climb. We, therefore, determined to depend
on our own investigation and on Dr. Cook's photographs
alone in our search for evidence.

Between these two tributary glaciers stood what we
called at our first glance "the great gorge." The
great gorge was formed by two lines of magnificent
peaks that rose in jagged lines above grim walls.
Through this aperture poured the main stream of the
big glacier, and under the heavy cloud banks we could
see the crushed chaotic seracs formed by the terrific
pressure of the ice against the cliffs.

The point of land between the great gorge and
glacier 2 we recognised from Dr. Cook's and Ed.
Barrill's description as the point on which they camped,
and we spoke of it as "Glacier Point." Between camp
9 and Glacier Point the glacier ice had formed a great
eddy. Large snow-covered hills of crushed rock had
been forced up by the pressure of the ice and between
lay deep hollows, some of which were filled with water
later in the season. Over this mass of glacial débris lay
a treacherous covering of soft snow. Herman Tucker
and I were carrying eighty-pound packs and in sliding
down and climbing up these steep hills we had many a
bad fall. More than once one of our party would break
through into the holes between the boulders, and become so hopelessly tangled with pack and snowshoes
that he needed assistance to get out. On one of the snow
slopes that swept down from the high peaks we saw a
big brown bear, possibly our visitor of camp 8B.

After an exhausting day's work we reached Glacier
Point. Our camp was pitched in a deep morainal
hollow, and we looked across the void to dim blue ice
walls capped by the serac of glacier 2.

"GLACIER NO. 2."

THE GLACIER ON WHICH DR. COOK TOOK THE FAKE PICTURES OF MOUNT
McKINLEY. THE SHORT ARROW INDICATES THE FAKE PEAK. THE LONG
ARROW INDICATES THE CLIFF SHOWN OPPOSITE PAGE 239 IN DR.
COOK'S BOOK. CALLED "McKINLEY CLIFF" BY THE 1910 EXPE-
DITION. THIS IS A DUPLICATE OF THE PICTURE OPPOSITE
PAGE 197 OF DR. COOK'S BOOK.

Photo by H. C. Parker.

"McKINLEY CLIFF" ON LEFT. "GLACIER NO. 2" IN FOREGROUND. "GLACIER
POINT" ON RIGHT. THE BIG GLACIER IN DISTANCE. McKINLEY CLIFF RISES
ABOUT 300 FEET ABOVE THE GLACIER, AND IS SITUATED 20 MILES SOUTH
OF MOUNT McKINLEY. THIS SAME VIEW IS PRINTED OPPOSITE
PAGE 239 OF DR. COOK'S BOOK AND IS LABELLED, "SCENE OF
GLACIERS, PEAKS, AND CLIFFS." "SHOULDER OF MOUNT
McKINLEY, A CLIFF OF 8000 FEET." RUTH GLACIER, THE
FREIGHT CARRIER OF THE CLOUD WORLD. THE GREAT
WHITE WAY, WHERE THE POLAR FROSTS MET
THE PACIFIC DRIFT OF THE TROPICAL DEWS."

Photo by Merl La Voy.

We intended to explore glacier 2 on the following day but it was stormy, so we returned to camp 9. In returning we held to the centre of the big glacier and found excellent travelling, and escaped the rough surface of the moraine; we therefore packed all our belongings from camp 9 to the centre of the glacier in order that we might profit by our new route. After forming the depot we returned to camp 8B for a third relay. We also needed "babiche" with which to mend our snowshoes, and we took this opportunity of leaving a letter for our companions, telling them which route to follow, as they had been gone a week, and we were beginning to get worried. I was attacked by snow-blindness while we were "filling" our snowshoes and we were forced to remain at camp 8B that night. We had left a mountain tent standing at this relay station and we found that it was necessary to move it as the exposed surface of the snow melted away so quickly that it left the tent standing on a high snow pedestal that would have collapsed eventually.

We carried heavy packs to camp 9 and Tucker and I exchanged them for our regular seventy-five pound relay loads and pushed through to Glacier Point. Our idea was to bring up at least a month's outfit in food and alcohol, and then we would be free to advance up the great gorge to Mount McKinley. The long stretch of glacier over which we did our relaying was as lonely and silent an expanse of country as I have ever tramped through. At night the fog would cling to the mountains so that from our dim trail you could see nothing but the blue snow melting away into the mist. After several hours of packing through this cold, blue solitude, the monotony would become almost unbearable. I remember trying all sorts of things to

keep my mind occupied. Probably the most successful
expedient was reciting poetry, in time to the clicking
of your snowshoes, for the faster you recited the faster
you travelled. The monotony of this kind of work
seems to have a hypnotic effect on the traveller. I
remember one night when Professor Cuntz fell into a
deep sleep during the short rests we made at half-hour
intervals. Talking, or yelling, did not have any effect
and I was forced to shake him into consciousness.

Several brown bears had wintered among these
great expanses of ice and snow, and we found their
tracks leading downward towards the lowlands.

On June 27th we intended to explore Glacier 2, but
the weather was cloudy and we devoted our energy
instead to moving our camp out of the hollow. We
established our twelfth camp on the edge of the great
gorge, making a rise of four hundred feet in altitude.
We were now worrying constantly about our companions, as they were several days overdue and we
feared that an accident had occurred.

We had packed to the edge of the great gorge:

> 19 6-lb. cans of pemmican
> 1¾ cases of hardtack
> 2 lbs. of Lipton tea
> 35 lbs. of Erbswurst
> 35 lbs. sugar
> 70 cups beef tea
> 22 lbs. raisins
> 12 gals. of alcohol.

In addition we had two mountain tents complete,
alcohol stoves, pots, ice axes, mountain rope, ice-
creepers, cameras, and a large supply of films, snowshoes, etc. This amounted to more than twice as.

much food, per man, as Dr. Cook and Ed. Barrill had
when they started from the Tokositna River, and we
were already half-way to Mount McKinley. Dr. Cook
said that he and Barrill carried forty pounds, and Barrill
told me that they carried less, as Dr. Cook's pack was
appreciably lighter than his. But accepting Dr.
Cook's figures we can allow them an outfit of eighty
pounds. An allowance of fifty pounds for food out of
the original eighty would be liberal, but we must
remember that out of this fifty pounds we must
subtract at least ten pounds for fuel. This would
allow them twenty pounds of food per man, at the
most, and the weight of cans, sacks, cooking utensils,
and a stove would reduce it still more.

On June 28th we made an early start to explore
glacier 2. But before going into the details of our
method of tracing Dr. Cook, a few words are necessary
to explain to the reader the photographic and topographical mistakes, or blunders rather, that Dr. Cook
had made. When his book, *The Top of Our Continent,*
was published, we found that it contained conclusive
proof that he had not ascended Mount McKinley.

Opposite page 227 is a photograph purporting to be
"The Summit of Mount McKinley, the highest mountain of North America, altitude 20,390 feet."

The camera that took this photograph was, as any
experienced mountain photographer can tell at a
glance, *pointing upward,* and yet in the right-hand
lower sky-line of this picture appears the dim outline
of a second *rock-capped peak,* which any mountaineer
would recognise as a mountain as high, or higher than
the rock called the summit of Mount McKinley.

Now as every sign of rock ceases a thousand feet
below Mount McKinley's summit, this photograph in

itself constituted absolute disproof of Dr. Cook's story, and yet he was careless enough to print a second photograph which shows this telltale "lower right-hand sky-line peak" in its relation to the surrounding mountains, *and Glacier Point!* Comparison showed that both of the pictures were taken from nearly the same point. Our knowledge of the country, therefore, enabled us to locate Dr. Cook's fake peak before leaving New York, and later events showed that we were only about one hundred yards out of the way in our reckoning.

It was four years after Dr. Cook's visit that Professor Parker, Cuntz, Tucker, and I arrived at Glacier Point.

Our food statistics were all that was necessary to tell us that we were close to the scene of Dr. Cook's mountaineering operations. Glacier No. 1 was, as I have before stated, eliminated from our explorations as there were no peaks there that resembled Dr. Cook's photographs. The perpendicular walls of the great gorge were ample evidence that he could not have made the pictures there. This left only the northern, or northeastern, amphitheatre glacier, or glacier No. 2, as the locality in which he could have taken his photographs.

With our eyes on this glacier, the great gorge, and the great peaks that rose above the gorge, we began to study Dr. Cook's pictures. We did not have long to wait, for in Dr. Cook's illustration which is published opposite page 239 in his book, was the answer to all our questions. This photograph showed the great peaks above the gorge including the second or telltale peak, the main serac below the great gorge, Glacier Point, and glacier No. 2 in the foreground. It was on June 22d that we reached Glacier Point and as we pitched our tent in the "morainal hollow" the view that we saw was the same as that shown in Dr. Cook's photograph opposite page 197, and we could tell by referring to this picture that he had taken the photograph from a knoll about three hundred feet above us.

Our mountain detective work was based on the fact that no man can lie topographically. In all the mountain ranges of the world there are not two hillocks exactly alike. We knew that if we could find one of the peaks shown in his photographs we could trace him peak by peak and snow-field by snow-field, to within a foot of the spot where he exposed his negatives. And now, without going out of our way, we had found the peaks he had photographed, but we had found as well from the photograph opposite page 239 that at the time that he took that picture he was not going towards Mount McKinley but that he was high up among the peaks at the head of glacier No. 2—*at least a day's travel out of his course!*

There was only one explanation for this fact and that was that close to where this photo was taken we would find the fake peak! From Glacier Point we could see several high mountains that looked as if they might prove to be the one we were looking for, and a cliff which stood above a saddle had a familiar look to us. The distance however was too great for a definite decision and we decided therefore to make a reconnaissance.

As we climbed the serac on glacier No. 2 we began to leave Glacier Point well below us, and by the time that we reached the upper snow-fields we had made two important discoveries. The first was that as we increased our altitude, peak No. 2 was not hidden by the intervening summits of Glacier Point.

This proved to us that if peak No. 2 was, as we believed, the same peak shown in the right-hand lower sky-line of Dr. Cook's fake photograph of Mount McKinley, we were travelling in the right direction to reach the spot from which he made his exposure. The second discovery was the confirmation of our suspicions that the cliff we had seen from Glacier Point was the same cliff shown on the left side of the photograph opposite page 239. The scent was growing warm.

There was one fact that puzzled us. We had been under the impression that the peak Dr. Cook climbed and photographed was a moderately high peak, and yet as we advanced we could see no peaks worthy of the name in the vicinity of the cliff. For we had decided that this cliff must be close to the fake peak.

It required but a short advance, however, to relieve our minds on this point, for turning to Dr. Cook's picture of the cliff with peaks 1 and 2 showing in the distance, we read: "Scene of Glaciers, Peaks, and Cliffs—shoulder of Mount McKinley, a cliff of 8000 feet. Ruth Glacier, the freight carrier of the cloud world. The Great White Way where the polar frosts meet the Pacific drift of the tropical dews."

Just what Dr. Cook intended by a "a cliff of 8000 feet" we can only surmise, but the top of the cliff actually rose about 300 feet above the glacier, and its altitude was only 5300 feet above sea-level! After this discovery we no longer expected to find that the Doctor had actually climbed a high peak—climbing with printer's ink was far easier. We had now reached the base of the saddle that led on its southern end to the cliff. We called a halt for luncheon, and as we ate our hardtack and pemmican we studied the country about us. Looking back at the cliff I was struck by a remarkable profile of William McKinley. The likeness was so perfect that on asking one of my companions what the outline of the cliff suggested to him, he replied without the slightest hesitation, "William McKinley." For purposes of identification, therefore, we named it McKinley cliff.

A few minutes later we began the ascent of the snow saddle on the way to the snow cornice on top of McKinley cliff. Professor Parker had started a few minutes before, and, as we neared the top, we saw him breaking down a small snow cornice that led to a small rock outcrop near the top of the saddle.

This cornice led in the direction of the summit of McKinley cliff, and as we turned to follow the saddle we heard Professor Parker shout, "We've got it!" An instant later as the cornice came into line with the rock we saw that it was true—the little outcrop of rock below the saddle was the rock peak of Dr. Cook's book, under which he wrote, "The Top of our Continent —the Summit of Mount McKinley; the highest mountain of North America—Altitude 20,390 feet."

While we stood there lost in thought of the dramatic side of our discovery, Professor Parker walked to the top of the rock at the point where Barrill had posed when Dr. Cook exposed the negative. His figure completed the picture. Then we gathered around the photograph that Dr. Cook had taken and traced the contours of the rock by its cracks and shoulders. As our eyes reached the right-hand sky-line there stood peak No. 2—the rock-ribbed peak on which we had based our denial of Dr. Cook's claim, and by which we had traced his footsteps through the wilderness of rock and ice. After taking a few photographs we sat down on the rocks in the warm sun. Avalanches were booming and thundering among the mountains, and the view of Mount McKinley, twenty miles away, across the blazing whiteness of the glacier far below, and up above the lines of grim knife-hacked ridges, was a picture of such sublime beauty that our powers of appreciation seemed benumbed.

Away and away to the south-eastward through the dim blue summer haze shone the snows of the inland plateaus that stretched from the Talkeetna Mountains to the end of the eastern horizon. On the north-east the horizon was broken by the tangled ice-armoured peaks of the Alaskan Range. Not a peak there was named and little did I think as I turned away that in two years to come we would be fighting the winter storms and unravelling the mysteries of that ice-bound wilderness. And yet, with all their grimness, the views held a hint of tender beauty, and the lowlands called to us with their promise of green meadows and hunting grounds as yet untouched by man.

The peaks about us were remarkable for their broken character; I have never seen peaks so seamed and disintegrated by the forces of nature. Rock pinnacles rose about us that looked as if a breath of wind would send them crashing and rumbling to the glaciers far below.

We rolled some big boulders over the cliffs and watched them leaping and spinning down, down, among the cliffs until they crashed with a great thudding splash into the snow-fields far below, and from the snow-fields in turn snaky snow-slides would slither down to the lower glaciers. Sliding snow has a nasty look and sound—there is something sinister about it—like the noise of a snake in dry grass.

The "fake peak" was covered with far more snow than it was at the time of Dr. Cook's visit. His pho-

THE AUTHOR PHOTOGRAPHING THE FAKE PEAK. TUCKER STANDING WHERE
BARRILL STOOD. THIS VIEW INCLUDING THE AUTHOR IS USED FOR A
SPECIAL REASON. AS SHORT A TIME AGO AS MARCH, 1913, A
GEOGRAPHER ACCUSED THE AUTHOR OF PAINTING (BY
HAND) THE VIEWS OF THIS PEAK WITH WHICH WE
CONVICTED DR. COOK!

Photo by H. C. Parker.

"THE GREAT GORGE" VIEW FROM "GLACIER POINT."

Photo by H. C. Parker.

tographs were made in September, while we visited the peak in June. On our return trip in July, we revisited the peak and obtained more photographs. The July exposures show the contours of the rock far better than the June exposures, but Dr. Cook's September pictures show that the snow cap had completely melted away and that some new snow had settled in the crevices.

CHAPTER XI

THE GREAT GORGE

La Voy joins us—News of the rear-guard—We advance up the great gorge—Hanging glaciers—Avalanches—The rear-guard joins us—La Voy's narrow escape—Aten leaves us—We enter the " big basin"—First near view of the southern walls of Mount McKinley—Reconnaissance trips—We advance toward the Southern North-East Ridge.

ON the way to camp I ran ahead to boil tea and as I struck into our old trail below camp 12, I saw fresh man tracks in the snow, which I found had been made by La Voy. He was waiting for us at camp. His eyes were tight closed by an attack of snow-blindness, and after treating them with boracic acid and cocain, he told us of his adventures since he had left us. Aten, Grassi, and he had had an uneventful and pleasant trip to Parkersburgh. They had at once begun the preparation of food, which consisted in boiling quantities of beans and drying them. The drying operations, however, had been postponed for several days by heavy rains and cloudy weather. The delay resulting from the bad weather had been augmented by the flooding of the glacier rivers, and they were unable to reach the big glacier until the waters had subsided.

While waiting at the last ford they had been overtaken by the Mazama expedition, who were just beginning their arduous relaying towards the big mountain.

As our men had comparatively light loads to carry
they had come through quickly to camp 8B. They
had then begun the relaying of the provisions that we
had left behind, while La Voy had pushed forward
alone to learn our plans and to tell us the news.

After his eyes had recovered and he had rested he
returned over the back trail.

We began at once to push relays of provisions up the
great gorge, and to escape the unlucky numeral we
called our next camp "Hanging Glacier Camp."

Our route led us along the foot of magnificent cliffs
that towered straight above us, grim and majestic.
Against the rocks pressed the stupendous ice-wall of
the big glacier—its surface broken and crushed into
countless crevasses and dazzling pinnacles. Sweeping
down from cloud-land we saw the first of the many
hanging glaciers that, like frozen Niagaras, bring down
the surplus ice harvests of the upper snow-fields. The
almost unearthly grandeur of these walls would have
made Doré throw down his brushes in despair, as
they were more weird and awe-inspiring even than the
pictures of his mind. As the setting sun lowered,
great, pointed shadows, such as cathedrals or enchanted
castles might cast, would zigzag across the cliffs, and
creep in deep blue ribbons across the lower snow-fields.
The lights changed constantly as one great peak after
another shut off the sunlight, and, very slowly as the
shadows joined, the great gorge took on the deep blue
mantle of night; it was then that the twisted towers
and broken masses of the seracs loomed like fantastic
frozen forms through the dusk, and added a weirdness
and wildness to the scene that I have never seen
equalled. As we moved cautiously across the cliffs
above the ice grottoes and dropped our loads below

the hanging glacier we were overcome with the wildness
and the silence of our surroundings; at times we had
heard deep cracking noises, as some ice-pinnacle was
crushed to bits by the pressure of the upper snow-fields,
but these sounds were swallowed up among the deep
grottoes and crevasses.

But suddenly, along the cliffs, a soft murmur ran
that swelled, and swelled, until the cañon was echoing
to a roar as of thunder, and a great cascade of snow
came sweeping over the distant walls, leaping from one
cliff to another, breaking into a thousand streams,
until it slid with a sighing sound far out onto the
blue floor of the glacier. This was the voice of the
great gorge, and we grew to know it well; for as we
pushed our way towards Mount McKinley, the sound
of avalanches became a part of our lives, and we never
ceased to thrill to the magic of this mountain music.

After bringing up all our belongings we made a
reconnaissance, on the rope, and without packs, to find,
if possible, a route across the rough side of the glacier
to the centre where the surface was smooth.

After worming our way among a maze of deep crevasses we were successful, and by the following day
we were camped in the centre of the ice river with an
open road before us to Mount McKinley.

We could now advance our entire outfit in three
relays, and after the second day in the gorge we had
reached the top of the long slope that begins to lead
down to the serac at the mouth of the gorge. Beyond
the glacier was fairly level and as the fog lifted we saw
a beautiful sight. The glacier stretched ahead of us
as level apparently as a floor for about five miles.
The snows of ages lay untouched, sheltered by the huge
cliffs that towered in long straight walls on either hand.

Through this great funnel we could see what we thought must be the base of Mount McKinley. We could see also that well ahead of us the cañon walls broke away and that there was a large basin of some kind, and then the mountain fog came creeping down and we pushed on by the loom of the side walls. I found two little birds that had died while trying to cross the Range. One was a warbler of some kind; it was mottled with black and grey, and it had a yellow topknot, and splashes of yellow on each side of its breast. The second was a smaller bird of the warbler family; it was yellow all over with the exception of a black-cap. The poor little things looked so out of place among those grim surroundings that it made one wonder at the power of that instinct which animated the tiny things and brought them to this lone spot over thousands of miles of mountain ranges. In a distance of about two miles we passed ten distinct cascading glaciers that swept down from heights of several thousand feet. These views we caught through rifts in the fog as we tramped back and forth over our relay trail; but the distant views were hidden from us and we could see nothing of the country ahead. There was an atmosphere of mystery in tramping forward through the dense fog; the uncertainty of where we were going, the uncouth loom of the men's figures as they rolled forward in single file, the death-like silence between the thunderous crashings and echoes of the avalanches, all combined to give a feeling of unreality and mysterious adventure to our toil.

In appearance we bore no resemblance to the party who had left civilisation only two months before. Our faces were burned almost black by the glare of the sun on the ice-fields, and were seamed and hard from the severity of our toil.   Our clothes too reflected the needs of our unusual calling.   Our legs were wrapped in puttees or bound with rawhide and our rubber shoe-packs were bound to the long, upturned Susitna snowshoes.   Wool or fur caps or hoods covered our heads, while every man wore snow goggles, or possibly, if the day was warm, a red or blue handkerchief with rough eye-holes cut in it. The fault in almost all of the glasses or goggles that one buys is that there is no ventilation, which results in the glass sweating and renders them useless.   The only satisfactory manufactured glass is also the cheapest on the market; it has a wire-net frame that fits closely around the eye socket, and for ordinary work it answers rather well.   The glare of the sun on the northern snow-field is terrific; it has to be seen—or felt—to be appreciated.

Although we were at comparatively low altitudes in 1910, I have seen the glare so strong that a man was afraid to step out of a tent, even for an instant, without first covering his eyes.

Trail-breaking under these circumstances is an ordeal, and as I did the leading for the advance party, my eyes were almost constantly affected by snow-blindness.   The slightest shadow or dark spot on which a man may rest his eyes proves a relief, as much of the trouble comes from being unable to find anything on the wide snow-fields on which to focus the eyes.   I have often tossed a burnt match or cigarette butt on to the snow in order to enjoy the relief of having something definite to look at.   For this reason the days when the sun is shining through a dense fog are the most dangerous, as the leader is forced to strain his eyes in trying to pierce the fog in the search for dangerous crevasses, or landmarks of importance.   On

A VIEW OF OUR " PROMISED LAND."

THE BASE OF MOUNT McKINLEY SHOWING FOR AN INSTANT THROUGH THE CLOUD BANKS THAT CHOKED THE " GREAT GORGE."

Photo by H. C. Parker.

LA VOY   CUNTZ   GRASSI   TUCKER   PARKER

THE 1910 PARTY IN THE " GREAT GORGE."

Photo by Belmore Browne.

foggy days there were times when, maybe for an hour, the only line I could get on our course was the light of the sun through the fog, and trail-breaking under these conditions invariably resulted in snow-blindness. Speaking from my own experiences I am of the opinion that no permanent injury results from snow-blindness. I have had more than twenty attacks without, so far as I have been able to discover, suffering any permanent harm. From personal observations on northern snow-fields I have learned to recognise two distinct forms of this unpleasant malady. The most common variety comes on slowly. The eyes water excessively and at the same time feel dry, as if they were filled with emory dust. The pain is sometimes excruciating and may in serious cases last several days. In bad cases I have noticed that the stomach is affected and the sufferer is unable to eat. Boracic acid and cocain, or boracic acid and zinc sulphate, are the best remedies known to me. The sufferer by bearing the pain that results can see by forcing his eyelids open; it is the pain that closes his eyes and renders him blind. The second variety comes on quickly and rarely lasts a long time if the patient takes the necessary precautions. No pain to speak of is felt, but total although temporary blindness results. One summer on the snow-fields of the Behring Sea coast my companions and I were attacked by snow-blindness. Having no medicines with us, we were driven to experimenting and secured some slight degree of comfort from placing tea-leaf poultices over our eyes. The care of the eyes in northern exploration is a question of the greatest importance, for, under certain conditions, a man's safety or possibly his life may hang on his ability to see clearly.

9

I have never met a man who was immune from this painful malady and so far as I have been able to discover the colour of a man's eyes does not affect his susceptibility to the glare of the snow.

On the 4th of July we were awakened by the crash and thunder of avalanches. It seemed as if Dame Nature was striving to make up for our lack of fire-crackers. The cañon walls had suddenly disappeared and although we could see nothing but grey walls of mist we had the feeling that something new had happened and that we had arrived *somewheres*. This strange sensation continued as we pushed our camp forward over the fog-draped waste of snow. After a hard day's work we succeeded in bringing up all our belongings and established our sixteenth camp.

Early the following morning we were awakened by "the creak of snowshoes on the crust," and then we heard a voice calling, "This is the Mazama party." We were all taken aback, for although the rivalry between us was a friendly one, we were nevertheless anxious to hold our lead. While we were unfastening our tent door, however, a suspicious whispering was going on outside and then to our delight we heard Grassi and La Voy laughing.

Aten joined us later and we had a great "pow-wow and potlatch." They had overtaken us with light loads from camp 14, and they had lots of news to relate. The last news of the Mazama party was that they had heard them shouting close to camp 8B, but they had not seen them.

La Voy had had an unpleasant experience between camp 9 and Glacier Point. He and Grassi were following our old snowshoe trail across the great plain of snow, and were unroped, and widely separated, for

our trail lying plain before them seemed a guarantee
of safety. La Voy, who had been plodding along for
an hour under his heavy pack, stopped to rest as he
was some distance ahead. When Grassi had approached within hailing distance, La Voy again started
ahead. He had taken only a few steps when the snow
broke under him, and he fell. The first thing he remembered was being under water, fighting for air,
and almost helpless in the tangle of his pack and
snowshoes. During the fall he had broken one of his
snowshoes, and his pack, consisting of sixty pounds of
beans in two waterproof sacks, and some odds and
ends, swung over his head. His nerve did not forsake
him, and after what to him seemed centuries, he reached
the surface and grasped a shelf that the water had worn
in the icy wall. To the fact that his pack consisted
of dry beans he probably owes his life, for the beans
being buoyant brought him to the surface; had his
pack consisted of sixty pounds of pemmican he would
have drowned. In the meanwhile Grassi was plodding
along with his head bent low under the strain of the
tump-line. Raising his eyes finally, he halted with
amazement—La Voy had vanished! Pressing forward
he saw the hole in the snow. Visions of the horror of
the crevasses they had passed crossed his mind, and
in an agony of fear he rushed along the trail. As he
neared the crevasse he heard La Voy's voice, and for
an instant was overcome by the reaction of the fear
that had gripped him. By this time La Voy had freed
himself from his load, and with the aid of the ropes
that Grassi now lowered to him, he sent up his pack
and scaled the fifteen feet of ice wall and stood shivering on the snow.

Now, on the big glacier there are three distinct

types of crevasses. First, crevasses that sink to the very bowels of the glacier—great blue chasms that are so deep that you can see nothing but a blue void; secondly, crevasses filled with icy stalagmites upon which a falling man would be impaled; and lastly, crevasses that fall sheer to subglacial torrents, the bellowing of which between the deep ice walls sends the cold shivers down a man's back. Some of the ice caverns were open, others were partly covered by snow cornices, while a few, and these we dreaded most, were completely hidden with snow. Usually there was a slight depression or discolouration of the snow that warned us of the hidden danger; but sometimes—as in La Voy's case—the snow lay smooth and white across the death-trap. Luckily the crevasse that came so near to being La Voy's sepulchre was the only one in the many hundreds that we saw that was filled with stagnant water. Had it been like the others he would have been ground to pieces by the subglacial torrents, or his body would now be lying frozen in the depths of the big glacier.

After a good rest at our camp the rear-guard returned to camp 14 for their last relay, while Aten continued his journey to base camp. As we had not expected to add him to our party we had made no allowance in special clothing or sleeping-bags for an extra man, and we were now beginning to reach an altitude where warm clothes and sleeping-bags were a necessity. Among other things that the rear-guard had left with us were fifty pounds of cooked beans. They were mouldy and sour so we spread them out on canvas sacks to dry. They had a peculiar taste, but by mixing them with erbswurst we were able to use a fair amount, although Grassi and Tucker were made ill by the sour bean diet and suffered from abdominal cramps.

It was not until our arrival at camp 17 that we were able to study any of the surrounding mountains, and then the fog only raised a few hundred feet. We could see a great plain of snow surrounded by mountain slopes that blended with the mist, but we were as yet unable to tell where the best point of attack lay. After a day's absence, Grassi and La Voy returned with their last relay loads. Aten had left them at camp 14 and departed for Parkersburgh. This reunion and the final relay loads placed us in a position to devote all our energies to the attack on Mount Mc-Kinley. In food and fuel we had:

      55 qts. of alcohol
      25½ 6-lb. cans of pemmican
      32 lbs. of sugar
      10 lbs. of good beans
      30 lbs. of sour beans
      30 lbs. of erbswurst
       3 lbs. of tea
       4 lbs. of bacon
      80 lbs. of hardtack
      21 lbs. of raisins
      Beef tea ad lib.
      Food total 228 lbs. or
        38 lbs. per man
      Fuel total 96¼ lbs. or
        16 lbs. per man

The above were the rations that we had carried to within two miles of the base of the southern cliffs of Mount McKinley, after thirty-six travelling days.

In comparing our food supply with Dr. Cook's own

figures, we find that on leaving the Tokositna River at the very beginning of his journey he and Barrill only had twenty-one pounds of food and two pounds of fuel per man. Dr. Cook is not a humourist or we could picture him smiling, while writing the following description of his equipment: "In preparing our equipment I had determined to break away from the established method of mountain climbing by reducing the number of my party and by changing the working equipment."

On the 7th of July we awoke under a clear blue sky and at 3 A.M. we were preparing for the day's work.

We had split the party into two working units. Each unit handled an equal portion of our equipment and occupied a separate tent. This system simplified the division of rations and added to our travelling efficiency. Professor Parker, Herman Tucker, and I formed the first party; and Professor Cuntz, Valdemar Grassi, and Merl La Voy completed the second. The second party was instructed to explore the base of the mountain on the western side of the glacier while we started over the blue snow-fields towards the eastern cliffs.

Dense cloud-banks still clung to the main cliffs, but the indications pointed to a clear day and we expected to discover the right line of advance before nightfall. As we plodded forward over the snow, Tucker began to complain of serious abdominal pains, and before long the cramps grew so severe that he was forced to lie in the snow until the attacks had passed. We returned to camp at once and left him well wrapped up in his sleeping-bag. As we left camp for the second time, the clouds lifted and we secured our first near view of Mount McKinley. We were awestruck at its immensity and grandeur and as we swept the giant cliffs with

RETREATING FROM THE "GREAT SERAC"
FOR FEAR THAT THE SUN WILL
START AVALANCHES.

Photo taken about 4 A.M. by Belmore Browne.

our eyes we began to search for promising climbing routes. We could also see the whole system of cliffs and glaciers that guarded the southern approach. The great gorge opened into a great piedmont glacier which lay in the form of a basin below the great peaks and cliffs that hemmed it in. The "big basin" was about 5000 feet in altitude and it stretched like a level floor to where the Mount McKinley glaciers brought down their loads of ice and snow.

Directly upon this level plain rose Mount McKinley —15,000 feet of rock and ice! and as the sun began to creep across its face the distant thunder of avalanches came to our ears. At the first glance we were overjoyed by seeing what appeared to be several climbable routes to the summit. But on using our binoculars we found that the intense glare of the sun combined with the similarity of colouring of the mountain rock, hid much of the bad climbing by making the nearby mountain masses melt into and flatten the approaches to the summit.

It was only by using powerful binoculars and the greatest care that we could see some of the great breaks between the huge snow-fields. After carefully studying the southern face we could see that it was unscalable. The great South-Western Arête looked climbable up to an altitude of about 15,000 feet, but at that point it joined the main peak below as savage and hopeless a mass of cliffs as I have ever seen. The north-eastern approach seemed to be the most promising. We could see a great ridge leading to the summit, and on this ridge we hung our hopes. As we did not know, at that time, that there were three north-eastern arêtes, we spoke of it as the North-East Ridge but it is really the Southern North-East Ridge. In order to study the country better, Professor Parker and I crossed the big basin and climbed a ridge that came down from a tangled mass of peaks that lay directly under Mount McKinley's southern walls. These peaks were attached by sharp ridges to a great dome-shaped buttress that forms one of the most important landmarks of that region. On reaching the top of the ridge I removed the rope which we had been wearing for our mutual safety. The ridge led up to a big snow-field and as I was crossing it the snow broke under me and I just caught myself on my outstretched arms. By feeling carefully with my feet I located one wall of the crevasse and Professor Parker gave me the end of his ice-axe to pull on. On looking into the hole that my body had made I could see a deep blue void with some dark rock masses far below. I reversed the proceeding a few moments later by helping Professor Parker out of another crevasse, and after that we always wore the rope. The country we were in was literally seamed with crevasses and it would have been criminal carelessness to have taken even a few steps without the protection of the rope.

From our lookout point on the ridge we could see that we would have to cross two jagged mountain ranges to reach the Southern North-East Ridge. As this was impossible from the food point of view alone, we turned our eyes farther east and there we saw two great snow *cols*, or saddles, that swept up gently from steep seracs to a height of about 11,000 feet. It was the only promising way out of the great amphitheatre in the direction of the Southern North-East Arête and we decided to attempt it at once.

While making these observations we had been sitting among some rocks at an altitude of 7000 feet. Directly opposite stood the great dome-shaped buttress that supports Mount McKinley's base and under the heat of the warm sun it presented an inspiring sight; from every cliff, snow-slope, and rock-runnell, avalanches were roaring down on to the glacier floor below, and the very air seemed to pulsate to the crash and thunder of the falling snow. In all of the well-known mountain ranges of the world the snow melts away during the summer. In cases where it does not disappear it becomes hard and packed under its own weight and gives a firm, safe footing to the climber. Mount McKinley, however, is so far north and the snow-fall is so great that the snow never gets in this desirable condition.

The cliffs are overhung and powdered with unnumbered tons of soft snow, and at the slightest touch of the sun the great cliffs literally *smoke* with avalanches. The sight is beautiful beyond words from a spectacular point of view, but when your object is the scaling of these selfsame cliffs the sight is not conducive to peace of mind. On our return to camp we were relieved to find that Tucker was feeling better, and we at once began our preparations for the advance on the great seracs below the 12,000-foot cols. While we were at work we saw our companions returning home across the snow-fields.

They were a long way off when we first saw them and it was a fascinating sight to watch the tiny specks growing larger and larger until they materialised into men. It was light almost all night while we were at the base of Mount McKinley; the advance and retreat of the night shadows went on with scarcely a pause, and sometimes we would be uncertain whether the alpine glow on the big mountain's icy crest was the light of the rising, or the setting sun. The dazzling whiteness of the snow-buried peaks made the contrast of sunlight and shadow the more beautiful.

CHAPTER XII

THE GREAT SERAC—FIRST RECON-
NAISSANCE

Explorations in the big basin—Night travel—Arrival at the base of the great serac—Avalanches—Fog—We fail to find a route—Return to main camp—News of the Mazama expedition—Puddings—Books—Short rations.

THE following afternoon found Professor Parker, Tucker, and the writer well up towards the base of the great serac. As we rose to the upper snow-fields the sun set. Deep shadows crept up from the distant lowlands, and the big basin turned into a deep blue sea of mystery. Mount McKinley rose between two giant peaks that framed it and as the shadows deepened its crest took fire from the distant sun. We pushed forward while our snowshoes began to sing on the frozen crust, and as the cold increased the silence was broken by the falling of ice on the cliffs.

There is a mysterious attraction about night travel on these northern snow-fields that is hard to explain; the clean, cold smell of the night air, the loom of great peaks against the night sky, the bigness and freedom of the everlasting snow-fields, and the excitement of the life, all combine to make a lasting impression on the minds of those who have travelled there.

As we approached the walls of ice their great size began for the first time to dawn on us, and we realised at once that even if we succeeded in finding an easy route to the snow-fields above, our food supply was scarcely equal to the magnitude of the task, for after crossing the 11,000-foot cols we would still have the whole sweep of the great ridge to negotiate.

We arrived at the base of the seracs after midnight and proceeded to make camp.

The serac rose sheer above us for 1000 feet, and we knew that beyond the first wall lay others that would bar our path. Against the sky stood pinnacles and spires of blue ice, broken into weird and fantastic shapes. As the biting cold of early morning crept downward we could hear the ice groaning and settling and now and then a deep cracking noise would run along the blue walls. Taking off our frozen packs and rope we broke and scraped away the thick crust, and began our mysterious "tent dance." In pitching our tents we always had to first stamp down the soft snow in order to insure a firm floor when the sun came out. Beginning with our snowshoes we would stamp out a circle in single file. When the surface was hard and smooth we would remove our snowshoes and stamp the snow down with our shoe-packs, and level it off finally with another snowshoe pounding. This operation resembled some heathen war-dance; seen through the frost-mist we must have looked like mountain elves engaged in a propitiatory dance to some glacier demon. When the floor was pounded flat we would stretch our tent and fasten the corners and sides with ice-axes and snowshoes.

Our beds and war-bags were passed inside, and the alcohol stove filled and lighted. After everything outside had been stowed neatly we would fill our pots with snow, and retire into our new home. Then the sleeping-bags were spread on top of waterproof covers, our bundles of damp socks were hung on the centre-pole above the purring stove, and pipes and diaries were brought out; in a few minutes, a warm human shelter would stand on the ice, and for the first time the silent glaciers would echo to the sound of human voices and laughter. By this time we had become experts at camp-making. I remember once noting the time when we began to make camp; no one was aware that I was timing the operation, and there was no un-usual hurry; yet only fifteen minutes elapsed before we were all inside our tents with our beds spread out and snow melting over the alcohol lamps.

After our arrival at the base of the "great serac" we ate a hurried breakfast and went outside in the hope of seeing a promising route over the ice wall. To our surprise we found that a dense fog had settled, and the crust was so hard and dry that we could run about on it in our sleeping-socks.

This was a novel experience to us after our weeks of snowshoe work and we enjoyed it to the full. After three hours' sleep we commenced preparations for our attack on the serac, but on opening the tent-door we again looked into a dense wall of fog. We waited an hour and just as the mist began to rise, a heavy snow-storm swept over us. After the snow had passed we began our climb, but on approaching the foot of the serac the sun broke through the clouds and in a few minutes avalanches began to thunder downward, and we retreated once more to our tent. We saw that nothing could be done until nightfall, and gave our-selves up to the rare delight of a day's rest. It was Professor Parker's birthday, and in honour of the event we made our first attempt at cooking pemmican. The result so far surpassed our wildest hopes that life

took on an added interest, and the concoction which
we named "Professor Parker's Pemmican Pudding"
became one of our standard rations. I have copied
the recipe from my diary in case the reader should ever
find himself in a similar position.

PUDDING FOR THREE MEN

First soak 3 broken hardtack in snow-water until they
are soft. Add 60 raisins and pemmican the size of $4\frac{1}{2}$
eggs. Stir slowly but energetically until the mess is
thoroughly amalgamated. Boil slowly over an alcohol
stove, add 3 tablespoons of granulated sugar, and serve in
a granite-ware cup.

During the afternoon we slept and played chess. We
did not need to look outside for the avalanches kept
up a steady war that told us that the seracs were
unclimbable. After hearing the noise one could not
but wonder at the terrific forces of nature. No foundry
or machine shop could be noisier than this great wall
of ice; avalanches breaking from the walls struck the
cliffs with a noise like artillery, and then crashed and
rumbled downward until you would have thought that
an army was firing small arms and rapid-fire guns.
The serac avalanches are distinctly different from the
great mountain avalanches, which start with a dim
murmur, that grows and swells until the cliffs echo to
the mighty roar, which slowly dies away among the
peaks until silence reigns again.

During the afternoon the sun beat down upon the
ice with such force that the heat was almost overpowering, and yet two hours later a snow-storm struck
us and I was suffering from the cold inside my sleeping-
bag, although I was clothed in two undershirts, two

woollen shirts, sleeveless sweater, sleeping socks, trousers, woollen hood, and gloves. The remarkable side of the temperature on Mount McKinley is the extreme changes of heat and cold that one feels without a corresponding change being noticeable in the thermometer. The maximum heat recorded by our party on the southern Mount McKinley glaciers was 52° in the sun, and the minimum temperature was 28°. Under a temperature of 50° the glaciers became blinding sheets of white light and the sun burnt like fire; it was unsafe to take a step without snow-glasses, and our skin peeled off like parchment. But the instant that you stepped into the shadow of a moraine, or mountain, you felt the chill of the ice creeping over you. I have seen fresh snow-shoe tracks frozen hard on the bottom and sides, where they were shaded, while the exposed snow was soft as slush from the heat of the sun.

We lay snow-bound under the great serac for one and a half days and finally at 3.45 on the morning of July 11th we began to chop our way up the face of the ice-wall. It was the most unpleasant and treacherous climbing that I have ever experienced, for instead of the serac being solid the ice was so rotten that you could bury an ice-axe to the head in ice blocks that looked perfectly safe.

Shortly after we left camp it began to snow, and after more than two hours of Herculean labour we came to a mass of ice gorges and grottoes below a high perpendicular wall. I was forced several times to hew doorways between the ice blocks with my axe. Skirting the wall to the right we came out on a platform that overlooked a deep gorge. Here we were halted by perpendicular ice-walls sixty feet high. While we were studying the problem, Professor Parker read his barometer and found that we were 1200 feet above our camp, although we had not yet reached the top of the first break in the serac. Turning to the left we began to follow the ice-wall but a dense fog shut us in and as the rising sun began to shine through it, we retreated as quickly as possible from our unpleasant surroundings. On the lower slopes the heat of the sun through the white mist began to send down avalanches. The heat was terrific, our clothes were wet with sweat, and yet to our surprise the temperature in the sun was only 48°!

We had only enough food for one more day so after a pemmican pudding luncheon we slept, in order to be fresh for a night attempt on the great serac, as our experience had convinced us that there was too much danger during the day. The night that followed will live long in my memory, for it was my first experience in night climbing in the north. We left camp at 9 P.M., with our complete mountain equipment, for a last attempt on the eastern end of the great serac. I led by as straight a course as I could hold until we had risen 600 feet above camp. At that altitude I was afraid that my steps would not hold, as the ice was rotten—in fact in the worst climbing condition I have ever seen. After a traverse to the right, we followed a good ice *couloir* that led between giant ice blocks, but above we had to pass under a sixty-foot ice cliff where we could see that avalanches had been falling during the day.

This climbing was too difficult to be undertaken with packs, but although we had given up hopes of finding a relay route at this point in the ice-wall our interest in our explorations urged us forward. At an altitude of 1000 feet above our camp we entered a glacial amphitheatre surrounded by perpendicular ice-walls—a frozen cul-de-sac, and as gruesome a spot as I have ever entered. One great block of green ice rose like a snake's head from a narrow base to a height of sixty feet and leaned drunkenly towards us. Fifty feet above us a rotten ice-bridge sagged from a shattered berg to the main wall, and as we looked a cold mist crept over us and everything was blotted from sight. It was midnight when we reached our turning point and as we sat fog-bound, an avalanche broke loose on an ice slope far above us. We could see nothing, and the roar grew louder and louder, like the sound of a fast approaching train. We were decidedly uncomfortable until it swept into a frozen gully beyond us, and we listened thankfully to the ice blocks crashing and thudding on the snow-fields far below.

On our return to camp we saw one of the most magnificent mountain pictures that I have had the good luck to witness. The fog had begun to fade away as we approached our tent. The main mountain masses were indistinct blue shapes looming against the dark sky. Along their great flanks films of clouds lay like frozen veils. High above the main ranges rose the dim majestic shapes of Mounts Hunter and McKinley, and as we watched McKinley's crest began to glow; at first with the merest tinge of warm colour, as if it was turning to gold from internal heat; then, little by little, the alpine glow crept downward until Mount Hunter was crowned with fire. Other peaks began to catch the sun in turn until above the great foreground of nocturnal gloom the great crests glowed like gems. We stood spellbound under the frozen cliffs and it seemed to me as if nature had for a moment drawn aside a veil and allowed us to look on one of the mysteries of the universe.

On our return to our companions we left our tent opposite a promising break in the western end of the great serac, as we had planned to return at once with more food and make another attempt to cross the 12,000-foot col.

During our absence the second party had advanced all our belongings well up towards the base of the serac, but as our outlook was so discouraging we decided to leave the bulk of our equipment there until we had completed our explorations. During our absence, Rusk, the leader of the Mazama expedition, had visited one of our rear camps. He had pushed forward without a pack and returned to his own party after a short visit. He reported that their food was nearly exhausted and that they would soon retreat to the Chulitna. He also stated that his party had been unable to locate "Dr. Cook's fake summit of Mt. McKinley" on account of cloudy weather, but he assured Grassi that since he had travelled over the big glacier, his sympathies were no longer with the Brooklyn explorer, and that finding the fake peak was superfluous evidence.

The following account of Rusk's meeting with our rear-guard was published by him, after his return to civilisation.

We had now made six camps in reaching this spot and the mountain (McKinley) was still unclimbed and, what was worse, unclimbable with our present equipment. We had only sufficient food left to last two or three days. There was nothing we could do but secure a lot of photographs and make a few reconnaissance trips, with a future ascent in view. We raised our tent at Camp Morden shortly before noon of July 12th. Rojec, while skirmishing for pictures, thought he saw figures moving about on the snow a mile or so to our north. With the glasses, I soon made out a camp to which I started. After travelling perhaps a mile and a half, I found Professor Cuntz, Grassi, and La Voy of the other expedition, who welcomed me warmly and opened a can of pemmican for my especial benefit. They intended to remain two weeks longer although their supplies, especially their alcohol, were running low. Parker, Browne, and Tucker had been gone for three days endeavouring to find a route by which to attain the north-east ridge of the mountain. Whether or not the expedition would attempt the ascent now depended largely upon the result of this reconnaissance. After a brief but pleasant visit I returned to camp, and we did not see the members of the other expedition again to talk with them while we remained on the glacier. Our relations with the Parker-Browne party had been of the most friendly character, and the best of feeling prevailed between us.

While Mr. Rusk's remark concerning our food supply was accurate in the light of the discoveries that we made later while trying to reach the Southern North-East Ridge, we still had as large a supply of fuel and food as I had thought necessary when undertaking the climb, for at our nineteenth relay camp, within one mile of Mount McKinley's southern cliffs, we had:

> 20 6-lb. cans of pemmican
> 2½ cases of hardtack
> 20 lbs. of erbswurst
> 20 lbs. of sugar
> Ample tea
> Ample beef tea
> 12 gals. of alcohol.

This would have lasted us twenty-five days, which would have been an ample allowance had we found a climbable route to the summit, but as it turned out, a

NIGHT CLIMBING ON THE "GREAT SERAC." THE RISING SUN CAN BE SEEN
STRIKING THE MOUNTAIN TOP ON THE RIGHT.

Photo by H. C. Parker.

"EXPLORERS PEAK," CLIMBED BY THE 1910 EXPEDITION.

Photo by H. C. Parker.

food allowance of fifty days would have made little or no difference in our attack by the south approach, as we were surrounded by mountain ranges that, from a freight transportation point of view, were practically unclimbable.

This brings to my mind a fact that is seldom realised, and that is that the most dangerous and difficult trips are usually those that end in failure. While things are going smoothly and the chances of success seem good, the mental satisfaction of the explorer eases the difficulty of the toil or the suffering of hardship. But when things go wrong a man is driven to taking risks in a frantic endeavour to win success, and the mental depression which follows failure is as hard to bear as bodily suffering.

In swimming the cañon at the head of the Yentna in 1906, and again in the serac climbing in 1910, we ran risks that were out of all proportion to the direct benefits to be gained, but we took these risks in a spirit of desperation while trying to surmount insurmountable obstacles, and wrest success from failure.

On trips such as ours the work is so arduous that at the end of the day or night's work you are usually too tired to talk much or play games. Occasionally during the delays caused by fogs or blizzards, we would summon enough energy to play chess or tell stories. But our principal diversion was reading for the one-hundredth time one of our travel-worn books. "Pig-skin libraries" or other luxuries permissible on exploring expeditions by ship in the Arctic, or caravan in the tropics, are out of the question in the rugged mountain ranges that we traversed. Early in the journey when we were cutting the covers from the few books we possessed to save weight, some wag referred

to the collection as our "Near-skin library" and the
name stuck. What few books we carried were public
property and were handed on from man to man in a
sort of endless chain. Our only hope was that we might
forget what we had read in order that we might enjoy
it over again when it returned to us. Nothing was
too commonplace to read; advertisements even were
acceptable and we read the list of instructions on the
kodak film wrappers until we could recite every para-
graph by heart. Our books had been collected in a
haphazard way, according to the personal choice or
caprice of each member of our party, and I must admit
that our list in no way resembled President Eliot's of
Harvard. Our two favourite authors were Shakespeare
and Omar Khayyam (Fitzgerald edition) and among
other books we had Epictetus, some of Browning's
poems, some of Emerson's essays, and *The Reveries of
a Bachelor*. I know of nothing in this world that will
produce a stronger attack of melancholia than reading
The Reveries of a Bachelor on a fog-draped glacier!

We lacked ordinary comforts even more than we
lacked amusements. Our tent floors were 7 x 8 feet,
and as the tents were only seven feet high and came to
a point there was practically no standing room. The
tent floors were always wet from the snow soon after
they were laid, and we were driven to all sorts of expedients in keeping our sleeping-bags dry. Extra covers or
articles to sleep on were extremely scarce, and mountain
rope, rubber-shoes, or anything that could be secured
was utilised in the construction of waterproof mattresses.

Keeping our belongings dry was perhaps the most
difficult of our many housekeeping problems. During
snow-storms, or the long days on the trail, our clothes
became covered with snow, which melted when we

entered our tents. As each man wore at least three pairs of the heaviest wool socks, and as there were three or four men in each tent, there were always eighteen heavy, damp socks to be suspended from the centre pole. After the socks were fairly dry, we usually put them in our sleeping-bags and dried them out by the warmth of our bodies. The principal benefit of this plan was that in case the socks did not become dry they were at least warm when we put them on in the morning. Alcohol was so precious that we could not use it for drying purposes, except in cases where it was possible to combine drying with cooking.

Our life in these tiny tents on the cold wastes of snow and ice was disagreeable and cheerless in the extreme. Quarrels and disagreements frequently occur in the wilderness under conditions far more pleasant than those we laboured under and it redounds greatly to the character of the men who composed our party that not a single unpleasant incident occurred to mar our pleasant relations. The two expeditions to Mount McKinley organised by Professor Parker and myself are the only serious expeditions that I have ever taken part in where no unpleasant incidents occurred. While this result is due largely to the type of men who joined our ventures, the management of an expedition is of the greatest importance in eliminating friction and producing *esprit de corps*.

Experience actually gained through hard knocks on many a long trip is requisite in a leader who handles bodies of men in the wilderness. This includes a knowledge of human nature, and the causes that produce friction. The fundamental cause at the bottom of all the dissensions that have occurred in the history of exploration is *selfishness*. There is only one way to positively eliminate unpleasantness, and that is by guarding absolutely against selfishness. The leader who refuses to recognise this fact is foredoomed to failure. Under the heart-breaking toil and brutal hardships of a life in the open the longing for comfort becomes an obsession; the craving for certain kinds of food—sweets in particular—becomes too strong for some men to resist; it is a well-known side of human nature that in Alaska is described by the term "Sugar Hog." While it was possible for us to guard against the "Sugar Hog" by using extreme caution in the selection of our men, I nevertheless devoted much of my time to seeing that the men shared equally in everything. It is an impossibility for any one who has lived the life of civilisation to realise the self-denial and self-sacrifice that men are called upon to show under primitive conditions. When a man has reached the stage of hunger where he would gladly fight for a lump of sugar, it requires the highest kind of self-sacrifice and honesty on his part to deal justly with his companions. The most liberal man in civilisation may be the most selfish under primitive conditions, for to be unselfish in the wilderness often means that you must actually undergo bodily suffering and discomfort, while in civilisation one often gains much by giving.

One of the best methods of insuring justice to every man is by putting the entire party on rations the instant they leave civilisation. Many men make the mistake of thinking that rations are ordered to save the food supply, but this is not necessarily true. The greatest benefit to be derived from rations is *that every man shares equally*. Any real man will starve when he knows that his companions are starving too. But the instant that the slightest whisper of suspicion runs

through a party, it becomes demoralised and the gaunt
spectre of the "Survival of the Fittest" becomes their
master. The instant a party goes "on rations" the
necessity for "fast eating" disappears, and an atmosphere of peace and security prevails.

In 1910 we worked on a very small food allowance.
Each man received one pound of pemmican and three
hardtack biscuit each day. In addition we had a
practically unlimited quantity of tea, but our sugar
was rationed at the rate of two flat teaspoonfuls
per man per meal. We existed and performed the
hardest labour on this allowance for fifty consecutive
days, but I can truthfully say that I consider it the
minimum food allowance permissible.

We reserved our raisins for the actual climb, but as
soon as we reached the big basin and saw the difficulties
that confronted us, I rationed the raisins in small
quantities. Our erbswurst was used as a luxury from
time to time and we usually drank it as a "night-cap"
before going to sleep.

While we would have been more comfortable had
we eaten more, it is interesting to know that we accomplished the severest toil on such a small amount, for the
average young man in civilization eats twice as much
without doing any physical work to speak of.

There was one amusing side to the food question
and that was the constant conversations on eating that
we carried on. To have heard us one would have
thought that we were an exiled party of epicures and
gourmands. The universal topic of conversation
was *food!*

We would be lying in our bags, resting up after a
hard day's pack, when one of the men would say—
apropos of nothing—"I went on a week-end visit in

the country once and I wolfed so much roast beef that later when some squabs on toast and salad came in, I was full-up and only made a bluff at eating them!"

After a long silence pregnant with sympathy and understanding some one else would regale us with a like harrowing tale, until our voices would grow weaker and weaker, and we would fall asleep—to dream possibly of ice-cream sodas and chocolate éclairs.

With these painful details in view the reader may form a faint conception of the tremendous excitement that swept over us on the discovery of the delights of cooked pemmican. Had we discovered a method of making diamonds we could not have felt more elated, and with feverish impatience we awaited the time when we should initiate our companions into the delights of "Professor Parker's Pemmican Pudding." The chance came at our reunion at camp 22. We had kept the discovery a profound secret, and as meal-time approached we could hardly control our excitement. At the proper time I entered their tent and told them that they were invited to a party, but that in view of our being in starvation country, they were called upon to make a contribution of their allotted rations. They demurred slightly at the last clause in my invitation, but eventually the rations were turned over, and I re-retired to our tent. Professor Parker, Tucker, and I at once began the preparation of our gastronomic secret. In the meantime, we had made a second valuable discovery. Professor Cuntz had brought (for medicinal purposes) a small flask of brandy as far as the big basin. The temptation was too great to resist, and after due deliberation, I commandeered it for the good of the whole. At the appointed time the pudding began to steam and we called to our mystified companions. It

was with the greatest difficulty that the six of us
crowded into the small tent. As the pudding was
ladled into our granite-ware cups it was covered with
sugar and a teaspoonful of brandy poured on top.
Professor Cuntz, La Voy, and Grassi ate the first few
spoonfuls in dubious silence, but soon an expression of
beatific contentment crossed their sun-browned faces,
and it was not until their cups had been emptied and
licked dry that they gave their enthusiasm free rein.
Finally, after a long, contented silence, La Voy said:
"No wonder you fellows stayed so long on the big
serac."

CHAPTER XIII

THE GREAT SERAC (SECOND RECON-
NAISSANCE)

We attempt the west end of the ice wall—Avalanches and crevasses—
Night climbing—We reach the top of the serac—Impracticability of the
route for relaying—We return to our companions—Report of the rear
party—We make the first ascent of Explorers' Peak—We climb 10,300
feet on the South-West ridge—We retreat to the Big Basin.

O N the thirteenth of July we started out for the
western side of the Great Serac, and at 11 p. m.
of the same day we were inside our tent below the
cold walls. During our absence the rear-guard were to
explore the central glacier on Mount McKinley's
southern side. We had no hope of finding a route from
this glacier, as it headed directly under the stupendous
ice walls of the big mountain. But a few great ridges
that hid the glacier's source gave enough uncertainty
to the venture to make it worth while.

Shortly after two o'clock of the morning after our
arrival at the ice-fall we were chopping our way up
the steep slopes of the serac. Eventually we found a
good cold-weather route to the top of the first ice-fall;
but avalanche tracks warned us to beware of the route
when the sun shone. Swinging towards the western
col we rose to an altitude of eight thousand feet only
to find ourselves thwarted by a second serac gashed by
immense crevasses. The great rents in the ice stretched
between almost perpendicular walls of rock. Across

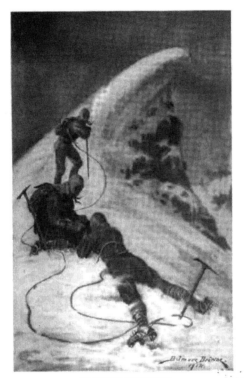

"BOILING THE HYPSOMETER."

ASCERTAINING THE TEMPERATURE OF STEAM ON A PEAK IN THE ALASKAN
RANGE.

From a painting by Belmore Browne.

the face of the western cliffs we could trace a large vein, but as the formation was not promising for valuable minerals we were glad to pass it by, for it would have taken nothing less than a mine of pure gold to tempt us under those avalanche-swept slopes. As we retraced our steps and studied the serac for a new route, the day broke, and the rumble of avalanches followed the march of the sun across the range. We turned at once, for we dreaded the steep slope that separated us from camp, and during the descent the snow began to get *greasy* and the noise of slides came from every side. We were glad when we reached our tent.

This failure to reach the left-hand col convinced us that there was little use in remaining longer at the base of the serac. But during the morning we had seen a very steep snow-slope leading up on the right-hand side of a wedge of rock that split the serac. It was out of the question to climb it in the daytime, but we thought that at night it might be possible. The route, even if we succeeded in reaching the top, would be too difficult for use as a relay route, but the desire to scale the serac had become a personal matter with us, and Herman Tucker and I therefore decided to have one more try.

As soon as the great white walls began to freeze, we left camp. We climbed quickly, except where snow-slides had swept away the footholds we had made in the morning, which had to be re-chopped. High upon the last big traverse, one thousand feet above our camp, we turned to take a last look at the tent, a tiny dark pyramid far below. Prof. Parker was standing outside watching our progress. Lowering my voice purposely, I said "Good-night," and such was the deathlike stillness of the frozen cliffs and plains below that he heard me as if I had been standing by his side, and his answering call of "Good-night and good luck" reached us like the strokes of a clear bell. We turned then to a snow couloir before us, a hidden crevasse broke under me, but Tucker was used to the job and swung back on the taut rope until I reached firm snow again.

Roughly our plans were as follows. This Great Serac leads to the only snow pass on the south-eastern side of Mount McKinley. The great terraced granite ridges that form the big mountain's southern walls are unclimbable. Our only hope then was to find a way over the high passes by way of the Great Serac. Twice we had tried earnestly and failed, at Reconnaissance Camp 1, to reach the right-hand col of the glacier.

Our third attempt had failed when we had encountered the crevasses, and the venture that we were now engaged in was in the nature of a forlorn hope. At first everything went well. We made a long traverse and found a deep couloir between ice walls that led us to a good elevation. Without knowing it, however, I had swung too far to the right, and suddenly we came out on a level snow ledge and found ourselves looking directly down the grim walls. One look into that frigid basin, with the dim blue snow-fields far below, sent us on a long traverse to the left. Here we found the route we had chosen from below. The climbing began to be very steep, and we were again forced to make a traverse that took us below a huge ice wall, over snow that was literally ploughed by the ice blocks that had fallen during the day. The night was very cold, and before we had climbed half way up the slope, our axes were encased in ice and our mittens were as hard as boards. At the head of the steep slope we entered a chaos of crevasse ends and intervening ice masses that puzzled us until

we turned a sensational corner above a deep cavern,
crawled below a ten-ton icicled overhang, and crossed
a rotten snow bridge that led us into the bottom of a
snow-filled crevasse. Here we were cheered by seeing
what appeared to be the smooth floor of the upper
glacier. After some more strenuous climbing we
came to an ice cavern that crossed our crevasse, and
we had to chop steps again until we reached the top of
the left-hand ice wall and then—we stopped. Below
us on both sides lay crevasses, one of which sank deep
into the heart of the glacier. There was only one thing
that we could do. Herman lowered me down the wall
of the largest crevasse, after we had crawled on our
stomachs across a narrow snow bridge from which we
could look down into the blue depths of the ice river.
As I went down I chopped deep foot-and-hand holds,
which Herman descended in. Then began the weirdest
pilgrimage of my life. Following the snow-smoothed
floor, we advanced between walls of ice that in places
rose seventy feet above our heads. We passed crevasses
end on, and looked far into their frigid depths. Blue
grottoes led into the ice glittering with stalagmites and
stalactites of blue-black ice, and one glance into these
caverns of deathlike cold and silence was enough to
turn one's skin to goose-flesh.

It was midnight, and the first cold blue sheen of dawn
was creeping along a distant snow dome that was framed
by the walls of our frozen roadway. We kept on until
we came to a second crevasse that wound away into the
snow-fields. We could see that there was an hour's
work ahead of us before we would be out of the crevasses, and the thought of the sun catching us on the
steep slopes far below sent us hurrying over our back
trail. At our highest point we were two thousand feet

above our camp, and we reached our camp at 2 A.M., after as strange a night's adventure as I have ever experienced.

After two hours' sleep we broke camp, and with our belongings on our backs started downward towards our companions.

The Great Serac had beaten us, but there was no regret in our minds as we snowshoed away over the hard crust, only a feeling of gladness that our hard toil on the treacherous ice walls was finished.

On the way to camp we stopped to admire the great central glacier that enters the big basin from Mount McKinley's cliffs. We were talking of exploring it on the following day when Tucker said, "There are some men on the glacier now!" Looking where he pointed we could see three tiny specks winding among the crevasses far away on the edge of the broken ice-fields. They proved to be our rear-guard, and as they joined us soon after we reached the tent, we had much to tell and learn. The central glacier, they told us, was broken by tremendous crevasses, and Grassi remarked that "to cross the glacier we would need a portable steel bridge with a span of 150 feet."

The reconnaissance work of our rear-guard and our own explorations on the Great Serac ended our hopes of reaching the Southern North-East ridge; the main southern cliffs, too, needed but a glance to convince us that they were impossible; the only hope left lay in the direction of the South-Western Arête. This great arête extends a long way from the big mountain. It rises steeply to a high altitude, possibly twelve thousand feet, and then extends for several miles, like a great wall, until it joins the main peak of Mount McKinley.

So far our chances looked fairly promising, but at the

point where the ridge joins the mountain, great cliffs
sweep down from the main summit, and these cliffs
are too dangerous and too difficult to climb.

On the western side of the great basin a narrow
glacier-filled gorge leads up to the lowest portion of the
South-Western ridge. On one side the stupendous cliffs
of Mount McKinley rise thousands of feet above the
glacier's frozen floor, while the opposite wall is formed
by a separate group of very steep and rugged mountains, whose steep cliffs are continually sending down
avalanches into the blue depths. We determined to
explore this glacier, and while we knew that our chances
of scaling the mountain were poor, we hoped to at
least attain a "respectable" altitude.

Before "turning in" for a much-needed sleep we stood
outside of our little tents and talked, and enjoyed the
wonderful mountain views that surrounded us. On
the eastern side of the big basin stood an isolated peak.
It was beautifully formed and rose to an altitude of
about three thousand feet above our camp. As we stood
talking, our eyes were drawn to this mountain. Its
steep snow and ice slopes called to us with the world-
old challenge, and Grassi—who had as a boy learned to
swing an ice-axe among the Swiss Alps—sighed as he
studied the mountain and expressed a wish to stand on
its corniced summit.

The idea was received with enthusiasms. For weeks
we had been doing the hardest labour yet devised by
man; furthermore, we had done the labour in hopes of
climbing Mount McKinley; our only reward had been
serac and glacier climbing, which is dangerous without
being sport; it was time that we had some fun. We
held a council of war on the spot and decided to attack
the peak after we had had some sleep.

We awoke late in the afternoon. The long blue shadows were beginning to creep eastward across the snows of the big basin. As night came on, the air began to bite, and we ate our pemmican in confidence of a good crust to travel on. We were not disappointed, and at 11:22 P. M. we moved out in a long line towards the peak we were going to attack.

We were divided into two parties of three men, only this time the rear-guard under the leadership of Grassi went ahead. We moved quickly through the cold air, our snowshoes making a fine noise on the hard crust. At the base of the first steep pitch of the western arête of our peak, we cached our snowshoes and began the climb.

Grassi worked hard from the start and from the start it was stiff climbing as the lower slopes were so steep that we had to traverse continually between a small serac and some rocks that lay to our left. After reaching a fair altitude the arête became corniced, and we gave the edge a wide berth until we reached a broad snow-saddle, where we ate a second breakfast.

The mere fact of climbing for pleasure exhilarated us, and so incessant were the jibes and jokes that were tossed back and forth between the two parties that if there had been any one in the silent basin far below they would have thought that an afternoon tea had been transplanted to the icy mountain side! We enjoyed the frolic to the full, and when Grassi, poised on a corner of solid ice, called down that there were two routes to choose from—"A safe, and a sporty route," we all clamoured for the "sporty" one. We advanced slowly over a very steep slope of nearly solid ice that swept downward two thousand feet. The tops of the great peaks about us were beginning to turn pale from

the coming of dawn and the big basin lay as still as
death, like a deep blue lake, far below. Grassi's step-
cutting gave us time to fill our eyes and minds with the
beauties about us. From the start the night had been
crystal clear. Mount McKinley had towered over us
since we left camp, and just above its crest a planet—
the only one we had seen for more than a month—
hung in the blue-black sky. Far below us now, across
the big basin ran the black walls of the great gorge,
whose gloom deepened the purple of the snows. We
had "raised" the Tokosha Mountains by our climb, and
their distant forms brought back memories of our boat
and camp far down in the spruce forests beyond.

We reached the snow-saddle at 2 A. M. and, turning
in our steps, we saw a sight that none of us will ever
forget: buried in gloom, as the ranges were, Mc-
Kinley's summit was catching the first pink flush of
the morning sun. Nothing could be more beautiful
than the glories that followed the march of the sun
across those icy mountains. As the pink deepened,
the higher snows seemed actually to burn, and deep
stately shadows began to creep across the giant walls.
We would turn in the still cold to our work of step-
cutting only to be stopped by an ejaculation of wonder
from one of the party, and turning we would see a
new peak burning in its sun-bath. Mt. Hunter began
to catch the sun next, and in an instant its stupendous
ice slopes were turned to yellow and gold.

Later a film of clouds sweeping in from Cook Inlet
added beauty to the scene, but fearing that Mount
McKinley would be hidden I made several exposures
of the big mountains between 2 and 2:30 A. M. The
fact that these photographs, as well as some that I had
taken previously on the Great Serac, at night, were

11

successful, will give the reader an idea of the strength
of the northern light. Finally, after what seemed
like hours of step-cutting, we reached the summit,
and our triumphant cheers were swallowed up in the
great silence about us. The summit was corniced, and
the wind made it necessary to shelter our hypsometer
in a rhuksack while we boiled it. Our barometers
registered an altitude of eight thousand feet. The fact
that we were twenty miles from timber, and that every
foot of our climb had been on ice or frozen crust will
give the reader an idea of the difficulties of mountaineering in the Alaskan Range. On casting about for a
name for the mountain we thought of the Explorers'
Club of which several of our party were members.
Our fellow-members of this club had made its influence felt from the North Pole to the Antarctic continent,
and in memory of their great work we called the mountain "Explorers' Peak."

On the return Professor Parker, Tucker, and I went
ahead. When we reached the ice corner above the
lower ridge I left the rope and waited with my camera
to take a photograph of the second party as they came
down over the steep ice slope. They had been detained
on the upper ice-field and it was bitterly cold where I
stood in the shadow of the peak. Finally ice and snow
fragments began to hurtle past me. One piece came
buzzing toward me, so I put my camera in an ice step
and caught it as it passed me. I will never be so fool-
hardy again! It seems inconceivable that so small a
piece of crust could gather such force. My hands ached
for hours afterwards, and to my added disgust the
picture that I waited so patiently to take turned out to
be a double exposure!

We arrived at camp after an absence of nine hours,

ON TOP OF "EXPLORERS PEAK" WITH MOUNT McKINLEY IN BACKGROUND.
FROM LEFT TO RIGHT: GRASSI, CUNTZ, LA VOY, TUCKER, PARKER.

Photo by Belmore Browne.

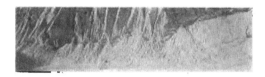

SNOW WALLS ON THE EDGE OF THE BIG BASIN.

Photo by H. C. Parker.

and our return to the arduous work of relaying was lightened by the memory of the day of sport.

On July 17th, we returned to the centre of the Big Basin and began to prepare for our advance on the South-West ridge. We had in provisions: 8½ gals. of alcohol (21 days for 6 men); 15¼ 6-lb. cans of pemmican (15¼ days); 14½ lbs. of raisins; 12¼ lbs. of sugar; 17½ lbs. Erbswurst (3 days); 340 hard-tack biscuits (19 days for 6 men).

preps

The reader will see that we could have remained on the ice twenty-one days longer—at a pinch—or as long as our fuel lasted. As it was we arrived at our base camp eighteen days later, and on the lower glacier we "ditched" some of our fuel when we got within striking distance of Parkersburgh.

After completing our preparations for the morrow we crawled into our sleeping-bags for a short sleep. But when we awoke we were dismayed by hearing the wind howling about us and the snow beating on our tents. Another long night and day dragged by to the accompaniment of howling wind and drifting snow, then a third, and a fourth. We lay in our bags, most of the time, resting and conserving our strength for the hard days to come. We played chess occasionally or checkers, or between fancied lulls in the storm we dashed hastily from one tent to the other. Our tents were so small that when one man went calling we usually exchanged him for a visitor so that every one would be comfortable.

While a short rest is always welcome to men who are working hard, these long periods of inaction were distasteful to us, for we knew that we would pay for it with tired backs and weary muscles when we began to carry packs again. One of nature's inexplicable laws is that while it takes weeks to get a man into good con-

dition only a few days of sloth or inaction are required
to spoil his wind and soften his muscles.

But every storm must cease and on the afternoon of
our fifth day the sun shone on a glistening world. The
Big Basin and the surrounding mountains were white
with their new covering but the bright sunshine revived
our spirits and we were a happy crew as we filed away
through the soft snow. We laid a straight course for
the deep gash in the western mountain wall, that was
to be our roadway to the great ridge.

At nightfall we entered the glacier-choked gorge and
as we began to climb the lower seracs Tucker and Grassi
complained of stomach and eye trouble, the result
probably of our enforced inaction during the storm.
As they did not improve we camped until morning.
With the break of day we continued and our advance up
the ice river was spectacular in the extreme. Stupendous rock walls rose on either side. I have never seen
cliffs of more grim and savage beauty. Where they
were broken they were incrusted with ice and snow, and
with the deep thunder of avalanches in our ears we
chose our route cautiously and swung wide of the
overhanging snow-fields.

The steepness of our ascent told us that we were
approaching the base of the South-West Arête and on
reaching a smooth step in the glacier we halted and
made camp, for a heavy fog hid the upper snows.

In the evening the fog lifted and through a rift we
caught a glimpse of a great wall of ice—the end of the
South-West Arête—blocking the end of the cañon. The
ridge was about three miles away and looked unclimbable.

The following day we awoke to the familiar sound of
snow and wind. On looking out we could see nothing

but wind-driven clouds of ice dust; but the deep roar of an occasional avalanche would tell us that the mountains were still there.

On the following morning we found that the bad spell of weather had at last broken.

Professor Parker, Tucker, and I left camp at 4.40 A.M. and the others followed us in half an hour. The travelling conditions were splendid, as there was a hard crust, but we carried our snowshoes to come back on in case of a thaw. There are four glaciers emptying into the northern side of the main gorge. They cascade down from the cliffs of Mount McKinley and head in huge *box-cañons* the walls of which rise in places to a height of five thousand feet above the glacier. About a mile above camp there was a serac which we "swung" to the left. At this point the main gorge was about one half a mile broad, and the largest of the tributary glaciers faced us on the farther side of the ice fall. We had just gained the top of this serac when an exclamation from Professor Parker halted us. We turned instinctively towards Mount McKinley's grim cliffs and then we were as men turned to stone. The whole of the great cliffs of the box-cañon appeared, at first glance, to be on fire. Unnumbered thousands of tons of soft snow were avalanching from the southern flanks of Mount McKinley onto the glacier floor five thousand feet below. The snow fell so far that it was broken into heavy clouds that rolled downward like huge waves. The force of the falling mass was terrific and as it struck the blue-green glacier mail it threw a great snow cloud that rose like a live thing for five hundred feet; whirling in the wind the avalanche had caused, the white wall swept across the valley, and almost before we were aware of it we were struggling and choking in a blinding, stinging cloud of ice dust. For a long time we crouched with our feet braced far apart and our bodies bent over our firmly planted ice-axes, and when the air finally cleared the walls were still smoking and rumbling under the masses of falling snow. It was a most impressive example of the terrific force of gravitation, and when we finally started onward we were thankful indeed that we had not ascended the right-hand side of the glacier.

We could now see that the glacier ended in a box-cañon. The side walls were formed by the great cliffs of Mount McKinley on one side, and the equally grim cliffs of a second mountain range on the other; the end of the box was formed by the South-West Arête. The arête dipped down, forming a col, but the walls were too steep to negotiate. If the climbing of Mount McKinley had depended on our scaling this slope, and if we could have counted on cold weather, we might have accomplished the feat. But the yawning *berg-schrunds* and particularly the overhanging fields of soft snow that scarred the lower slopes with avalanche tracks made the risk too great.

Below the final basin we travelled through a maze of huge crevasses, and while crossing one of them on a long snow bridge, Tucker broke through. I had already crossed, on my hands and knees, to distribute my weight, so that Tucker was between Professor Parker and me and we held him easily until he extricated himself. Many of these crevasses were so deep that although the walls seemed perpendicular we could see nothing but an inky blue void below.

Once below the col the travelling was safe, but a high wind had arisen that blew clouds of snow from the upper ridges, which settled in soft drifts into which we sank to our knees. It was regular winter weather and long "mare's-tails" of snow streaming to the leeward of the higher ridges added to the arctic aspect of the scene. We stopped below the col for a second breakfast, and after chopping a hole in the ice and sheltering it with our bodies we succeeded in boiling a hypsometer. Our barometers placed us at ten thousand feet.

Before long the wind had begun to moderate and by the time we attacked the col, the weather was quite pleasant.

We rose five hundred feet over avalanche tracks and finally came to a halt directly below the lowest point of the great ridge. What would n't we have given to rise five hundred feet more and look out over the other side! Beyond, just out of our sight, was an absolutely unknown mountain wilderness. Mounts Foraker and Hunter we knew would be in sight, and could we have only climbed a little higher we would have secured a view that no man has ever looked on, or probably will ever look on. We were at an altitude of about 10,300 feet when we stopped. A *bergschrund* stretched across the ridge above us, and the constant sound of falling ice warned us from the cliffs on either hand. This was the end of all our labour—10,300 feet; it seems like a small thing on paper, but we knew what every foot of the 10,300 had cost—and were content.

As we stood looking off across the tangle of jagged peaks and gleaming snow-fields I was conscious of a feeling of reluctance to leave it all. The glacier we had climbed wound downward in a deep gash to the Big Basin far below and as a final payment for our toil every peak in that alpine wilderness stood clear cut against the sky. We stood there a long time drinking it all in,

Failure

and then Tucker said, "Every step that we take from
now on, means green grass, trees, and running water!"
With his words the longing for the lowlands swept over
us; Mount McKinley and its everlasting snow-fields
were a thing of the past, and we started downward
from our last climb with light hearts. As we tramped
along we swung towards a small shelf of rock that broke
through the ice on the glacier's edge. It was "pink
McKinley granite," an actual part of the great mountain, and we broke off samples with our ice-axes to
take back over the long trail. As we rested our companions passed us on their way to the col—tiny black
specks, they looked, against the immensity of the
mountain masses that rose about them. Climbing out
of the snow gully below the rocks we could place our
hands on the cold granite slabs and as we passed we
each patted the old mountain on the back, as it were,
in farewell.

We reached camp at 1 P. M. having made 3500
feet of altitude during our climb. We snowshoed the
last mile through the slush the northern sun had made
and I ended the morning with a snow bath, which is the
only luxury that the snow-fields have to offer. After
the return of our companions we lay down for a short
rest, and then a long steady "hike" brought us to our
old camp in the centre of the big basin.

Everything was bustle and confusion as we prepared
for our final tramp to the lowlands. Each man's
belongings were thoroughly overhauled and each useless
article thrown aside after the closest inspection.

The instant anything is thrown aside it becomes
public property; each frayed sock and worn shoe-pack
is carefully balanced against its mate, and every ounce
of unnecessary weight is eliminated. I remember an

MOUNT HUNTINGTON AND THE GLACIER THAT WE FOLLOWED TO THE SOUTH-WEST RIDGE.

Photo by H. C. Parker.

amusing incident that occurred in 1910 which I have often seen repeated. While breaking camp one morning Professor Parker regretfully discarded an old pair of trousers. On reaching the spot I was overjoyed to find that they could boast a solid seat and untorn knees. I made an exchange on the spot, and as I looked back some minutes later I saw Printz marching proudly along in my trousers while what remained of his former pair decorated a willow bush. The condition of Printz's original pair is too awful to contemplate!

Before leaving our last camp we made a careful survey of the surrounding mountains. Professor Cuntz had been busy taking the angles and elevations of the surrounding peaks and as the great number of mountains made it difficult to describe with accuracy the individual mountain masses we decided to name three of the most important peaks that rose above the big basin.

On the east stood a magnificent mountain that rose in the shape of a rock-ribbed, ice-incrusted throne, above a broad base whose lower snow-fields had been carved into buttresses by the glacier winds. This peak we named Mount Hubbard after General Thomas H. Hubbard, president of the Peary Arctic Club, whose lifelong interest in exploration has been of such great benefit to mankind.

The highest peak on the eastern edge of the Big Basin we named after Professor Huntington, president of the American Geographical Society, under whose auspices we had undertaken the exploration of Mount McKinley's southern glaciers.

Directly under the southern cliffs of Mount McKinley stood a third peak that we wished to name. It was a magnificent cliff-girdled pile that formed in itself

the main southern buttress of the McKinley massif.
The naming of this peak rested with our entire
party and the name chosen was that of Daniel Carter
Beard, the father of the world-celebrated Boy Scout
movement, and a man who has endeared himself to
every American man and boy through the pages of
The American Boy's Handy Book.

We conferred proper names on these peaks as it was
impossible to choose descriptive names that would
not be confusing among such a chaos of unnamed
mountains, and the names chosen were in each instance
those of men who had either directly or indirectly
contributed towards the exploration of this region.

Our last hour in the big basin was celebrated by the
first bonfire that has ever reddened those lonely snow-
fields. By gathering together each infinitesimal piece
of wood from our pemmican and chocolate boxes we
succeeded in making a respectable fire and we joyfully
gathered around to enjoy the grateful warmth.

On the following day we said farewell to the trampled
area of snow that had, for so long, been our mountain
base camp. It had been a hard pull. In reaching it we
had endured many hardships. We had given our best
efforts and every foot of progress had been won by
the sweat of our brows, and by this toil we were un-
ashamed—yes, even proud in a small way of our work,
for we had mapped and explored a part of what is
probably the grandest mass of rugged peaks on the
North American continent.

Every man had done more than his share, and after
forty-two days on the ice we were living in greater
comfort and amity than we were on that day so far
away when we had said good-by to the lowlands.

CHAPTER XIV

THE RETREAT TO CIVILISATION

We leave the Big Basin—We re-photograph the "fake peak"—
Changes along our route—The joy of running water and wild flowers—
We reach timber—Remarks on packing and physical condition—Arrival
at Parkersburgh—The feast at "Wreck Island"—Talkeetna Station—
The man hunt at Susitna Station—We arrive at Seldovia.

WE left our old camp with seventy-five pound packs
and in two hours we reached a point well down
between the walls of the great gorge. The travel was
all downhill, and as we picked up and passed our old
relay camps, we realised to the full the difference
between relay travel and straight packing. We sometimes travelled in one march a distance that it had
taken two days to cover when we ascended the glacier.

On the second day we reached Glacier Point and
camped by a snow-water lake that had formed during
our absence. We crawled into our sleeping-bags at
1.30 P. M. and at 4.40 we were up again as we wanted
to revisit Dr. Cook's fake peak while the weather was
good.

The day was perfect, with no wind and a bright sun
for photographing. While crossing Glacier Point we
encountered some sun-bared turf where moss, grass,
and purple lupine were growing luxuriantly, and the
very look of the beautiful spring carpet to our snow-
worn eyes acted as an intoxicant. Dropping onto the
ice again we pushed on steadily to the fake peak. We

found that the snow formations had changed considerably during our absence. But there was still a good deal more snow than Dr. Cook's September photograph showed. We secured the photographs without delay and the following morning found us on the march again.

On the lower glacier everything had changed and instead of blinding sweeps of snow we now found bare ice seamed with countless crevasses. During our midday's rests we brought out a worn pack of cards and played bridge whist for candy, to be paid when we reached civilisation, but the craving for sweets from which we all suffered was aggravated instead of appeased, and even the winners drew small consolation from their good fortune. On August first we found grass growing in considerable quantities among the rocks of the glacial moraines and we derived a considerable amount of satisfaction from eating the soft stems. We were "vegetation-mad" and to us even the poorest little wild flower was a thing of exquisite beauty. As we neared the glacier's snout we were greeted by the dim greens of the nearby mountain slopes and by an alpine lake we found the fresh tracks of a small band of caribou that had come up out of their summer retreats in the foothills.

At last the great day came when we dipped down over the last ice-field and found ourselves on the bank of the glacier stream that swept the base of the ice. We did not hesitate before taking to the water, for on the farther bank we could see the gleam of dead willow branches and as the warm flames leapt about our steaming clothes we laughed with joy and chattered like children, for we were once more in "God's country" and our fifty days of glacier travel had come to an end. In the deepening dusk the glacier's form loomed black against the night sky. There was something sinister and repellent in the grim loneliness of the scene, and we turned with thankful hearts to our willow fire. As La Voy said, "Looking back at the dead ice walls was like looking back on a misspent life."

At this time, with base camp only a day's march away, I wish to say a few words about our physical condition after our long ordeal. In the first place we were in magnificent condition and yet according to civilised standards we looked weaker than when we first reached the ice. In civilisation when a man's cheeks are full and smooth and his body also runs to curves people say, "Does n't he look *well?*" On the trail we could say with greater truthfulness, "Does n't he look ill?" Our faces were hatchet-thin, our eyes sunken and wrinkled from days of squinting over blinding snow-fields, and our bodies worn down to bone and sinew. But every unnecessary ounce of flesh *and muscle* had been burned away in the fire of constant toil, until each tendon worked as smoothly and evenly as the well-greased parts of an engine. One would naturally suppose that our lower limbs in particular would have shown a noticeable increase in size, but, if anything, they were smaller than when we left civilisation.

A fact of even greater interest is that we were living comfortably on a smaller food allowance than we consumed on our march up the glacier.

With these facts in view the work accomplished on the following day will prove of interest. When we broke camp on our last "drive" to Parkersburgh, La Voy, Tucker, Grassi, and the writer shouldered packs weighing between ninety and one hundred pounds. After going about a half-mile, we came to a food cache left by Aten and Thompson in case of need, and knowing that

there was no food to spare at Parkersburgh we picked up
this cache, which included a tent, axe, tin buckets, beans,
etc. This raised the weight of our packs to between
ninety-six and one hundred and twenty pounds, weighed
with scales on our arrival at Parkersburgh. With these
loads we travelled through alder thickets so dense
that we were forced to chop out a trail, and over bogs
where we sank to our knees in the sticky mud. High
water had washed away our bridges and we forded swift
water waist deep and climbed gravel banks on our hands
and knees, and yet we reached camp as fresh and happy
as a band of children. We could have repeated the
journey with ease, and yet it was in covering this same
stretch of country, under far better conditions, that
we became so tired on the first day of our arrival. In
stating these facts I am not holding up our labours as
an example of weight carrying—under different conditions we could have carried much more; the point of
interest is that we accomplished the labour more
easily on a small food allowance, and after weeks of
toil, than we did when well fed and fresh from
civilisation.

Our arrival at Parkersburgh was a joyful event. To
us the green cottonwood groves and flower-spangled
river banks were a paradise, and the cosy tent with its
log walls a veritable palace. Our food supply was
low, but the evening meal of baconless beans, sugarless
tea, and sour-dough biscuits was a Lucullan banquet.
That night as I lay in my warm blankets listening to
the familiar roar of the Tokositna the two previous
months seemed a strange jumbled dream—bitter cold
camps in the snow—the roar of avalanches—dreary
hours under a tump-line—and dim stretches of blue
snow under the night sky came back to me in queer

THE "COL" OF THE SOUTH-WEST RIDGE OF MOUNT McKINLEY.
Photo by Merl La Voy.

THE SNOW WALL THAT PREVENTED OUR REACHING THE TOP OF THE SOUTH-
WEST RIDGE.
Photo by Belmore Browne.

disjointed pictures; but the whole was already an intangible blend of memories that had faded away to form what men call *experience*. Now our minds clung eagerly to the future: the song of "glacier glutted rivers," the smother and roar of the cañon we would "shoot"—but above all to our treasure trove— our cache on the gravel island hard by the Talkeetna. The last thing I remember hearing before falling asleep was La Voy's voice beseeching an all-wise Creator to keep our potatoes from spoiling until we reached the cache.

Our last day on the Tokositna began with "the crack o' dawn," and by night we were encamped well down towards the mouth of the Chulitna. We tried frantically to reach our cache but the river gainsaid us. In the swift water we had to come down backwards, letting the current do the work while Thompson gave a "kick" with the propeller now and then to keep steerage way. The gravel bars, too, gave us trouble. When you are ascending a river and run aground it usually occurs at the foot of the shallow, and the current will help you to get off. But in descending a stream when you strike a gravel bank you usually lodge on the upper end and at every movement of the boat the current forces you into shallower water. In cases of this kind we reached deep water by "sluicing." Several men would carefully sound the shallows about us for the deepest channel. Having once decided on a route we would move the *Explorer* in the following manner. Taking the bow we would either move or lift it to one side of the current. This would deflect the rushing water and in a short time it would make a channel on the exposed side of the boat. When the water was deep enough to suit our purpose we would push the *Explorer's* bow in the opposite direction and as the current cleared away the gravel under her she would slip into the new channel and move downstream a foot or two. In this slow manner we would sluice a channel through the shoals until we reached deep water. We moored the *Explorer* to the bank well after dark.

It was a peaceful spot and yet before the night wore through we were destined to have one more adventure.

In the inky blackness La Voy zealously attacked an "adult" dead spruce for firewood, which breaking side-ways, as dead trees can, came crashing down on the *Explorer's* bow. The majority of the party were aboard wrestling our supper from a brace of oil stoves. Luckily a coil of cable on the bow saved the boat from damage, but in the resulting kick of the *Explorer's* stern our hot cakes and beans went skyward.

Now our party included men of many diverse temper-aments. In moments of excitement Grassi depended on volcanic outbursts of Italian to sooth his feelings. Professor Cuntz boasted a deaconship but in moments of stress he has been known to say "My gracious!" as we can all bare witness. Professor Parker being a scientist was coldly accurate in his remarks, while Tucker's speech flowed along with an *abandon* that was positively refreshing! Thompson's diction in moments of mental exhilaration resembled the purr of a contented motor. La Voy and I, being safe in the gloom of the forest, could give our entire minds to the ensuing babel and when silence at last reigned he turned to me and said, "It's an education to travel with a bunch like ours; when anything *good* happens you can listen to a whole dictionary!"

We needed no alarm clock to wake us next morning

for the luxuries in our cache called to us with a voice that drowned all other thoughts. We slipped quickly downstream and soon a gleam of white among some cottonwood trees told us that our hour of joy was at hand. We moored the *Explorer* by a gravel island but the Chulitna had eaten out some new channels and our canvas canoe was launched and sped away through the rushing water. We stood on tiptoe watching the retreating figures, and as they reached the cache our anxiety was boundless; but soon the welcome hail of "Everything's O. K.!" came across the river to our eager ears, and in an instant we were all at work gathering firewood and preparing for the coming feast. By the time that our stove was going, the boat arrived and we unloaded the treasures it contained in the same ecstasy with which children empty their Christmas stockings! We were actually ravenous, and as jars of chow-chow, cans of maple-syrup, and tins of meat appeared we hugged them in our arms and danced delirious dances on the sand! One of the great truths of life that one learns to understand in the north is that it is well worth while to go without the things one wants, for the greater the sacrifice the greater the reward when the wish is consummated. I have eaten with all manner of hungry men from the sun-browned riders of the sage to the bidarka-men of the Aleutians, and I have feasted joyously on "seal liver," "seagull-omelets," and "caribou spinach"; but never have I seen men eat more, or better food!

We started standing up, and wiped the stove clean; then we refilled our pots, pans, and oven, and made a clean sweep of that—sitting down; we ended conservatively—*on our backs!* Then we lay "as we had fallen," and with the sound of glacier water in our ears and

12

the warmth of the northern sun in our faces we slept the whole day through.

Now we knew that Talkeetna Station would be populated, for in addition to Dyer who ran the A. C. Co. store, there would be Indians coming in from their summer camps. One detachment had passed us while we were repairing the *Explorer* on our way up the Chulitna. They had drifted past us in boats made of the green skins of moose and caribou. The primitive canoes were loaded to the gunwales with men, women, children, and dogs, and in the bow of each sat an Indian man tapping the river bottom with a slender pole and searching the channel for dangers that might wreck his frail craft. Your northern red man is a master of the craft of travel. After the salmon-run on the lower rivers have filled their caches with food for man and dog they await the freezing of the waters. When the icy covering has formed their dogs pull their belongings to the moose pastures and caribou ranges of the interior. Here they hunt and trap the long winter through, and after the spring sun has sent the ice booming towards the sea, they sew up their winter skins into boats and drift with dignity to their summer homes. Here the boats are dismantled, and the skins—none the worse for their immersion—are tanned. When their winter's fur catch is traded they can await the autumn salmon run in peace, and so their lives run, sliding gently from spring to winter and from winter to summer, until they take their last long journey to "the happy hunting-ground."

We were not disappointed in our expectations, and when we drew in to the bank at Talkeetna the shore was lined with Indians that had been drawn by the sound of our exhaust. Among them stood our good friend Dyer and some prospectors whom we had not as yet met. The prospectors were headed towards the gravel bars of Valdez Creek in the interior, where gold had been found in paying quantities.

While our stay in Talkeetna Station was short we made up for lost time in communion with our fellow-men. The Rusk Mount McKinley party had departed for "the outside" some time since. We heard, too, for the first time, that some Indians on whom they had depended to bring them provisions had refused to make the trip, and one who acted as a river guide had been averse to ascending the Tokositna, being obsessed evidently with the olden legends which people the Mount McKinley region with devils and hobgoblins. I had many an interesting talk with old Talkeetna Nicolae, chief of the Talkeetnas. Sitting cross-legged on the floor of his cabin with the smell of tanning moose-hide in my nostrils, I listened to weird stories of the olden days, and it was there that he told me of the Russian trader—possibly one of Malakoff's men—who died in the Kichatna swamps. Later he posed proudly before my camera, his chest liberally decorated with watches—that had long since ceased to work!

A long lazy run took us down to Susitna Station. When the river broadened out sufficiently we could turn the *Explorer's* head loose and let her go, and we did, with the river pushing behind us while the miles flew by.

We found Susitna Station in a turmoil. A man had been lost in the swamps behind the town, and a searching party was being organised to find him or his remains. We took our places in the long line that filed out into the back-country. A rifle shot was to be the signal of success in our quest.

All day long we moved fan-wise combing the swamp and spruce groves, but the expected rifle shot was not heard, although we strained our ears in the monotonous drone of the mosquito hordes. Later we heard that the man, half-crazed, had reached the banks of the Susitna.

At Beluga we picked up a prospective buyer of the *Explorer* and turned the old boat's bow towards Seldovia. Kussiloff we entered through schools of belugas that were harrying the salmon hordes and stopped at the cannery. On visiting the bunk-houses we found that the scenes of more civilised "Chinatowns" had been transplanted to this northern beach. A night of freezing spray and heavy seas followed, but with the sunrise we came in between the sheltering points of Seldovia harbour, and one more summer of toil and pleasure was finished.

THE "EXPLORER" STRANDED ON THE GREAT "FLATS" FORMED BY THE SILT CARRIED DOWN BY THE SUSITNA RIVER.

Photo by Merl La Voy.

CHAPTER XV

THE 1912 EXPEDITION

Plans—Difficulties—Preparations for a winter trip—We choose the Seward route and determine to cross the Alaskan Range—Gathering dog teams—Aten and La Voy commence freighting—We reach Seward—The first days on the trail.

IMMEDIATELY after our second failure to climb Mount McKinley Professor Parker and I began to plan a third attempt. We were through with the southern approach—that much we knew—and our next attempt would have to be made from the northern side of the Alaskan Range. The question therefore was which side of the northern approach was the most promising, and we could answer it with our own first-hand knowledge of the great peak. During the night in 1906 that I spent with Dr. Cook on the mountain top west of the Tokositna glacier, I had been able to look along the south-western end of the big mountain. From this point and from the Mount Kliskon country even farther westward I had carefully studied the mountain's contours. Throughout this whole sweep I could not see one promising route. I studied the profile of the Western ridge which dips downward to Peters Glacier. It was at this point that both Judge Wickersham and Dr. Cook had unsuccessfully attacked the big mountain and I could see indications of the cliffs which render this arête difficult.

The northern face we knew was unclimbable, as we had seen both Brooks's and Dr. Cook's photographs of these forbidding ice cliffs.

By a process of elimination therefore our minds centred on the Southern North-eastern Ridge. As I have before stated we did not know as yet that there were three ridges on the north-eastern side, but from what we could see of this approach we were convinced that it offered the best chances of success.[1]

After deciding on this line of attack the next important question was how we were to reach the ridge. Fairbanks on the Tanana River is the nearest town to Mount McKinley and with the aid of dogs, in the winter time, the journey offers no difficulties, consisting as it does of only 160 miles of excellent snow-travel. Fairbanks is easily reached from the seacoast via the Copper River Railroad and a well travelled trail that crosses the low pass at the head of the Tanana River. This then was our logical route.

But as we thought it over our minds filled with memories of the magnificent stretch of mountains that form the Alaskan Range east of Mount McKinley. Many times we had looked yearningly at the great line of snow peaks, and it was our hearts' desire to explore their unknown cañons. If we could find a pass through the high range we would explore a magnificent mountain wilderness that otherwise might remain unknown for years. The very thought thrilled us and we at once began to perfect our plans.

Now about sixty miles from Mount McKinley the Alaskan Range breaks away, and the mountains become lower and more rounded as you approach the Tanana River. In these lower mountains, eighty miles from Mount McKinley, there is an easy pass called Broad Pass, which has been crossed by a good many prospectors and one survey party.

The only authentic crossing of the range between

[1] For note see page 191.

Broad Pass and Mount McKinley was accomplished by Dr. Cook's expedition, in 1906. In describing it he fails to place it accurately, but states that they crossed it in a single day with pack horses, and that the pass was drained by a large tributary of the Chulitna River.

This description places Dr. Cook's pass in the low part of the Alaskan Range close to Broad Pass, as the only river that enters the Chulitna from that region is the west fork of the Chulitna.

We knew moreover that we would find no pass worthy of the name in the high, ice-bound portion of the range close to Mount McKinley. If we could force a way through we would be satisfied. In the glimpses of the range that we had caught from the country south of Mount McKinley we had noticed one promising fact— the range, even in the summer time, was covered with snow. This fact meant that the valleys and cañons would be filled with glaciers which in turn would discharge streams into the Chulitna, and on the frozen surfaces of these rivers and glaciers we hung our hopes of finding a route across the range. While it would be possible for a small party of strong men to ascend the Chulitna during the summer in boats and then pack light loads through the range, the transporting of a large outfit in this manner would require too much time and the accomplishment of this feat in addition to the climbing of Mount McKinley would be an impossibility. We were forced therefore to make a winter trip of it, and to depend for our transportation on the Alaskan dog.

Now the value of dogs in the north fluctuates with the seasons. When the trails begin to harden and winter throws its mantle of snow across the land there is a corresponding boom in the dog market, while in the springtime when the dogs' usefulness vanishes with the melting snows they can be purchased for a song. In order to profit by the spring "slump" we commissioned Arthur Aten to buy dogs for us, and when the summer of 1911 arrived we possessed a strong and well-trained team.

But plans are made but to be broken. With the coming of spring came a call of "Gold" from the north. With feverish haste we packed and stood ready. Then followed travel-worn letters that told us that "strikes" were being made along the glaciers, of Prince William's Sound. Mount McKinley was for the time, forgotten, and we spent our summer among the ice-fed fiords.

With the coming of winter our thoughts drifted back to the big mountain and when the first snow flurry came down from the Kenai Mountains we were ready to advance. Aten and La Voy were the only men of the old party to join Professor Parker and the writer. Our journey was to be entirely different in character from the work we accomplished in 1910, for speed in dog travel depends on a small party, and we no longer needed the large number of men necessary for relay packing. It was with the keenest regret however that we started on the long trail without our old companions.

As we were to enter the Alaskan Range just east of Mount McKinley our route would lead us up the familiar waterways of the Susitna and Chulitna rivers. But as Cook Inlet was choked with ice during the winter time, we were forced to leave the steamer at Seward.

Seward lies at the head of Resurrection Bay on the south side of the Kenai Peninsula. It is from this port

that the incompleted railroad, so often mentioned in
the newspapers, starts on its long journey to the interior.
Striking directly through the heart of the Kenai Peninsula the railroad winds and tunnels for eighty miles
through magnificent mountain scenery to tide-water
on Turnagain Arm at the head of Cook Inlet. At this
point construction has ceased, but a winter trail leads
from the end of the line to Susitna Station via
Knik Arm. Beyond Susitna Station a winter trail
now leads over the Alaskan Range at the head of
the Kichatna to the Kuskoquim and the gold fields of
the Iditerod. This three-foot strip of foot-hardened
snow is the only link now joining the village that will
some day be a city with the wilderness that in days to
come will be an inland empire. The road is not
operated in the winter time but the grade is too valuable to stand idle, and after the ties and tracks are
covered with snow the scream and rumble of the
locomotive gives way to the jingle of dog bells.

At intervals of about ten miles, road-houses stand
offering food and rest to man and dog. They are one
of the most important of Alaskan institutions, and on
all the winter trails that criss-cross the great land, one
will find these resting-places which make rapid travel
possible.

Now only one man can drive a dog team. When
"the going is bad" an extra man can *help*. But the
Seward trail was supposed to be a good trail.

For that reason Professor Parker and I turned over
our outfit to Aten and La Voy in October. They were
to relay our supplies to Susitna Station and then up
the Susitna as far as they could, returning to Susitna
Station to meet us in February. At Seward La Voy
met a "sour-dough" fresh from the Iditerod. He had

come over the long trail bound for "the outside" and
sold his dogs, sled, and fur sleeping-robe for a ridicu-
lously low price. This addition gave us fourteen dogs
for the heavy hauling, and each one had more than
earned his cost before our freight rested at Susitna.
A telephone line that connected the road-houses was a
great help to us. Our companions 'phoned the news of
their progress to Brown & Hawkins—the leading mer-
chants of Seward—who kindly forwarded the messages
by mail. In this way we were able to keep track of our
companions until the day arrived when we too were to
start on the long trail.

It was during the last days of January that our
steamer drifted in between the fog-draped cliffs of
Resurrection Bay. Only ten years before I had been
in the same harbour; but now a bustling Alaskan town
was scattered over what had then been a green spruce-
covered point, and along the water front I could see
the trestles of the new railroad whose right of way we
were going to follow with our dog teams. The mountains alone were unchanged and looked down through
the fog rifts as they did in the old days. To me this
is one of the most striking facts in our great country—
the rapidity of growth. I have heard an Englishman
earnestly comparing (unfavourably) the transportation
facilities of a Western city with those of London when
I could remember the days when the stumps of forest
trees were still obstructing the main avenue of that
city! When I first saw Resurrection Bay it was little
more than a wilderness fiord. When our little steamer,
that, in any other land, would long since have been con-
demned, came to rest, a canoe came gliding from the
shore. The man who paddled it was calling aloud
for a minister. The minister was wanted by one Bill

MOUNT McKINLEY—NORTHERN APPROACH.

VIEW FROM THE HEADWATERS OF THE KANTISHNA RIVER. THE NORTHERN, AND CENTRAL NORTH-EASTERN
RIDGES ARE SHOWN ON THE LEFT. THE SUMMIT IS HIDDEN BY THE NORTH PEAK.

From a painting by Belmore Browne.

or Tom and "he wants to get married *bad*" the canoe-
man added, "for he has two kids already!" Such was
Seward in the old days, but even then it was historical
ground. The Russians had settled there when Alaska
belonged to the White Bear, and the first wooden man-
o'-war ever launched on the Pacific coast was built by
them in this sheltered harbour.

On our sail along the Alaskan coast we had been overcome with forebodings of trouble through the mildness
of the winter. No winter like it could be remembered,
even by "the oldest inhabitant." Our wildest fears
were realised as we walked to our hotel along the
Seward streets for the thin glare of ice that covered
the ground was melting perceptibly.

Our first task was to find a traveller with a dog-team
who was going to Susitna Station, for besides our
personal duffle of fifty pounds to the man the invariable
forgotten or left-over things had swelled our belongings
to a weight of three hundred pounds. Fortune led
us to the United States mail-carrier, Vause by name,
who was starting over the trail in a few days.

He turned over his second team to us, partly loaded
with second-class mail matter—which under his con-
tract he is not forced to deliver. This raised our load
to five hundred pounds while he carried an equal bulk
of letters on the lead-sled. For a number of days we
kicked our heels about the streets of Seward, waiting
for the weather to turn cold. In the meanwhile the
town was stirred by the arrival of the Iditerod gold
shipment.

The gold was packed in small wooden chests—one
hundred pounds to the chest—which were handled with
grunts and groans by the bank clerks who took them
from the dog sleds. The populace stood packed about,

but fully one half of their interest was centred on the two magnificent, perfectly matched dog teams that had pulled the treasure from the banks of the Kusko-quim, four hundred miles to the north.

The dogs were owned and driven by "Bob" Griffith, better known as "Dog" Griffith among the trail men. He knew dogs better than a Kentucky horsemen knows horses, and had participated himself in the greatest sporting event of this world—"The Nome Sweepstake" —when men race an unlimited number of wolf-dogs over four hundred miles of frozen Alaskan trail.

We met him later as he wanted tallow to feed to his dogs and I had an over supply to trade. From his lips and those of Mitchell, the driver of Griffith's second team, we heard picturesque but awful things concerning the condition of the Susitna trail. On the theory that the longer we waited the worse things would be, we set the following day for our time of departure.

An earthquake—the precursor possibly of the Katmai eruption that buried Kadiak Island in ashes—rattled the frame houses as we prepared our outfit for the trail.

We said good-by to Seward and its hospitable citizens on the first of February. We crossed a piece of rough trail through the waste of burnt and slashed timber common to Alaskan towns before reaching the shelter of the woods.

In the shelter of the timber we found snow enough to grease our sled runners and before long we were trot-ting along the line of the railroad.

Vause led with a five-hundred-pound load of mail lashed on a Nome sled, drawn by five dogs. Professor Parker travelled with the lead-sled, while I followed them at the gee-pole of the second Nome sled loaded

also with 400 (four hundred) pounds, and drawn by
four dogs.

Unless one has been in the north it is hard to realise
the importance of the "broken trail." In the winter
time the whole country is covered with several feet of
soft, powdery snow. This snow is seldom crusted
until the spring thaw sets in, and in consequence it
is difficult to travel through; even a man on snowshoes
may find it arduous work. But after a man has walked
over it his snowshoes leave a broad path that freezes
hard, and on this narrow strip of frozen crust dogs
can pull a loaded sled. As the trail is used it grows
broader, firmer, and smoother, until in time it becomes
in reality a "winter trail."

After a snow-storm, or a heavy drifting wind, the
trail must be rebroken, and at times when it becomes
completely effaced you feel your way with a sharpened
pole lest you lose the trail and the benefit of its firm
foundation.

Now dog-driving, when you have a heavy load and
the going is bad, is about as strenuous a job as a man
can tackle. Even one week of idleness will allow hardened muscles to become soft, and after many months
of city life, no matter how conscientiously one has
exercised according to civilised standards, the body is
in no condition to stand the demands of the trail.

On our first day's run we put twenty-one miles of
soft snow behind us. The trail was in execrable condition. The warm weather had rotted the snow, and
the sleds in consequence were continually breaking
through and turning over into the soft snow beside the
trail. Now when a sled turns over or "killapies" its
outside runner has a fiendish way of catching under the
hard lip of the trail; put five hundred pounds on top

of the sled and it is a man-sized job to lift it back onto the trail again. When you have trotted twenty-one long, soft snow miles punctuated frequently with these sled episodes your very bones cry out against your past months of idleness.

Another source of bruises and bad language that we encountered were the numerous trestles. There was a drop of about three feet from the surface of the trail to the ties.

The snow had fallen through between the timbers which were capped with cones of hard ice. We would nurse our dogs as gently as possible to the edge of the trestle and then give them the word to "Mush!" Vause's dogs being under his constant supervision and at the head of our line took the bridges quietly,— a thing which few dog teams will do. As I was a stranger to the dogs I drove and as they were behind they took the bridges with a rush. The "gee-pole" or steering-pole is lashed to the right-hand runner of the sled in such a position that the end comes level with your right hand when you stand six feet in front of the sled. When the sled slid from the level of the trail the gee-pole first swept out into space and then plunged down to the level of the ties. As it is absolutely necessary to hold on to the gee-pole to guide the sled, we had to take the drop-off on the run, leap out into space, land, somehow, on the ice-capped ties, and *keep running* while the ice scraped the skin from the knuckles of our right hands. It was dashing, bone-breaking work, and would have made good moving picture "stuff," but when you are wedged between ice-capped ties with the steel runners of a four-hundred-pound sled grinding your back, it's hard to appreciate the picturesque side of things!

About twelve miles from Seward stands the first road-house, and here we got a bite to eat and rested the dogs.   Some miles beyond we came to our first trouble; the bridge over Snow River had been washed out by a freshet and the rails and ties hung in midair, held only by the spikes and fish-plates.   One look at this aerial route was enough, and we descended to the naked gravel bars of the river bed and by doubling our two dog teams relayed the sleds over a jury-bridge of logs.

When we reached the railroad again it had been transformed by the late freshet into a ridge of ice. On the top of this "ice tight-rope" we juggled with sleds and dogs.   Once, my foot slipped and I landed with my sled and dogs in a tangled heap at the base of the ridge.   Night overtook us beyond Snow River, and it was inky black when we saw the lights of our night's shelter.

Vause was trail-hardened, having carried mail since the first snow, and to him our day had been only a moderately strenuous one.   But to me—fresh from the flesh-pots—it savoured of "hard labour."

With all this work however there goes the invariable recompense; back of all these aches, and strains, and cuts, and bruises lies the knowledge that you are being made over; it is only nature's way of doing the job. It is always hard when you first "hit the trail," but as you think of the days to come, when, with a body as hard as those of the dogs you drive, you can trot unwearied the long day through, the game seems well worth the candle.

Note for page 182.—Before our departure we heard of the Central, and Northern North-east Ridge, from Thomas Lloyd of Fairbanks, Alaska; we also gained a general idea of this side of the mountain from a photograph shown to us by Charles Sheldon.—AUTHOR.

CHAPTER XVI

THE SEWARD TRAIL

"Mother White's" road-house—Bad condition of trail—We cross
Trail Lake—We reach Turnagain Arm and find it clear of ice—We try
the water route—Failure—Crow Creek Pass—Eagle River—We reach
Old Knik—News of our companions.

THE road-house where we rested was known as
"White's" as it was kept by a nice old couple of
that name. "Dad" White supervised the outdoor
part of their domain, filling the generous wood-boxes,
bringing in the ice-cold water from the mountain
streams, and, in the summer time, mending boats and
tending the little truck-garden that sloped down to the
shore of Kenai Lake.

In the house Mrs. White, or "Mother White" as
she was called by all who knew her, reigned supreme.
Dressed in the costume of the day she might have
stepped from the frame of a Copley or Sir Joshua.
Her snow-white hair was the only hint of the weight
of years she bore, for her mind and figure were those of
a young girl.

They tell the story along the trail of how, in the
early days of the railroad, when travelling rates were
high, Mother White used to walk the twenty miles
to town. But one day an official of the railroad, who
was inspecting the track, passed her, and in her next
mail she found a pass to Seward.

"BOB" GRIFFITHS' DOGS PULLING OUR FREIGHT OVER CROW CREEK PASS.
Photo by H. C. Parker.

OUR OUTFIT LEAVING SUSITNA STATION. ALL THE INHABITANTS SHOWED
THE GREATEST INTEREST IN OUR JOURNEY AND DID EVERYTHING
IN THEIR POWER TO AID US.
Photo by H. C. Parker.

When we awoke the next morning we looked out over the steel-grey surface of Kenai Lake. In the distance the water blended with the mountain mist. No ice was to be seen, and Dad White told us that it was the first time in the memory of man that the lake had not frozen.

While we were finishing our hot cakes a suspicious murmur from the roof drew our eyes to the windows, and to our dismay we looked out into sheets of warm rain. Nothing in this world is more disheartening than trotting through rain-rotted snow in a steady downpour, and besides the mail must be kept dry. I own, too, to having felt a secret joy at this unexpected rest. The following day, however, was cooler and we made up for our delay by an early start.

The day was remarkable for the fiendish travel we encountered. Once only were we blessed by a good bit of trail. This was at Trail Lake where we found a mile of clear ice. Jumping on the sleds we went sailing along, and in verity it was more like sailing than sledding, for the dogs were splashing along in several inches of water, and our sleds left long ripples behind that broke the clear reflections of the surrounding mountains. At the end of the lake we paid heavily by running into a piece of trail where we worked for an hour and only made one mile. The trail itself would not bear our weight and we broke through sometimes to our waists.

The conditions held us down to a fourteen-mile day, but the fourth day we trotted eighteen miles, crossing the Kenai Divide and dropping down to the road-house at "Mile 52." The travel was through splendid mountain scenery. We followed, as usual, the railroad line which led us along the timbered mountainsides. When

13

the pitching, sliding sleds allowed us to turn we could look through the ragged tops of the spruce trees to the distant mountainsides that glittered under their mantles of snow and ice.

At the road-houses we learned day by day the history of Aten's and La Voy's trip across the trail. The miserable winter had changed their trip into a terrific struggle against adverse conditions. At one road-house we would hear that a heavy snow-storm had destroyed the trail and that they had spent two days "breaking" a new one to the next shelter. Farther on we heard that Aten had spent the night, snow-blind in an abandoned cabin, with nothing but the dogs to keep him warm. And again we were told that a fight had occurred among our "huskies" and that our best lead-dog was dead.

As you come out of the Kenai Mountains onto the Cook Inlet side a broad valley opens before you. On the farther side you can see one end of Portage Glacier which runs in a broad ice road across the neck of the peninsula and dips into the Pacific on the southern side. On the left the railroad begins to climb down to the valley floor in a series of curved trestles like a "scenic railroad" at Coney Island. There was a firm crust on the snow—for a wonder—and so we left the line and prepared to coast down to the tracks that we could see winding in big loops below us.

Under the body of a Nome sled there is a thin board capped with steel claws. When you stand on its projecting end and heave up on the handle-bars the steel claws grip the snow and, sometimes, stop the sled. We took our sleds down one at a time. Vause held to the gee-pole with his feet braced straight in front, and I swung on the brake behind. We swept

down the long hills in a cloud of snow—our dogs racing
madly to escape the leaping sled.

There was little travel at the time we used the trail.
Once we met a man who trotted steadily along on long
upturned snowshoes. "Going to Seward for medicine
for a sick woman at Glacier Creek," he said as he jogged
by. We met him six days later at Glacier Creek and
found that he had covered the one hundred and fifty-
two miles of bad trail in less than five days. On
another occasion we saw black specks on the trail ahead
that materialised into a team of dogs aimlessly pulling
an empty sled. The lead dog had in some manner
loosened himself, and as we approached he tried to lead
his truant companions around us. We headed them
off, however, and tied them firmly to a dead spruce while
the surly leader sat at a distance and howled out his
sorrow and chagrin. A half-hour later we met a sturdy
Swede whose "A ban loose my dogs!" we answered with
an account of their capture. From the determined
expression on his face as he started after the runaways,
it required little imagination to picture what would
happen to the lead-dog when our Swede friend caught
him.

Beyond the road-house at "Mile 52" the trail leads
recklessly along the edge of a precipice, now plunging
through tunnels where the dogs panted as they drew
the sleds over the bare ties, then hanging over straight
drop-offs, where water from the cliffs above had frozen
into icicles weighing tons. Here we had to chop
grooves in the glare ice lest our sleds should start sliding
and drag our dogs into space. Once through the
tunnels we dropped down to the Flood River flats at
the head of Turnagain Arm and were at sea-level once
more.

On the "flats" the glacier winds had been playing
their old game, and we were confronted by miles of
bare track. But the old saying, "It 's always darkest
before morn," proved true for we found a battered push-
car on a siding. With light hearts we hoisted our two
sleds aboard and climbed on top, while the combined
dog teams swept us majestically along. "Dog driving
on a freight car!" Vause called it, and smiled gleefully as the miles flew by. At nightfall we reached
Turnagain Arm and a cabin occupied by a man with a
boat. He told us that we could go no farther with
the car as rock-slides had covered the track, and that he
would take our sleds around the obstructions in his
boat the following morning. Unhitching the dogs we
led them onward in the darkness. Once they broke
away in a strip of timber and chased a wild animal of
some kind, but eventually we reached the road-house
at "Mile 71" which is "the end of construction."

The road-house at "Mile 71" is on the shore of Turnagain Arm. A rough trail leads along the shore from
there to Glacier Creek, a little settlement a few miles
farther on. At this point we picked up Muckluck, the
right wheel dog of Aten's team, who had been left behind
to recuperate from injuries received in a fight. Turnagain Arm was open, and the weather so balmy that a
large brown bear had left his hibernating den and
wandered to the railroad track, where he was shot by a
chance traveller. Early in the morning our friend with
the boat arrived and we caught the strong tide and
rowed to Glacier Creek.

As far as we could see the "Arm" was open, and the
ease of water travel put an idea in my head. If
Turnagain Arm was clear, Knik Arm should be open
also, and if we could reach Knik by water it would save

us hauling our sled over Crow Creek Pass, a 3500-foot gash in the mountains, where we would be forced to back-back our duffle to the summit. It was well worth considering, and later when I met an old friend at Glacier who had a twenty foot boat, the plan began to crystallise. Naimes thought that we could reach Knik without difficulty, so we loaded his boat with Vause's second-class mail matter and our own duffle and put to sea. Vause hitched both teams to his sled and started overland for Knik where we would be reunited. In conception the plan was perfectly feasible, but Cook Inlet has a malevolent temper that cannot be reckoned upon.

At first Naimes's gasoline engine refused to work, it was too cold, but under sail and oars we caught the tide that ran like a river, and made good headway down the "Arm." Then as there was no ice to be seen and the weather was clear we headed for Fire Island twenty-five miles away.

After darkness had settled down we began to see dim masses of ice, and finally when we were only a short distance from Fire Island the floes became so numerous that we could go no farther. As we were afraid of being caught in the ice and swept out into the inlet we had to return to the mainland. This move forced Naimes and me to row all night. After a short rest we started in daylight for our last attempt to reach Knik Arm. After rowing about ten miles we began to encounter more ice-floes, the sky grew black, and snow began to fall. If a storm had come up our chances of escape would have been small. When the floes began to freeze together our failure was written, so we turned and pulled frantically for shore. We rowed for hours in the inky darkness. It was bitterly cold and

the snow turned the water to slush. Professor Parker
was attacked by a severe chill, and but for a bottle of
"hooch," which Naimes had brought, he would have
been in a serious predicament. We reached the mainland late at night and a large fire and liberal quantities
of moose meat restored our spirits. On the following
morning we pulled back thirty miles to Glacier Creek,
and our attempt at winter boating was ended.

The important question now was getting a dog team
to haul our possessions to Susitna Station. Vause
was well on the way, and there were not many dogs for
hire at Glacier Creek. With Muckluck as a nest-egg
I began to gather a dog team, but my efforts were
stopped by joyful news. Bob Griffith and Mitchell,
with their two splendid teams, were approaching on their
way back to the Iditerod.

MacDonald a Yentna gold miner and a friend of ours in
the old days brought the happy tidings. He was on his
way to Susitna Station accompanied by his wife, and
he added Muckluck to his team until our ways parted.

On the appointed day Griffith arrived and after
throwing our freight onto his big sleds we began the
climb to Crow Creek Pass. The railroad was now a
thing of the past and we followed a regular wood trail
that wound steeply upwards through thick groves of
Alaska spruce. High above us we could see the snowy
crests of rock-ribbed mountain peaks, and on a steep
shoulder that had been swept bare of timber by a snow
slide, we entered a snow-filled mountain valley. The
desolation of the scene was added to by huge piles of
worn boulders that choked the frozen bed of a mountain stream. These were the handiwork of man as the
coarse gravel held its share of gold.

Travelling behind Griffith's dogs was a different pro-

A FIGHT BETWEEN RIVAL DOG TEAMS.

From a painting by Belmore Browne.

position from ordinary dog-driving. In the first place the big Nome sleds were lightly loaded and there were nine dogs in one team and eight in the other. They were all heavy dogs—too heavy for very fast travel, but splendid workers on a long hard pull. Their harness was perfect from the silver bells that jingled so sweetly to the red pom-poms that bobbed gaily on each furry back. The teams were hitched in the regulation Alaskan trail manner—two by two with a single leader.

They pulled on a long pliable "tug-rope" of squared walrus hide which is a luxury on the trail as it does n't freeze, or cut your moccasin tops into pieces. Almost every dog had been with Griffith since the days of puppyhood, and in handling them he treated them more like children than dogs. On the few occasions when I saw him use a whip he merely pulled it from the bag between the handle-bars and then put it back again——the dogs *knew*, and behaved!

On the level mountain benches we could jump on the sleds and take a whiff or two at a pipe or swap a yarn before the trail steepened again. At last on the ragged edge of timber line we came to rest before a snow-covered cabin. This was Sam Capper's road-house and it stood at the mouth of the icy valley that led steeply to the pass.

We took this trail early the next morning. A United States game warden helped us. He had lost most of his fingers on both hands in a winter storm in the Kenai Mountains, but with the stumps he could do more than an average man. After manhandling the sleds over the snow-covered avalanche debris in the valley bed, we came at last to the snow-filled amphitheatre under the wall of the pass. Six hundred feet it rose above us, so straight that it was all we could do to stand in our shoe-packs. "It's here that we begin to sweat," said the game warden. "The dogs *may* be able to pull the empty sleds—but no loaded sleds have crossed the pass this year." But Griffith was studying the slope and made no move to unhitch the dogs. Then turning to the second sled he said, "What do you think, Mitchell?" and Mitchell answered, "Let's take a chance." And we did. First the teams were hitched in one long line, and then came the question of which dog should lead. Now among Griffith's seventeen dogs there was one puppy, a splendid intelligent animal whose fine head and big bones promised well for the days to come. He ran loose a good part of the time, frisking along in the soft snow beside the dignified working dogs. Griffith had taken him on the long trip "just for the experience and to see the world." The puppy at that moment happened to be sitting near by gazing at our activities with the vacuous stare peculiar to puppies, so Griffith, laughing, hitched him at the head of the long line. If we could have understood canine talk we would undoubtedly have heard some indelicate and sarcastic remarks from the old dogs, but the puppy was already leading up the steep slope, and we were engrossed in the task that confronted us.

Griffith went first—with the dogs; Mitchell and the game warden wrestled with the sled and kept it from swinging pendulum-like on the hard snow; I followed with a shovel poised to brake the sled when it came to rest, while Professor Parker, camera in hand, snapshotted our progress from the rocks above.

During the rests we gasped for breath, and the panting of men and dogs filled the air. When our breathing

had returned to normal, Griffith would shout, "Mush!"
Sixty-eight furry feet would tear madly at the snow and
the sled would lurch upward, to an accompaniment of
gasps and flying snow. In this way with our tendons
cracking in the mad rushes we won to the top. Then
came a wild slide to the base of the mountain for the
second sled. Noon found us eating a light lunch on the
top of the pass and shivering in the icy wind. According to Professor Parker's barometer we were 3500 feet
above Turnagain Arm. Around us rose a frozen
desolation of mountain peaks, the home of the white
sheep and goat.

The game warden's eyes were vainly searching the
mountainsides for a sled that had been left on the summit, but it had disappeared—blown into one of the
rocky gorges below us by the winter wind.

We wasted no time on the summit but said a hasty
good-by to the game warden and started downward
through a long valley that stretched bare of timber as
far as we could see. It was a long, hard, downhill
fight. On the first steep pitches we had to double
"rough-lock" our sleds or they would have overrun
the dogs. We used heavy dog-chains for the purpose
and even then we used the brakes freely. But it was
in the lower valley that our real troubles began as we
found miles of smooth "sideling" trail, where it was
impossible to keep the sleds from swinging downhill.
Frequently we were forced to shovel or chop a deep
rut for our uphill sled runner in order to hold it in
place on particularly steep stretches. But more than
once, despite every precaution, the big sleds "killapied"
and we landed men, sled, and dogs in a tangled heap
below the trail. Chopping trenches for the runners
and the general bad conditions held us until night over-

took us on the top of the steep hill that slopes down to
the valley of Eagle River. Professor Parker had gone
ahead, and we knew that food and warmth would be
awaiting us in the Raven Creek road-house below, so
we left our sleds on the mountainside and stumbled
downward with our dogs.

At the "crack o' dawn" we were back at the sleds,
and by nightfall we had pulled them twenty miles to
the Eagle River road-house. We had crossed the last
high divide between Seward and Susitna Station, and
the day's travel followed the course of Eagle River
towards Knik Arm. Eagle River ran unfrozen and
at many of the fords we had to pull our sleds through
the water. At first the trail was rough, but as the valley
broadened the "going" improved. Soon we began to
reach stretches where we could sit on the sleds and enjoy
the views about us. These rest "spells" were a relief
after the labours of the previous days.

Contentedly puffing our pipes we would watch the
country fly past. The aches and bruises of the early
days were almost forgotten. Griffith would tell me
snatches of his years on the northern trails; of men
frozen on the Behring Sea coast; of the great race at
Nome, when with victory almost in his hands a blizzard
struck him, and his dogs froze stiff in their harness; of
the hunt for gold in the early days of the Yukon, and
of the old days in the Rockies, when he had driven
a stage coach on the turbulent frontier.

Now and then moose tracks in the deep snow would
make us search the thickets, but the jingle of the dog-
bells was a warning to the forest folk. Stevenson has
said that there is no paradise comparable to the deck of
a wind-jammer in the "trades," but I have tried both
and I would always choose the back of a Nome sled on

a northern trail when you can smell the tang of evergreens in the frosty air, and the dogs are running
smoothly with ther tails tight curled.

Beyond Eagle River we made an easy eighteen-mile
day to Old Knik at the head of Knik Arm. Every
view now was like a smile from an old friend, for I had
hunted in that country before the trail was built. From
the sled I could show Griffith the wind-swept tops of
snowy mountains where I had followed the white sheep,
and several times the dogs smelled moose and we swung
hard on the brakes, our ears ringing with the crash of
wolf music that followed.

The trails in general were in miserable shape. In
the road-houses at night, when we sat around the big
stoves drying our steaming clothes, the talk revolved
around the mildness of the winter. The belief was
general that the Japan current had changed its course,
and wild tales of a tropical Alaska filled our evenings.
One old prospector with an active imagination said,
"Wont it be hell when we have to 'chop-trail' through
rubber plants!" But the principal subject of conversation was the trail that we had just crossed on Crow
Creek Pass. It had been built, so the trail men told
me, by a "government man" at a cost of $50,000.

Now there is not enough travel over the Pass in
summer to warrant an expenditure of five thousand
dollars, as there is a good water route direct to Knik,
and any man who has ever done a winter day's work
in the open would know at a glance that no trail could
be built over the pass that would not be drifted over by
the winter snows.

As you approach Old Knik you drop down to the
flats of the Matanuska River. In the summer time it
is a beautiful stretch of woodland, meadow, and salt

marsh. As you wander through the cotton-wood groves you are transported to the farm country of the New England States until you raise your eyes—then the towering snow-capped mountains of the Chugach Range bring you back to Alaska.

The salt meadows were frozen and we "boomed along."

As we entered a strip of familiar woodland the hair on our dogs' backs began to rise and the jingle of our dog-bells was soon answered by the wailing cry of a pack of Indian dogs. "Caches" and scattered cabins began to appear, and as we passed the Indian inmates came to their doors to see us. On seeing the pinched half-clad forms, the rough cabins, and the starved dogs one could not help pondering on the difference between the white and red man.

We white men were all the product of civilisation, and everything about our sleds and equipment had been built along the lines laid down by the Indians, and yet what a difference. Our great dogs were sleek and strong and their coats rippled like martin fur over their iron muscles. Our sleds were in perfect condition, varnished against the weather and without one broken brace. We ourselves were warmly and strongly clad and we shouted for the pure joy of life as we flew along the trail. And yet the Indians were products of this wilderness and had taught the white man how to live. As I thought, I remembered the Indian graveyard behind the woods, and the number of fresh graves that I had seen there.

Tuberculosis was their curse when I first visited them, and I still remembered the hopelessness of their struggle. I had called on the Chief of the tribe for aid in finding some goat meat that one of his dogs had stolen from

A SUSITNA INDIAN VILLAGE SHOWING "CACHES" FOR STORING FOOD, AND
THE CABIN WHERE WE SPENT THE NIGHT.

Photo by H. C. Parker.

me. The day was bitter cold and as I opened the door of his cabin the thick fetid steam from the interior dimmed the air. The heat was terrific and yet he joined me in the open with a single cotton shirt covering his chest and his legs showing bare through the rents in his trousers. I did not wonder that his body was racked with coughs as I followed him. He was dead when I returned to the village. Again when I was camped by their village a man came to me with a sick child. I have never seen a silent person show more sorrow. The child was in the last stages of consumption, so I gave it bread and maple syrup to make it happy. As the Indian left he said, "White man say Indian sit down long time in cabin get sick—maybe sit down in tent get strong?" I answered in the affirmative and told him that hot cabins were unhealthy, but later when I visited his tent I found it pitched on the *mud* at the edge of a *marsh!* If the missionaries who go among the Indians would talk hygiene in place of religion they could do a great work.

Leaving the Indian village we crossed a second narrow strip of woodland and then the great open flats of the Matanuska lay before us. In the distance we could see Brown's road-house, our shelter for the night, and the dogs raced madly across the level ice and brought us up with a flourish before the door.

The place seemed like home to me. Some years before I had camped close to the spot where the road-house now stands. At that time the only white inhabitant of Old Knik was a man called "Scotty" Watson. It was he who had built the road-house, and I had put in my leisure hours helping him. In return for my services he taught me to play "Seven up," and to make catsup from the mushrooms that grew on the marshes.

While we were eating supper a man arrived from Knik who told us that La Voy and Aten had returned from their trip up the Susitna and were waiting for us at Knik, which was eighteen miles away across the arm. "Red-Jacket," second chief of the Susitna, paid us an official call. I had met him some years before on the Susitna and he told me the gossip of the Indian camps. Talkeetna Nicolae was well and "was looking for a new wife!"

CHAPTER XVII

THE END OF THE SUSITNA TRAIL

The mouth of the Matanuska—Scarcity of dog-salmon—Improvidence of Indians—Knik—We rejoin Aten and La Voy—Good travelling—We reach Susitna—We leave Griffith and Mitchell—Preparations for the big trip.

EARLY to bed and early to rise is a maxim of the trail. As the dogs are fed only once a day, and then at night, it does not do to travel late. Going to sleep early in civilisation may be difficult, but after twenty miles of soft snow travel you need no urging from the Sandman. In fact this sleep-dispensing individual is a tyrant in the northland, and brooks no opposition; when you feel the first touch of his magic wand you fly to your blankets lest sleep overtake you on the way. You notice, also, a difference in the amount of sleep that you need, and you will be surprised to find after the first few days of physical exhaustion are over, that you require less after a hard day on the trail than you do after a strenuous day in your office.

When we left Old Knik it was the beginning of our fourteenth day on the trail, and I was just beginning to feel those first joyous hints of the approach of good physical condition. The really distressing stiffness and soreness resulting from the first pitiless days in the soft snow was just beginning to wear away. Soft muscles were beginning to harden, useless tissue was burning away, raw places on tender feet were being covered with a protecting callous, and sore and swollen hands were beginning to toughen. I knew that many days would pass before I was "fit" according to wilderness standards, but the worst part of this necessary metamorphosis was past. The old trail-hunger, too, had gripped us—that ravenous desire for food that sweeps over one when nature calls aloud for fuel with which to build up the tissues which are being burned up in days of toil. This is the hunger of a famished animal, when table manners are but a dim memory, and table conversation a waste of valuable time.

We swung out over the Matanuska flats in the grey dawn. In places the hard beaten trail was the only snow left, and we could run on the frozen marsh alongside, while a slight pressure of the left hand on the geepole kept the sleds on the trail. Men and dogs were in fine fettle and the miles flew by. While we were crossing a salt water "slew" on the rotten ice, we heard the sound of a floe splitting, and turned in time to see Professor Parker struggling in the ice-cold water. During really cold weather this would have been a serious accident, and we would have rushed him to the nearest timber and thawed him out over a spruce fire. As it was he scrambled out before his clothes were wet through, and his warm wool clothing held the heat of his body. On the edge of the marsh we passed two cabins, and a man told us between the howls of a pack of Indian dogs, that we could purchase dog-salmon at a cabin a half-mile from the trail.

Mitchell and I accordingly left the sleds, for there was a dog-food famine throughout the Susitna country, and there had been a corresponding rise in the price of this necessary commodity. Under the circumstances the grumbling of the dog-men was excusable, for in a country where every river is a salmon stream the failure of the Indians to catch enough fish for trade was due to laziness alone. Had any of the Indians who lived along the trail laboured with even the slightest degree of energy, they could have made enough money to supply them with every luxury for the coming year. As it was they were living in want and poverty. The needs of these natives go deeper than a lack of religion or medicine, for I have seen them eating refuse from the beach, when only three days of bidarka paddling would have taken them to mountain ranges teeming with white sheep.

The sight of so many cabins scattered along the Knik shore was a surprise to me, as on my last visit the flats were the uninhabited edge of a great wilderness. In fact the only time that I have heard timber wolves in any numbers was on these same flats six years before. I was camped at the time close to the junction of the Knik and Matanuska rivers and during the evening I heard wolves howling all about me. A tale is told of a prospector who made a trip cross-country from the Matanuska to the Talkeetna. As he was travelling "light" he swung up into the Talkeetna hills and drifted along above the timber. When he had reached the uplands, so the story runs, a pack of timber wolves joined him. While they did not attempt to harm him they dogged his footsteps day by day. At night he would make his "tea-fire" in an isolated grove of spruce, retiring to the protection of the branches before sleep overcame him. For several days he was followed by his unwelcome escort until at the head

14

of Big Willow Creek they crossed the trail of more promising game and left him.

Another story is told of a dog-driver who was freighting in the Matanuska Valley. He had dropped behind his dog team to roll a cigarette and the team had jogged ahead until about one hundred yards separated them. Suddenly, a pack of wolves broke out of the brush that bordered the trail, and before the man could reach them they had killed, cut out of the traces, and carried off his lead-dog.

While I will not vouch for the truth of these stories, I know that cases somewhat similar have happened in this region. An intimate friend of mine was freighting with dogs on the Skwentna River. On several occasions he was followed by wolves. Usually he was warned of their proximity by the terror of his dogs, for the wolves never showed themselves, but in places where the brush was thick they would approach so close that he could hear them forcing their way through the undergrowth. While he felt uncomfortable at times he was convinced that the wolves were after his dogs and meant him no harm, although the question of what they would do in a time of famine interested him greatly.

Where the Matanuska flats "peter out" you follow the beach under the bluff shores of Knik Arm. At this point the warm winds had turned the trail to ice and we enjoyed excellent travelling. At times even we could ride the sleds and talk or smoke our pipes. The dogs on these occasions seemed to glory in our added weight and would respond to Griffith's cheery commands by curling their tails tighter and pulling with added enthusiasm.

From the tops of our sleds we could look across the ice-packed neck of Knik Arm to the glistening peaks of

A CAMP ON THE UPPER CHULITNA SHOWING HOW WE BROKE A YARD AROUND
OUR TENT, AND TRAILS TO FACILITATE HANDLING OF SLEDS.

Photo by Merl La Voy.

IN THE CAÑON OF THE UNNAMED TRIBUTARY OF THE CHULITNA RIVER.

Photo by Belmore Browne.

the Chugach range, and across the foothills we could
recognise the rugged country through which we had
laboured two days previously.

In this way—now riding where the trail was good,
then running at a steady dog-trot across the bad
stretches—we came to Knik. The "town" is a tiny
settlement of white men and Indian cabins. George
Palmer runs the only store, and there the traveller can
purchase all the necessities for a wilderness trip. The
settlement's excuse for existence is in its location at the
entrance to the Matanuska Valley where the Susitna
trail crosses.

As we approached the town we were greeted by the
howls of countless dogs, and after passing scattered
cabins we came to rest among a crowd of men who were
gathered outside of the combination store, hotel, and
restaurant.

In the tangled mass of dogs and humanity we found
Aten, La Voy, and Vause. It was a joyful reunion, and
after answering and asking countless questions we sat
down to a hurried luncheon.

Aten and La Voy each had a team of six dogs. I
had known many of them during the previous summer,
and we greeted each other affectionately as befitted
old friends. They were in magnificent condition,
hardened by their work on the trail and full of fire after
their short rest.

Aten and La Voy had accomplished a lot, for under
the most difficult conditions they had advanced the
bulk of our outfit to a point several miles beyond the
mouth of the Tokositna River on the Chulitna. In
general they had encountered execrable travelling conditions, but fate at last relented and on the Chulitna
River they found miles of glare-ice where they loaded

everything onto the sleds and rode behind the leaping dogs. Leaving their outfit on a *supposedly safe* cache they had returned with empty sleds to Susitna Station and thence to Knik.

The easy return journey had hardened our dogs without taxing either their strength or vitality. They were of the small or native variety known as huskies and malamutes. For heavy freighting, such as Bob Griffith was engaged in, the heavy dogs were superior to the small type, but in every other respect the small dogs are more satisfactory. They are faster, quicker on their feet, and will work on less food than the big half-breed dogs. Nature works along certain distinctly drawn lines. In her wisdom she has cast dogs in a certain mould, and when man attempts to improve on it the result is a dog who lacks strength and "snap."

After these northern dogs have had a few days rest they literally radiate strength and vitality. Ours were so obstreperous that we had our hands full when we started to hitch them up. We had to begin operations by anchoring our sled with a bight of rope to the pillars of the store verandah, for as soon as each dog was hitched in place he would begin to howl and pull with all his might on the tug-line.

Vause's, Griffith's, Mitchell's, and our two teams were all bound for Susitna Station, and they made an imposing picture when they were ready for the trail. Vause being the U. S. mail carrier was given the head of the procession, and as he swept down the trail our dogs howled and threw themselves with savage envy against the traces. When our turn came Professor Parker got into Aten's sled and I into La Voy's and the straining ropes were loosened. We were off like the wind, swinging around corners on one runner, bouncing over bumps, and sweeping over the straight stretches in a smother of snow. All we could do was to hold on and pray that we would n't hit a tree. The man who handles the team holds on to the handle-bars with one foot on the brake and the other on a narrow platform at the rear of the sled. He swings the sled with the brake and by heaving on the handle-bars with all his strength.

I was just beginning to congratulate myself on having escaped without a broken head when the trail plunged down-hill into a wood. The trees flew past in a blurred line and suddenly we saw our Waterloo awaiting us! The dogs were wild with excitement and beyond control, their powerful bodies level with the snow as they dashed along, and beyond was a six-foot drop-off where the trail descended to a lake and turned at a right angle. When the sled bounded into space the dogs turned instantly on the trail and over we went—men, dogs, and sled in a jumbled mass! When we finally got the snow out of our eyes and ears the other dog teams had dwindled to small specks, and above the distant jingle of dog-bells we could hear roars of laughter.

The dogs, chastened by the experience, settled down to their steady trot and we could begin to take in the beauty of the winter landscape. The country between Knik and Susitna Station is flat and our trail took us across the smooth surface of many lakes. The ragged spruce, common to all the muskeg country of the north, added to the desolate aspect of the scene. The trail for some unknown climatic reason was hard and smooth. Hour after hour we slid along, the five teams winding in a sinuous line, while jokes and laughter passed back and forth above the jingle of dog-bells. The miles of bad trail that we had passed were forgotten, for we were at last enjoying winter travel at its best.

As the afternoon wore to its close we struck into a frozen watercourse hemmed in by solid lines of black spruce. It was the Little Susitna River, and the word was passed down the line that there was a road-house close at hand. Vause, Griffith, and Mitchell stopped, as Susitna Station was still twelve miles away, but we kept on as our dogs were fresh and we had no loads. As night came on the cold increased and the jingle of our bells and the grating of the runners were the only sounds in all that great expanse. The sun went down in a deep red sky and still the dogs trotted on. Soon the spruces loomed weirdly against the night sky and the steam of the dog's breath showed light against the blue snow. La Voy sat behind me on the handle-bars while the cold wind sang past. At times like this, when you have the leisure to think, the spell of the wilderness takes a powerful hold on you.

The spruce-fringed horizons stimulate the imagination, and the monotonous song of the wind and bells has a lulling hypnotic effect on you. You feel as if you had always travelled as you are doing then and always will; that civilisation is only a jumbled dream, and the only things that count are adventures, hard muscles, and food for man and dog.

But suddenly the dogs struck up a faster gait until their trot had changed to a run; faster and faster they went, while the sled rolled drunkenly over the broadening trail. Then a light appeared and flashed behind; others came into view and the dogs making a final spurt brought us up before the houses of Susitna Station.

Even in the darkness the houses had a familiar look, and as the doors about us opened we saw the faces of many old friends. Mindful, however, of the hard days to come we saved the news of the trail for the morrow, and after seeing that our dogs were comfortable, we turned in for a much-needed sleep.

We had covered fifty-five miles during the day but the day had been an easier one than any of the days that we had spent on the trail. The brutal, soul-trying days are those when you labour from dawn to twilight and fall asleep with a paltry ten miles to show for your toil.

Our last days in Susitna Station were filled with a thousand interesting details of our coming trip. Odds and ends of every description had to be attended to; ice creepers for river running, raw-hide for mending snowshoes, and letters written, as it was the end of civilisation.

We were joined by Vause, Griffith, and Mitchell on the following day. Vause was planning a trip towards the Talkeetna to recover the body of a man who had drowned in the Susitna the year before. Griffith and Mitchell were resting for a day before beginning their long hard pull to the Iditerod. Among many old friends we met a prospector who gave us the last chapter in the lives of the horses that we had lost at Tyonik in 1906. He had been prospecting the rivers that entered Cook Inlet west of Tyonik. It was in the early part of the winter, and the streams had just been covered with a firm sheet of ice. As he was passing a small Island he was surprised to see a dead animal lying in the snow. On reaching the island he found the carcasses of the other horses and the story of their death was written clear. They had reached the marshy island while searching for fodder and when the ice began to form they were unable to escape. Broken and re-frozen scars in the ice showed where they had attempted to force their way landward, but they had quickly given up the attempt and had died before the ice would bear their weight.

Now Susitna Station is the nearest settlement to the Alaskan Range on the Susitna side. It also forms the only port of entry and departure for the men who have penetrated the great wilderness between the Susitna River and the Tanana. If we could find any knowledge of a pass close to Mount McKinley it would be at Susitna Station. We therefore asked all the prospectors in the town concerning our chances, and Vause, our trail-mate, was the only man who could give us any information. His knowledge, however, was indefinite, and all he knew was that there was a river flowing north below the Chulitna forks, and that he had heard of a prospector who had crossed the range. Vause gave me a rough map of the country as he remembered it which showed the approximate location of the stream that the prospector had described, but as I have never been on the headwaters of the Chulitna I am to this day uncertain as to whether or not the stream we eventually followed was the one indicated. We learned in addition that there was a party of three prospectors freighting towards Talkeetna—two brothers by the name of Wells and their partner Coffee. Coffee and the Wells brothers, we were told, knew more about the Chulitna country than any other men, and La Voy who had met Coffee told me that it was he who had crossed the range. While it would have added to our peace of mind to have known just where we were going, the uncertainty of our plans made our task the more alluring.

Every one at Susitna Station showed the greatest interest in our venture. We were invited to a "civilised dinner" by McNalley, the A. C. Co., representative—the last we were to enjoy until we reached the Yukon.

OUR FIRST VIEW OF THE ALASKAN RANGE AFTER EMERGING FROM THE CAÑON OF THE UNNAMED RIVER.
SHOWING OTTER TRACKS ON LEFT BANK OF OPEN WATER

CHAPTER XVIII

THE BEGINNING OF THE WILDERNESS TRAIL

We leave Susitna—Rabbits—Arrival at Kroto—"In an Indian Lodge"—We arrive at Talkeetna—We ascend the Chulitna—We meet Stephan and Talkeetna Nicolae—We trade successfully for moose-meat —View of Mount McKinley—We pass the Tokositna River—We arrive at our cache—Wolverines.

ON the 19th of February we were ready for the trail. We drove our dogs into line above the high bluff beneath which we had battled with the churning eddies in our motor-boat days. As we were saying our last farewell an old friend presented us with four quart bottles of rum. Now on all of our previous trips we had placed a ban on alcoholic drinks, and for an instant I thought that it would be wiser to return the gift, but suddenly the memory of Professor Parker's pemmican pudding and the commandeered pint of brandy in 1910 crossed my mind and I thankfully placed the present in a safe place. I am glad now that we took it, for during the months of snow travel that we experienced this rum was the only luxury that we possessed, and used in very small quantities it proved a welcome addition to our evening meal. We used it in our tea, at night only. The first bottle was rationed at the rate of two tablespoonfuls per man per day, the second bottle went at a single tablespoonful a day, the third was dispensed in two teaspoonful lots; while the fourth and last we finished at the base of Mount McKinley by a daily allowance of one teaspoonful a day! While alcohol in any quantity is harmful to men who are leading an active life, we found that rum used in small quantities after a long hard day in the snow acted as an aid to our digestion and circulation.

As we had always left Susitna Station by boat it was a new sensation to slide down onto the frozen surface of the great river and jog away on snowshoes.

In our journey up the Chulitna and Susitna we were always passing places that we remembered from our previous trips—now a smooth snow-covered point where a bad rapid had bothered us, or a spruce-covered island where we had camped in the old days.

We had at last said the final farewell to civilisation, and were dependent on our own resources. The well-travelled trail, with its road-houses was a thing of the past, and we were following a trail that led to an Indian settlement called Kroto, about fifteen miles away. We had reduced our teams to five dogs, respectively, as we had no way of procuring dog food, if we should run short, until we reached a big-game country.

Where an Alaskan town ends the wilderness begins. A short way from Susitna Station the winter silence shut down on us; no sounds but the straining of the dog harness and the rhythmic clicking of our snowshoes broke the absolute silence. Even our dog-bells had been cast aside, for while their jingling was pleasant to hear they were an added weight and might alarm big game. Erratic snowshoe trails grew fewer, and dotted lines in the smooth sweeps of snow told where rabbits had dared the unprotecting opens in frantic leaps.

Knowledge

Had it been a better rabbit year we could have counted on them for dog food and carried less on our sleds. But the Alaskan rabbits die off about every seven years. The character of this epidemic is not known for certain, although I was told by a prospector that an army doctor at Fort Gibbon had found it to be tubercular. The fact remains, however, that the rabbits are practically exterminated at regular intervals, and a man can travel for hundreds of miles without seeing a track in the snow. Were it not for this wise provision of Nature there would not be a willow bush left in Alaska inside of fifteen years. At the time of our journey the rabbits had been on the increase for only three or four years, and yet in favoured localities we saw whole thickets of willow that had been killed by the long-eared pests. When they are really numerous the amount of damage they do is beyond belief, and it is difficult even to get snow with which to make tea, without its tasting of rabbit!

The rabbit crop likewise plays an important part in the economy of the wild, for with the increase in rabbits there is a corresponding increase among the fur-bearing animals. This being particularly true of the lynx. The birds of prey also take their toll of the rabbit hordes, and we often saw the trails of rabbits that ended in a wing-brushed circle of snow with a few drops of blood to show that the cruel talons had reached their mark.

Night began to close in on us as we neared Kroto, and we debated the question as to whether we would invite ourselves into some Indian's cabin or pitch our own tent in the snow. Professor Parker was slightly pessimistic about Indian hospitality in general and Kroto hospitality in particular. But the rest of us rather welcomed the adventure, and after touching on the ethnological value

of our proposed call we halted our dogs before the most
pretentious cabin. Forcing our way through a yapping
rabble of stunted dogs we entered the outer compartment of the cabin and were met by a stalwart Indian by
the name of Shilligan. He readily agreed to our demands for a night's shelter, and after bringing our sleds
into the outer compartment to protect them from the
Indian dogs we entered the inner compartment or
"living-room."

The ensuing night can best be described by the word
hectic! What with prowling Indian babies and puppies
our ethnological studies were rudely interfered with,
and none of us had to be urged into the open on the
following morning!

All day long we jogged over the great flats of smooth
snow. Far away lines of black showed where the spruce
forests met the river banks. Then new snow came to
cover the dim trail, and late at night we camped under
a high bank where a fallen spruce furnished us with
boughs and fuel.

Our days on the Susitna were much alike. We travelled always over blinding snow flats that stretched
away to the black regiments of spruce. Now and then
a bluff relieved the monotony, or the snow clouds
breaking away would give us glimpses of the icy peaks
of the Talkeetna Mountains.

Two days from Susitna we ran gleefully into a fresh
broken trail, and a new cache told us that we had
overtaken the Wells brothers and Coffee. Following
came the call of a dog-driver, and black specks that
grew into two men riding empty sleds, who drew aside
into the soft snow to let us pass. It was the elder Wells
brother and Coffee. They were freighting to Broad
Pass they said. Coffee said that he had been across a

pass in the Alaskan Range; that he had just gone to take "a look-see"; the pass was short as he crossed over and back, but that "coming back was a damn sight worse than going over!" He had travelled light in the summer time. This was all we heard as our dogs were impatient for the trail and we had a long day ahead of us. As we said "so long," Wells told us that his brother was "keeping camp" a mile up the trail, and later he welcomed us with the splendid hospitality characteristic of the Alaskan prospector.

These men represented the finest type of the Alaskan frontiersmen. Freighting their supplies in the winter time, the spring "break-up" would find them in some distant range of "the interior." Here they would build their cabin, prospect and trap for a year or more, eking out their food supply the while with rifle and fish line. When their food was gone they would raft down some wilderness river, sell their catch of fur at a frontier post, and outfit for another venture. Having found good quartz prospects near the Alaskan Range they were freighting in a two years' outfit, counting optimistically on "the coming of the railroad" to make their embryonic mines valuable. This is the best type of the men who are "opening up" Alaska.

While we were eating a snack with Wells he turned to me and said: "If you tear off anything for the papers about this neck o' the woods tell 'em we need a railroad and need it bad." I promised, and the reader is the witness of my relieved conscience. We left Wells with regret, but it gave us some pleasure to know that they would have the benefit of our trail for many days.

We had little in the way of camp duffle with us; all our regular outfit was in our cache beyond the Tokositna, and we got along as best we could with a tiny mountain

tent and a frying-pan or two. We "siwashed" it for
two nights until we reached the main fork of the Susitna. Here the upper Susitna, the Talkeetna, and the
Chulitna rivers combine to form the main Susitna.
The Talkeetna sweeps northward from the unknown
fastnesses of the Talkeetna Mountains, while the
Chulitna rushes southward from the Alaskan Range
and Mount McKinley. In 1910 when the trading-post
built by the A. C. Co. was new, there was a tiny
settlement at the forks, but now as we trotted into the
familiar clearing the cabins stood cold and deserted.

It was at this point that we began our arduous trail-
breaking towards the Alaskan Range. We were
steadily creeping away from the seacoast, and already
the still, intense cold was noticeable. The snow was
dry and powdery under our snowshoes and steam was
rising from men and dogs as we swung along. We
could now see the Alaskan Range standing like a
wall of ice against the northern sky; while Mount
McKinley's mighty buttresses blended with the haze of
distance, so that the great mountain seemed to float
cloud-like above the foothills.

Early in the winter an Indian or two had used the
Susitna route and left a dim trail, then Aten and La Voy
had broken a relay route through the white drifts.
Since then no teams had passed that way, and as we
drove our dogs up the Chulitna we had to rebreak our
trail. We were encouraged in our added toil by the
thought that the wilder the country was, the more
interesting it would be.

It was on the Chulitna that we saw the last signs of
human habitation. A cache and fresh snowshoe tracks
led us to an Indian camp. Pushing through the
invariable ring of snarling dogs I entered one of the

MOVING UP TO OUR LAST WOOD CAMP ON THE SOUTH SIDE OF THE RANGE. SUNSHINE BREAKING THROUGH THE CLOUDS AFTER A THREE DAYS' BLIZZARD.

Photo by Belmore Browne.

tents and to my delight found myself in the presence
of (Talkeetna Nicolae) and his two wives. We greeted
each other joyfully, for we had met and traded to our
mutual benefit in 1910. One of the women thanked
me in the sign language for a photograph that I had
taken of Talkeetna Nicolae and sent to him. Sitting
among a litter of malamute puppies we exchanged the
news of the trail. Stephan, Nicolae's son-in-law, had
killed a moose, and would trade, I was told; so repairing
to the open I began bargaining with the successful
hunter. To my question of "How much ketchum moose-
meat?" Stephan replied, "Ketchum two bits pound."
Now twenty-five cents a pound was next door to piracy,
and in addition I had once given Stephan's wife a liberal
outfit of food when he had left her destitute and had forgotten to return to her. Stephan's lack of appreciation
hardened my heart and I laid the matter before La Voy
who had just joined me. Money is usually a useless
encumbrance on a wilderness trail, but we each had a
small amount that we had forgotten to spend before
leaving Susitna Station. So La Voy gave Stephan
fifty cents, and said, "Let's see if he knows how much a
pound is." To our joy Stephan's mind was hazy on
weights and he gave us about five pounds of meat. La
Voy then tried again with all his worldly wealth which
consisted of forty-five cents, and secured in return an
equally large slab of meat. It was now my turn and
I tried a piece of "frenzied finance" by giving my only
dollar to Stephan and asking him to return the ninety-
five cents to La Voy and give me meat for the difference. Without hesitation he handed the ninety-five
cents to La Voy and gave me about five pounds of
hind quarter for my five cents. When we swung out
on the trail again we left Stephan chuckling slyly over

his business acumen, but we waited until a point of spruce hid the camp before giving vent to our triumphant laughter.

It is not often, however, that the white man comes off victorious in these financial skirmishes, for the Alaskan Indian can, and usually does, drive a hard bargain.

A short distance above the camp we came to the spot where in 1910 the narrowing valley walls had warned us of our approach to the Chulitna cañon. But how different the scene looked now! In place of the rushing waters of the river there lay a smooth expanse of untrodden snow; where, on our first visit the air had trembled to the sullen roar of the rapids we now jogged along through an almost oppressive silence; and where the river banks had been hidden in a tangle of vegetation we looked on rolling snow-drifts and naked rocks.

As we rounded the rock bluff, where on the day long past we had tuned up the *Explorer* for her fight with the rapids, gusts of icy wind began to buffet us. The trail soon disappeared and with heads down we felt our way slowly along. Soon I was forced to use our tent-pole to find the firm foundation, and our progress became so slow that night overtook us between the cañon walls, and we made camp.

The wind subsided during the night and we made faster time the following morning. The cañon had acted as a funnel for the wind and snow, and as soon as the walls began to draw back we began to strike little patches of ice. The "good going" encouraged the dogs and we began to reel off the miles. Soon the cañon bluffs fell behind and towering high into the winter sky stood Mount McKinley. The fact that all the foot-hills were buried in snow gave the mountain an entirely different aspect from the views that we had obtained

in the summer time; the principal difference being that
the snow caused the great ridges that run towards the
mountain to blend with the southern buttresses; and
in consequence we looked with amused surprise on
what appeared to be several climbable routes from the
southern approach. Our intimate knowledge of every
detail of the mountain's southern formation, alone
enabled us to unravel the optical illusion.

The travelling improved as we trotted along, and soon
the sight of the frozen entrance of the Tokositna awoke
memories of the old days. It seemed that if we were
to turn aside and ascend the river we would find our
old camp of 1910 standing in the shade of the cottonwoods and hear the voices of our old companions, and
the familiar hum of the mosquito horde. As it was
we were moving through a land of as savage grandeur
and frozen desolation as this world can boast. Our
roadway was the mile-wide icy bed of the Chulitna
River. It ran flat as a billiard table to the very foot
of the Alaskan Range; there the snow smothered foothills began to roll up, two, four, six, eight, and ten
thousand feet into the sky, and then behind an interval
of blue haze the towering, gleaming form of Mount
McKinley rolled up nineteen thousand feet above us.

The Tokosha Mountains, Foraker and Hunter,
loomed gigantic to the westward—each one by itself
a king but for the overwhelming grandeur of old
Bulshaia.

Under the spell of all this beauty we were running with
our heads turned towards the range, when suddenly
an ominous crack came from under the first sled, and
in an instant Aten and the dogs were wallowing ankle
deep in the icy water. It was an "over floe" common
on all the northern rivers. After a river has frozen

solid it often happens that the water will force its way through some weak or open place in the ice. This upper layer of water then freezes, but in our case the new ice was not yet strong enough to bear our weight. It was not very far to the point where Aten and La Voy had cached our main outfit and we quickly sized up the situation. The cold was not severe enough to render a wetting dangerous, and the only other alternative was to retrace our steps and break a new trail through the soft snow on the edge of the timber. We all decided in favour of the wet route, and for the better part of a mile we dragged our sleds through five inches of water.

In loading a sled a long canvas tarp is first placed on the sled body. The freight is then placed on the tarp whose edges are folded over the load which is then lashed down with much grunting and heaving. These canvas tarpaulins protected our freight from the water, and when we finally reached the grove of spruce that sheltered our cache our dunnage was none the worse for its wet journey.

Now this cache had been our Mecca since the day we had left Knik. For it contained all the pemmican, fuel, and equipment that we were to use in our struggle with the big mountain; but in addition it stood for comfort, warmth, ease, food, and everything that makes life worth while in a snow-bound wilderness. There rested our big tent, stove, axes, bacon, beans, flour, tea, sugar, guns, ammunition, and all the little odds and ends that in civilisation we call necessities but which in the wilderness become luxuries. To protect this treasure trove from wild animals (a cache is sacred to northern men—red or white) Aten and La Voy had placed it on a platform of logs suspended from a number of trees.

As an added precaution one usually sheathes the

trees that hold up the cache with two or more feet of
tin from kerosene cans, as it offers no foot- or claw-
hold for that Archfiend, the wolverine. This animal
boasts the distinction of being the most hated and
despised beast on the North American Continent.
Woodsmen have a yard long list of descriptive epithets
for this animal and of these only two—"Glutton," and
"Indian Devil"—would pass the censorship of even the
most reckless publisher! For its size it is perhaps as
powerfully built an animal as nature has produced.
Its iron jaws will splinter the strongest box and its
razor-edged claws will carry it up the tallest tree. Its
mental attributes consist of a ravenous appetite, a
hatred of everything in general and mankind in particular, and a perverted passion for wholesale and wanton
destruction.

With the thought of wolverines in a far corner of
my brain I had asked Aten and La Voy when we first
met if they had taken the precaution of "tinning our
cache." They answered that they had not in view of
the fact that the smell of man would linger about and
protect the cache until our return. Now the "smell
of man" idea will work with *any* animal but a wolverine,
and when, as we were approaching our cache, we saw
wolverine tracks in the snow we were all decidedly
uneasy. On reaching it our worst fears were realised,
for the snow was padded down with the tracks of these
animals and the canvas covers of several pemmican
packages lay in the snow. Closer scrutiny showed that
the trees that formed the posts of our cache were scarred
with the claw marks of the Indian Devils. We lost
no time in making a thorough investigation, and after
lifting off the canvas tarpaulin that covered our provisions we found that a goodly amount of our dog-

salmon and bacon had gone. We were cheered by
the thought that the damage might have been greater—
but there was more to come! I have already spoken
of the wolverine's passion for vindictive's and wanton
destruction and in a moment we made a discovery that
will illustrate why this animal is hated above all other
animals.

On starting on our long journey La Voy had invested
in a beautiful and expensive Graflex camera. To protect it on the trail, he had purchased an expensive
leather box of the best workmanship. Feeling that
it would be perfectly safe in the cache he decided to
leave it during his return trip to Susitna. The heavy
leather cover being weather proof he hit on a novel
plan to protect it from damage. Cutting down a slender cottonwood about thirty feet in length he rove a
rope in its end. After lifting the pole into an upright
position alongside of the cache he lashed it firmly in
place, then tying his camera to the end of the rope
he hoisted it to the very top of the pole. Now any
one would think that a camera inside of a heavy leather
case swinging at the very tiptop of a thirty foot pole
would be about as safe as man could make it. A
wolverine, however, had climbed the pole, cut off the
corners of the shoe-leather case as cleanly as a razor
would have done, and then gnawed his way into the
camera case! If La Voy could have corralled the entire
wolverine clan the Chulitna Valley would have run
with blood! For months afterward when we wanted
to rouse his "fighting blood" all we had to do was to
mention the word *wolverine!*

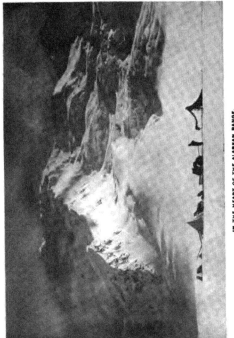

IN THE HEART OF THE ALASKAN RANGE.

CHAPTER XIX

BEGINNING OF THE LONG RELAY

Reorganisation at Wolverine Camp—Method of relaying—Trail-breaking—Indications of a pass—The first big glacier—We pass the Chulitna gorge—We find the Chulitna gorge—Advance up the cañon—Dog food—A moose hunt—We find a break in the range—We discover the "unnamed river."

DESPITE the visitations of the devilish wolverines our arrival at the cache was a great event in our lives. Outside of the material comfort gained it meant that we were at last "under way" and on a working basis. Heretofore we had been travelling straight away, as we were able to pull all our belongings on the sleds at one time. But from Wolverine Camp onward we had 2500 pounds of duffle to wrestle with which meant that we would have to relay. Furthermore we had no longer even an excuse for a trail, which necessitated the construction or "breaking" of every foot of the path over which we pulled our freight.

No one can realise, without having travelled through a trackless wild, the importance of even the slightest marks to show you the way. On several occasions we lost a full working day by not knowing the lay of the land. The first experience of this kind occurred while breaking our first trail from Wolverine Camp. The main channel of the Chulitna had not frozen in places, and as I was confident that I would soon find a frozen area large enough to allow us to cross with our teams I kept on the edge of the valley. Now one of the most reliable facts about a river is its unreliability. As soon as I had gotten well within its power the river began to squeeze me towards the bluffs. Finally at the base of an almost perpendicular wall I was forced to stop. One look at the snow cliff sent me on a run to camp for a shovel and then La Voy and I went to work. At the end of two hours back-breaking work we had shovelled a deep trail around the steep point, and just when we were congratulating ourselves on a clear road we saw a second and steeper bluff come into view ahead, with the perverse river rushing around its base. There was only one thing to do—go back and begin over again. Thereafter we held to the centre of the valley, and just as soon as an unfrozen stream began to lead toward either side we would cross it at all costs and hold to our straight course. By the sweat of our brows we bought experience, which, luckily, is the only way, for in the wilderness, of all things under the sun, human labour is the cheapest!

We were now following the great valley of the Chulitna. It was several miles broad in places and as level as a floor. When unfrozen streams did not compli-cate our advance our trail would lead as straight as a ruled line for miles. Aten and La Voy gave all their time to moving our freight, and I shouldered the duties of surveying and breaking our trails. In the broad expanses of the Chulitna one could save an immense amount of time and worry for the dog drivers by break-ing an absolutely straight trail, and in this seemingly simple labour one will find that there is lots to learn. A straight trail can be gained only by constant mental

concentration. If you let your eyes or mind drift, even
for a minute, from the point of spruce trees miles away
that you have chosen as a sighting mark, your trail
will not run true. It is as if the snowshoes were an
electric needle that recorded on the white snow-fields
every slight change of the mind. If your mind wanders
it will be written in the snow for all to read, and when
on your way home you can see your trails stretching
away across the snow like a tautened wire you can
nod your head in approval at a job well done. There
was a great satisfaction in these long cold days on the
snow-fields. First came the long tramps straight away
when you concentrated your whole mind on the trail
and swung your whole weight onto each snowshoe to
pack the soft yielding snow. Then came the easier
return when your feet flew of themselves treading down
automatically the humps left between the snowshoe
tracks. Now you could look about you and see the
country or follow the flight of great flocks of ptarmigan
that rose from the willows as you advanced.

The Chulitna led us always parallel to the Alaskan
Range, and on clear days we looked eagerly to the
eastward, for it was there that we were going to try to
find a way through the ice-bound mountains.

In the abstract, hunting for a pass through an un-
charted mountain range might be likened to finding a
needle in a haystack, but in reality the finding of a
break in the range gave us little worry. Any break
would be glacier filled and the ice-fields would of
necessity throw off large quantities of water which
would form rivers. The clew to a pass therefore would
be any river of sufficient size to indicate large snow-
fields. The finding of a break, however, was in no way
a guarantee that we could make a crossing, and it was

in the uncertainty of the *kind* of break that we would
find that we found cause for worry.

The first indication of a pass east of Mount McKinley
is a huge glacier that lies east of the "big glacier"
which we followed to Mount McKinley in 1910. It is
the largest glacier of the Mount McKinley region;
heading under the cliffs of the north-eastern ridges of
the big mountain it flows in an easterly direction to
the valley of the Chulitna.

Had we been successful in our attempt in 1910 to
climb the "great serac" and cross the "12,000-foot col,"
we would have dropped down onto the upper ice-fields
of this great glacier close under the Southern North-
East Ridge.

When Doctor Cook made the trip around Mount
McKinley in 1903 he rafted down the Chulitna and saw
the huge ice river. He gave it the name of "Fidele
Glacier," but the name was not adopted by the United
States Government.   As this body of ice and snow
discharges more water into the Chulitna than any other
single natural feature an appropriate name for it would
be the Chulitna Glacier.

At the time that we were approaching this great
river of ice we were hugging the timber on the left-hand
or Alaskan Range side of the Chulitna. It was at
least a mile to the opposite side of the valley and I took
it for granted that the Chulitna ran past close to the end
of the ice.

We were having good travelling at the time, and
finally succeeded in moving all our duffle up and building a new camp within about five miles of the glacier.

Then came a clear day and La Voy and I pushed
ahead on a combination reconnaissance and trail-
breaking trip.

As we approached the glacier we began to search for the opening in the bluffs where the Chulitna came through. The closer we got the more surprised we were, for as far as we could see there was no place where a river could come through the walls. Pushing on ahead I at last reached the eastern wall of the glacier and the truth of the matter lay before me—there was no room for a river as large as the Chulitna between the bluffs; we had passed the cañon where it entered the valley!

At times like this a sense of humour is invaluable and after a lunch around a fire of dry spruce we were able to laugh over our wasted efforts. Looking back across the valley we could see about five miles away, and opposite our camp the merest suggestion of a wooded point that blended cunningly with the higher bluffs behind. "That's her," said La Voy, "she comes sneaking out behind that point!" And we both drew a breath of relief when we realised that we had only moved up 250 pounds of freight. As we had come so far we decided to take a look-see and we accordingly climbed a part of the terminal moraine. We could not see very much, as the swell of the ice hid the distant horizon, but from the curve in the mountain walls we could tell that the glacier curved towards Mount McKinley. I would have given much to explore its great ice-fields, but it was too big a job to undertake as a side-trip, and the chances of being caught in a huge amphitheatre as we had been in 1910 decided us in pushing farther eastward.

Dame Fortune is always a good old soul at heart and that night she sent a cold frost down from the mountain gorges. It turned the surface of the snow-fields into a hard crust over which we could pull moderately loaded sleds. With light hearts we began freighting our supplies across the valley. As we neared the low timber-screened point that had caused my blunder I saw a low place that promised a route across the neck to the Chulitna. If we could find a good trail across, it would save us about a mile of travel around the point, so Aten and La Voy waited with their sleds until I could investigate.

It was one of those wonderful winter days when the snow glitters like cut glass and distant snow-covered mountains stand clear-cut against the deep blue sky.

In all that great land there was not a sound to be heard except the creaking of my snowshoes on the dry snow. The stream I was following was spring fed. It ran deep and crystal clear and its bed was green with a kind of aquatic grass. Suddenly I heard a slight noise, and turning quickly I saw a large otter ascend the bank and stretch himself full length in the snow. He was only forty feet away, but he watched me quietly until I began to move forward, when he slipped with scarcely a ripple into the clear stream.

After I had gone a little way, I happened to look back and saw him watching me from the shelter of the bank, craning his long neck from side to side as a sea-lion does and making a sniffing noise.

After I had looked the country over, I went back and got La Voy, with his Graflex camera, in the hope of securing a picture of the otter. When we reached the stream the otter was not in sight, so we sat down to wait. Before long he appeared swimming up-stream, and then he crawled up the bank and began to roll over and over in the dry snow. Finally he saw us and slipped back into the water. La Voy did not make an exposure as he hoped for a closer view and I did not shoot the otter, although I had my .30–.40 trained on his

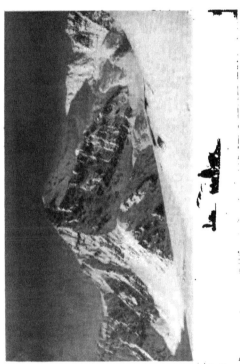

shiny body, as I was waiting for the click of La Voy's camera. ~~He owed his life to our being "camera fiends."~~

On the edge of this clearing I found a great spruce whose trunk was covered with the claw and tooth marks of the Alaskan brown bear. It was evidently a salmon-fishing spot for the bears, as the tree was still covered with bear hair and dry mud where the great brutes had rubbed themselves after coming out of the river.

The change from open to cañon travel was a relief in some ways, for the scenery was more impressive, although the trail-breaking was more arduous. ~~Aten and La Voy~~ were the official dog-men. Dogs are far more susceptible than horses to the influence of their drivers, and for this reason it is imperative that each team should be handled by one man. A team driven by different men, even if they are all expert drivers, soon becomes demoralised.

We carried with us two types of snowshoes: the long, graceful, upturned shoes made by the Indians, and the short, strong, "bear-paw" variety made in New Hampshire. The latter we used in rough, steep, climbing, such as we found on the Mount McKinley glaciers, while the long, upturned shoes were used for "breaking-trail" in soft snow.

When Aten or La Voy accompanied me on my trail-breaking trips I would go well ahead and give the snow a preliminary pounding with my snowshoes. Aten or La Voy would follow me on snowshoes, with the dog team. We would advance in this order about five miles, when, after dropping our load, we would ride back on the sled, as our weight on the runners improved the trail. These rides to camp were splendid sport.

As we turned the eager dogs' heads towards camp

they were yapping with excitement, and the instant the sleds were straightened out in the trail they were off like a shot and we had to jump on quickly or stay behind. After a time they would settle down to their rapid, trail-eating trot, but later when camp came into view they were off again and we would dash up to our tent in grand style. It seemed to be a regular game with the dogs. They would bark and frisk about when their harness was taken off as if to say: "Well! we certainly 'went some' that time!"

The following day, if wind or snow had not damaged our trail we could haul about five hundred pounds to the team over it. We would make two trips in a day, or about twenty miles in all, until our equipment was five miles ahead of our camp. Our camp and personal duffle made a light load for the two teams, and on the following day we would advance ten miles, or five miles beyond our cache, breaking the last half of the trail as we advanced.

If we were uncertain as to our route, both teams would work on the "back-trail," and I would go ahead on a long reconnaissance and trail-breaking trip. It was in this way that we worked our way steadily through the silent wilderness. Everything was done with system; every man knew what his duties were without being told; and, of course, in a life of this kind every one must strive to do even more than his share.

Especially in "making camp" after a long, hard day, does willingness and a knowledge of what to do prove of benefit. When we decided to camp there were two things that we looked for: a *straight*, dead spruce, close to the river bank, and a water hole in the ice. When these two important factors were found, we tramped down a camp-site, flat and hard, with our snowshoes, and went to work. The dogs were fed once a day, at nightfall.

As a rule, smoked salmon—dry feed, as it is called—is the favourite food when fed with tallow. But salmon is too bulky a food for a long wilderness trip.

We were forced to feed corn-meal and "dog-rice," seasoned with salmon and tallow, for the meal and rice swell in cooking and go farther. We cooked it in a large iron pan, and after the mess had cooked we set it in the snow to cool and weighted the cover down to keep the hungry dogs from stealing it. One of our dogs claimed the duty of watching the pan, and any other dog that approached did so at his peril.

The dogs were splendid animals—hard working, faithful, affectionate, and lovable; but among themselves they were savage brutes. Each team was held together by the frail bond of daily companionship and when a fight started each team would back its favourite to the death. We lost some of our most valuable dogs in these savage fights, which were of frequent occurrence.

The upper Chulitna was a beautiful river. Now and then the spruce-crowned walls would draw apart, forming snow-filled amphitheatres, and it was in one of these deep basins that we found our first signs of big game.

It is impossible to convey in words the avalanche of emotions that sweep over a man in the wilderness when he finds himself on the fresh trail of a big game animal. When a man has lived the hard life of the trail for a month or two he not only thinks of and longs for fresh meat during the day, but he dreams of it at night as well. All the camp-fire talk revolves around this one word—*meat!* Now, when you add to this craving the overwhelming excitement of the chase, it is small wonder that your heart beats audibly between your

teeth, and that your hands tremble as you pull your
rifle from its case.

The track that we saw was made by a fairly large
bull moose. Under ordinary conditions I would have
waited for a fresh snow or a windy day to stalk him,
as there was a thin, brittle crust on the snow. But we
were travelling rapidly, and I had to take the chance
or leave it. The bull had wandered across the flat,
feeding on willow buds, and had then followed a small
stream below the towering bluffs that rimmed the
valley. In one place he had ventured on to thin ice
and then backed slowly off on discovering his danger!
Then his trail turned and ascended the bluffs.

Hunting the Alaskan moose was an old story to me,
and I was conversant with the wonderful climbing
ability of the animal, yet this time I could scarcely
believe my own eyes, so steep and impassable were the
places this moose had climbed. I had to throw my
snowshoes ahead of me and dig steps with the butt
of my rifle until I reached them. Finally I left the trail
where a growth of alders clung to the hillside and drawing myself up, hand over hand, I reached the top after
an hour's hard work. As I lashed my snowshoes on
I looked over as beautiful a stretch of moose country
as I have ever seen.

Rolling, spruce-dotted hills swept away to the very
foot of the Alaskan Range, which rose in snowy steps
to a line of ice-capped peaks. To the eastward I was
overjoyed to see a break in the range that promised a
possible route through the mountains. After carefully
locating its position in my mind I found the moose trail
and began the hunt. But no matter how carefully I
advanced the crust broke under my snowshoes. Knowing that I had no chance under these conditions I left

the trail, and kept a sharp watch ahead. After some time had passed a murmur swept through the spruce groves and a slight breeze began to shake the ice from the trees. Slowly the rattle of falling ice increased and, overjoyed at what seemed an intervention of providence, I swung back to the bull's trail. Keeping among the spruce trees I again advanced and after going about three hundred yards I came upon the bull's fresh bed. How the beast heard me I will never understand; but hear me he did, for after rising to his feet he had moved slowly away, keeping behind every piece of cover until he had crossed a low ridge, and then he had struck into a slashing run that had sent the brittle crust flying.

Day after day we pushed up the Chulitna River. We never knew monotony, for men who have reached the perfect physical condition that we had attained would find pleasure and enjoyment in anything. The bends of the cañon too beckoned us on, and stimulated our imagination. We always wanted to see what was around the next bend or beyond the next amphitheatre, and we were thinking always of the break in the range which I had seen while following the moose. "Perhaps the next bend will bring us to our river," we would say, and trot onward optimistically, only to find the same stretch of frozen river running between the same unbroken walls.

A few days later I succeeded in breaking a long piece of advance trail and, while Aten and La Voy were advancing the freight, I made a second attempt to secure meat. Leaving our camp on the Chulitna, I crossed the rolling country to the north until I reached timber line on the Alaskan Range. From this point of vantage I secured a magnificent view of the eastern face of Mount McKinley. During the day I snowshoed about twenty miles through the still snow-smothered woods, and secured a magnificent view of that mountain. It was the first time that I had seen it from the east, and as I studied it through my binoculars I could trace every contour of the eastern side. The Southern and Central North-Eastern ridges joined at an altitude of about 16,000 feet and formed the main Eastern Ridge of the southern or highest summit. The Northern North-East Ridge came down directly from the northern or lower summit. Tracks of wild things dotted the snow—of ermine, wolverine, marten, hare, squirrels, and ptarmigan. Once I saw a marten watching me stealthily from a bole on a gnarled spruce. Great round balls of snow covered the evergreens like turbans and, strange to relate, I heard some bird—a finch, I think—singing as if its throat would burst. I saw no moose sign. The track of the bull that had evaded me was the only sign of big game which I saw on the southern side of the Alaskan Range.

While my moose hunt was a failure from the meat point of view, it was successful as a reconnaissance, for I secured a nearer view of the "break" in the range to the eastward, and I could now see indications of a large stream flowing from the depression, and joining the Chulitna River a few miles above our camp.

The next day Professor Parker and I pushed ahead. The wind was blowing a gale and the river ran alternately through deep cañons and circular amphitheatres. At last we saw some noble peaks of the Alaskan Range topping the timber, and finally we reached a point where the gorge split. The northern or left-hand cañon crossed the line of the valley and turned straight towards the Alaskan Range. Breathlessly we advanced

APPROACHING THE PASS IN THE ALASKAN RANGE.
FOR 17 DAYS WE WORMED OUR WAY THROUGH THIS CHAOS OF ROCK AND ICE.
Photo by Belmore Browne.

OUR HIGHEST CAMP IN THE ALASKAN RANGE, 6000 FEET ALTITUDE. IT WAS
IN THIS CAMP THAT THE STORMS AND COLD WERE ESPECIALLY SEVERE.
Photo by Meri La Voy.

until its size and importance told us that it drained a large part of the range, and that it came from glaciers that might offer us a route to the Yukon side. It was the river of our hopes and fears!

Our thoughts of the future, whether or no we could break through the mountains and where we would come out—if successful—were forgotten. Every anxiety was obliterated by the challenge of the unknown river and the thrill of impending adventures. Racing back to camp we stamped the trail flat and poured out our joyful news, and the following day found us camped in the new cañon.

16

CHAPTER XX

THE "UNNAMED RIVER"

Reconnaissance of the "unnamed river"—Beauty of the cañon—We reach the end of the cañon—We see the Alaskan Range—The timber begins to disappear—"Camp-making"—We eat owl—Reconnaissance of the head of the valley—We find a big glacier.

AFTER we were settled Aten and La Voy went back for our freight, and I for a long trail-breaking scout ahead. The walls of the cañon were beautifully coloured in warm sienna and umber. Tons of soft snow hung on the cliffs and carpeted the narrow stream bed. Now and then I passed holes in the ice through which I caught glimpses of clear, cold water; the strange snake-like tracks of otters ran here and there and coveys of snow-white ptarmigan flew ahead of me as I advanced. The stream bed was now climbing perceptibly, and large boulders told me that the mountains were near.

There is an indescribable charm in this kind of exploration. In the depths of the cañon I could see no distant landmarks—my compass alone told me that I was going towards the Alaskan Range. I drew a chart of the cañon on the butt of my rifle with a nail and found that it made forty-seven sharp bends in a distance of about five miles. As the time passed the desire to see the mountains grew almost irresistible. From the view that I had secured on my last moose hunt I knew

242

that the cañon was leading me into a great gash in the Alaskan Range—but that was all. I felt like a child at its first theatre party waiting for the curtain to rise. I travelled steadily until my watch told me that I had broken five miles of trail. It was time to find a camping place which was an easy matter as a grove of dead spruce stood on a near-by point. Then there was the stamping down of a tent site to be done so that we would have a firm frozen yard when we arrived on the following day. In hunting for a water hole I advanced to a point beyond our camp, and as I raised my eyes from the snow I saw that the cañon walls were breaking away, and that some of the snow peaks of the Alaskan Range were topping the timber ahead. This was all I wanted to know—that the cañon was leading us *somewhere*, and with a feeling of relief I trotted back to camp.

Our advance up the wild gorge was the pleasantest part of our long journey. I have never seen a spot that symbolised more perfectly the pleasant side of the spirit of winter in the wilderness. Tucked away, as it was, deep down under the protecting flanks of the side ranges it lay steeped in cold sunshine, and silence. Our camps in the tinder-dry spruce groves were protected from every wind, and the still stabbing cold that crept down at nightfall from the ice-capped peaks accentuated the comforts of our warm tent. We had left the unpleasant damp winds of the Pacific behind us and were enjoying for the first time what we called "real winter weather!"

For the first time, too, since leaving Knik we were beginning to encounter rough travel. The mile-broad river flats were giving way to snow-covered rapids and huge drifts that brought our shovels into play.

In the account of our journey over the Susitna-Seward trail I purposely mentioned the use of "Nome sleds." Where one travels over flat snow-fields, or a broken trail, there is no sled superior to the rawhide-lashed basket sleds from the Nome coast. But in a rough journey such as ours the small prospector's, or "Yukon sled," proves its superiority. These are small iron bolted sleds without handle-bars. As they are not large enough to carry a very heavy load we used two sleds behind each team, hitched tandem. When they "killapied" it was easy to right them one at a time, and in particularly steep places we could cast off the rear sled and return for it later, which saved us the unpleasant task of unlashing our loads. The runners being closer together than those of a Nome sled made it unnecessary to break a broad trail.

When we established a camp at the edge of the cañon the snow was firm enough to push on with light loads, so we took our complete camp outfit and moved into the mountains. A mile of snowshoeing took us to a point where the cañon had disappeared for good, and the whole majesty of the Alaskan Range rose before us.

On each side of the valley great side ridges swept down, and through the hollow that they formed we could see a chaotic mass of ice-capped peaks—the "back-bone" of the range—blocking our path.

The whole land, peaks, mountain slopes, and valleys were one gleaming sheet of snow, except where the rapidly thinning groves of spruce broke the white mantle in dark lines. In grim solitude and desolate grandeur the scene could not be surpassed by the mountains of the moon. After one look ahead we realised that we were in for a rough time, but as we were expecting a hard trip we could only grin and solace

ourselves with the thought that the more difficult the
crossing the greater our pleasure would be when we
reached the Yukon side.

The thinning spruce told us too that the day was not
far away when we would be brought down to alcohol
stoves and a pemmican diet. With the idea of enjoying the wood while it lasted we devoted special attention
to choosing a camp site.

In the abstract one would naturally suppose that
camping in a tent during a northern winter would be
cold, uncomfortable work, but I can say in all honesty
that I have never enjoyed such rest and comfort as our
little Yukon stove and 10 x 12 tent supplied. After
we had stamped down a firm foundation in the virgin
snow, each man would go to work—there was no
division of work as you see among "campers"—but
each man did unconsciously the task required at the
time. First a large dead spruce would come crashing
down into the snow, followed by numerous smaller
spruces. The green spruces were quickly stripped of
their boughs, and the poles—we used six full lengths
and four half-lengths—raised the tent. The boughs were
then "woven" into a deep soft mattress and a smooth
"foot-log" placed across the tent to divide the beds
from the stove and "kitchen." A crib of green logs
was then placed under the stove to keep it from melting
its way into the snow. Then the kitchen boxes were
brought in, containing all the necessary foods and
cooking utensils. Each man's "war bag" and "bed"
were placed in a row at the head of the tent; and the
snowshoes and everything else eatable—from a dog's
point of view—were hung out of reach on the tent-poles.
The boughs were then covered with a tarpaulin.

While these activities were under way one of us

would be sawing the dead spruce into stove lengths and splitting it, and a generous wood-pile would be ready by the time our tent was pitched.

While the cook was at work trails would be broken to, and water brought from, the nearest water hole, and an out-door kitchen built for cooking dog food. More boughs were brought on which to pile our freight which was covered with our sled-covers.

With the dog food cooking merrily and everything outside stowed away we would repair to the tent. A rope would be stretched along the ridgepole for our wet clothes to dry on, our beds unrolled, and we could surrender to the enjoyment of peace and warmth.

Strangely enough the fur robes in which we slept were all made of a different kind of fur. Professor Parker's was made of the skins of summer killed Lapland reindeer, La Voy's was made of Australian wombat, Aten's was composed of both summer and winter killed white sheep (*Ovis dalli*), while mine was made of timber wolf skins. For ordinary winter travel they were all equally good, but in extremely cold weather the wombat was inferior to the other skins, and during our explorations on Mount McKinley La Voy left his wombat bag with Aten and used the sheep skins.

They were all sewed in the form of a bag. Professor Parker's was arranged with a complicated opening that buttoned over flaps; it was made (at great expense) by a New York outfitter, after the regular New York way. The other three bags were simply sacks with an open end. When you were cold you doubled the top under your head and breathed through a small hole which you made by pushing your hand out of the opening of the bag and withdrawing it. This

LOWERING SLEDS BY HAND TO THE TOP OF THE "1000-FOOT DROP-OFF" BELOW THE PASS.

Photo by Merl La Voy.

simple arrangement is warmer, simpler, and cheaper than the New York way and is used almost universally by the men who live in the north. For a hard trip the reindeer and white mountain sheep bags were superior to my wolf skins for the reason that they weighed less. My wolf skin bag complete, including a balloon-silk cover, weighed seventeen pounds, while the sheep skin bag weighed only ten pounds, and the reindeer even less. But weight for weight and warmth for warmth the white sheep bag, roughly made by the Knik Indians, was by far the best. Besides being light and warm the hair on a sheep skin does not hold moisture to any extent, and as our bags were covered with ice, from our breath freezing during the night, this fact was of great value.

While we were making camp Professor Parker had gone ahead to a point of spruce and brought back word that he had seen a glacier winding downward from the centre of the range. We were thrilled by the news, for we knew that we were now on the verge of our struggle with the Alaskan Range. At this time we began to feel the effects of the near-by ice-fields. The streams even in the rapids were frozen from the bottom up; our water pails froze solid beside the stove; and in the mornings our dogs were white with frost.

Knowing that there were hungry days ahead we ate ravenously while there was still wood enough to cook with. Our provisions were of the simplest kind: beans, bacon, flour, sugar, tea, and dried fruits; but in addition we had a liberal supply of sago, and as Aten numbered among his other virtues the ability to concoct savoury dishes from unpromising ingredients we revelled in puddings and deserts. Our breakfast consisted always of the classical sour-dough hot cake, which by the way

is superior to all other hot cakes. With a little bacon
and liberal quantities of tea they "filled our bunkers"
until lunch time. The sour-dough pancake "makes
the northern world go round"; it is the universal food
of the Alaskan prospector and from it he has received
his name of "Sour-dough." As they say in the north,
"it sticks to your ribs" and makes an excellent food
"to travel on." Lunch was always a potluck affair,
and at night we had our big meal of beans, bacon,
biscuits, and fruit.

Aten, La Voy, and I divided the doubtful honour of
lighting the fire in the morning. The chilling plunge
from the warmth of our sleeping-bags into the frigid
air was accomplished with lightning speed, and as
each man's turn came around he spent the previous
evening in the most elaborate preparation of shavings
and kindling wood. When, early in the morning our
old battered alarm clock would "go off," the unlucky
man, whose turn it was, would leap from his bag, "choke"
the alarm clock, open the stove, throw in the bundle
of shavings, pile on the kindling, set it afire, put on the
water pail, and leap back into bed within the space of a
few seconds. No sprinter ever followed the report of
the starter's pistol with more feverish energy!

Despite the large quantities of ptarmigans we had
secured little or no meat. These birds had, as is usual
in the winter time, banded into large flocks, and they
were extremely hard to approach. Unless we were
able to secure a large number or enough for all hands
it was a waste of time. With the Alaskan Range straight
in front of us our thoughts clung to the big game
ranges of the northern side, and we talked constantly of
the meat of sheep, caribou, and moose.

One night we were talking about food in general

when Aten stated that owls were good to eat. We
listened rather sceptically, but when an owl began to
hoot behind our camp I picked up our 22 cal. rifle and
went in pursuit. Now a few days previously the ejector
of the little arm had broken and without another
thought I had put it in my pocket. After locating the
owl I took a careful sight and fired. The report of the
piece was followed by a heavy blow on my eye and
everything went black. Putting my hands to my eyes
I could feel blood running through them and I could
hear the dogs gathering about me and eating the red
snow. After washing my eyes with snow I could see
with the left one, and later the surgical ministrations
of Aten and La Voy developed a deep gash beside my
right eyeball. A fraction of an inch would have meant
the loss of an eye.

In a trip such as ours accidents are bound to happen,
and for this purpose we carried one of the Burroughs &
Welcome folding surgical cases. It was light and
remarkably complete and in the few cases where it
was needed it more than paid for its weight. The owl
also had been wounded, and later I had the satisfaction
of eating some of it, and found it very good. The dogs
were very fond of human blood and they fought eagerly
for the blood-stained snow whenever we bled from an
accident. Their actions at these times have led me to
believe that all the tales one hears of men being attacked
by their dogs in time of famine, are not fiction.

On the following day Professor Parker and I made a
reconnaissance of twenty-five miles. We followed the
valley to its head, and found that it split. The western branch wound away between two towering peaks.
The eastern branch ended in the glacier that Professor
Parker had seen from our camp. It led far into the

mountains like a huge white roadway. We could not tell where it went to, although its surface promised a possible sledding route, and I determined to prospect the left-hand cañon before committing ourselves to the glacier route. On the way home we located the last grove of timber, which were cottonwood trees, and broke a straight trail to our camp.

CHAPTER XXI

CROSSING THE RANGE

The last timber—Blizzards—The long reconnaissance—A possible "pass"—We move onto the ice—More blizzards—Dog-fights—The Summit—Adventures with our freight on the "big drop-off"—The new glacier—More blizzards—A crevasse—We see timber to the east —Another reconnaissance—We find the Muldrow glacier—Crossing the last pass in a storm.

TO facilitate our reconnaissance trips we advanced our camp the following morning to the last grove of cottonwoods, and their gnarled and twisted trunks bore witness to the savage storms which swept the bleak valley we had entered. Great mountains shot up for thousands of feet and their sides were sheathed with snow and ice. It seemed as if the mountains and elements had joined hands to keep us from going forward.

We were awakened the first morning by the wild shrieking of a mountain gale. The wind sang a grand, deep song among the sharp peaks and desolate gorges, and great spouts of snow shot high into the air where the narrowing mountain walls confined the wind. Aten and La Voy fought backward through the blizzard to bring up our last relay before the trail was lost. I tried to break a trail ahead to the glacier but my tracks disappeared as soon as I lifted my snowshoes from the snow.

On the following day the "pouderie," as the old *voya-*

251

geurs would have called it, still continued. I hunted a
possible pass through a deep gorge, where in the choking
clouds of snow I had to turn my back to the gale to fill
my lungs. My journey was unsuccessful, however, as
I saw no indications of a break in the range. This
left only the unknown glacier on which we could hang
our hopes of reaching the Yukon side.

Aten and La Voy had urged their frightened dogs
through the cutting ice-dust, and dropped their loads
by some willows below the glacier's snout. This was
a good deed, for during the following day and night
the blizzard raged so fiercely that we did not leave our
straining tent. Finally, as the storm continued, we
moved our duffle between blizzards, as it were, and
having sledded up some tent-poles we pitched our tent
in the last thicket of willows.

We were becoming inured to storms and flying ice-
dust, for on the following day we advanced six hundred
pounds of equipment to the top of the first steep pitch
on the glacier's snout, and it was difficult work, as in
places the walls were so steep that the dogs could
scarcely keep their feet. Coming down, Aten led the
dogs and I coasted on the sled; it was blowing a gale
at the time, and I had to shut my eyes against the
cutting snow-clouds, but I dropped down to the valley
floor like an arrow from a bow—it was exciting sport.

The following day the storm again increased to a
blizzard. All day long we lay on our fur robes and
listened to the shrieking of the wind between hotly
contested games of dominoes.

At last a clear day came, and with the break of dawn
I was off in light marching trim to see if I could find
where our glacier went to. I climbed the glacier snout
slowly, breaking a well-graded trail for the dogs to

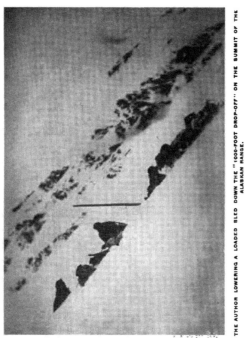

THE AUTHOR LOWERING A LOADED SLED DOWN THE "1000-FOOT DROP-OFF" ON THE SUMMIT OF THE
ALASKAN RANGE.

freight on, and then I hit a fast pace up the glacier. The ice river ran like a Gargantuan road between towering mountain walls; at its head a forbidding line of ice-encrusted precipices barred its course, but to the left, or south, long golden splashes of sunshine slanting down across the blue cliffs told me that there was a break in that direction. This fact cheered me slightly, although I was terror-stricken at the thought that our glacier might prove to be impassable.

As I advanced, a suggestion of a glacial basin on the north, or right, came into view, and I noticed that the main glacier had swung around in a gentle curve until it was running due west. This put an entirely different aspect on the desirability of the left-hand break as a route, for it would lead us south and away from the northern foothills.

The same change made the right-hand basin the only avenue of success, but I had little hope of finding a pass there, as the mountains seemed to rise in perpendicular ice-covered cliffs.

Never in my life have I been filled with such conflicting emotions. If there was no pass our expedition was already an absolute failure, for we would be forced to use our mountain food before reaching Mt. McKinley.

As I advanced through the soft snow more and more of the barrier range came into view. Sometimes the skyline would begin to sweep downward as if it were going to break away, and I would run in my eagerness until the range would begin to climb upwards again, and, panting, I would drop into a walk and curse the snow that made me move so slowly. Close to the northern basin which was still hidden by a mountain shoulder I ate some dog pemmican, and one hardtack biscuit washed down with some water which I melted over a candle in my tin cup. From this point I could see that the left-hand route, where I had seen the promising slants of sunshine, was impossible, while the only break in the barrier range was a mighty glacial amphitheatre with perpendicular walls of solid ice. My only hope was the right-hand basin and, after a short smoke, I started onward. Slowly the mountains broke away and suddenly, as I mounted a moraine, the right-hand basin stretched before me and there lay a smooth snow-field *leading gently to the summit of the range!*

Mad with joy I ran faster and faster, my heart hammering from the exertion and excitement. What would I find on the summit—another impassable range? These and other wild thoughts ran through my mind. As I neared the crest of the range I was almost afraid to look, so much depended on what I would find. I thought of the day in 1906 when Barrill and I reached the summit of this same range one hundred miles to the westward, and then had to retreat after feasting our eyes on the northern "sheep-hills." Here I was again on the very crest, but alone in the blinding glare of unnumbered snow-fields, while on that other day we had toiled upward over sheep pastures spangled with wild flowers.

When only a few feet from the top, I stopped and removed my fur cap—to propitiate the mountain gods—and then I stepped up to the summit. Only a blue void lay below me. I took another step—the void deepened, and with my heart in my mouth I drew gently back—I was standing on a snow cornice that overhung a precipice! For a minute I was completely bewildered, but I finally pulled my scattered senses together and began to think clearly. The first thing to do was to find a place where the cornice was broken so that I

could study the country below me. Turning to the
left I followed the ridge until, to my delight, I found a
point where the cornice broke away, and sitting down
on the very summit of the great range I looked out over
a gleaming sea of unnamed peaks.

The scene was one of stupendous and awful grandeur.
Far below me I saw a tangled system of ice rivers that
drained the mighty mountainsides. To my left a narrow arête dropped downward from my eyrie; on the
right was the deep glacial basin that I had looked into
from the snow cornice; on the left of the arête was a
second ice-filled gorge; and both these glacial basins ran
northward—separated by the arête—until about four
miles beyond they joined a large glacier whose course
was hidden by projecting mountain shoulders. The
first thing to do was to settle once and for all time
whether or not it was possible to descend into either
of the glacial basins. Luckily I had my ice axe with
me. Taking off my snowshoes I made a *traverse* below
the cornice, chopping steps in the hard ice until I reached
the crest of the arête.

I could now see that a descent into the left-hand
hollow was impossible, as the ridge broke off into
great *schrunds* and ice walls. Following the arête I
descended to the top of a very steep but climbable
pitch, and below me I saw gentle snow slopes leading
downward to the snowy floor of the right-hand basin
—*we could cross the pass!* I tried to yell but the silence
of the vast range choked the sound in my throat. I
remember wishing that my voice could reach to our
camp so that my companions could hear the glad tidings.
The next best thing was to hurry home, so reaching the
summit I lashed on my snowshoes and started on the
ten-mile run to camp.

Now that we had found the pass all our energy and resourcefulness were needed to cross it. During my absence Aten and La Voy had hauled about 1200 pounds of duffle to the top of the glacier, and on the following day they pushed 350 pounds five miles up the ice river. Then another blizzard came sweeping across the mountains; our trails were wiped out, and again we spent long hours listening to the noise of the storm and playing dominoes or checkers. But our fighting blood was beginning to rise and we decided to advance despite it.

It shows what mountain equipment can do, for with our alcohol stoves and silk tents we were able to make camp high up on the wind- and snow-lashed back of the glacier. Professor Parker and I slept in our little mountain tent, while Aten and La Voy swung our old wall tent on a rope stretched between the two trail-sleds. They took the dog teams into the tent with them, thereby securing both warmth and diversion, for a big fight started and the noise was tremendous until the hostile teams were torn apart.

During the night the wind blew with such savage fury that we thought our tents would go to pieces at any moment, but they held splendidly and we soon felt confident of riding out any storm the mountains might send against us. The altitude of our first glacier camp was 3000 feet, or 600 feet above brush line.

The days that followed were a continuous round of toil. I would break trails ahead only to have them lost by a new storm. Aten and La Voy stuck doggedly to their freighting, and slowly—relay by relay—our pile of freight was moved upward toward the pass. Our second glacier camp was at an altitude of 4200 feet.

While the sun was shining and we were working, the

temperature often felt as warm as a sunny spring day, but the instant that the higher peaks began to cast their deep blue shadows the temperature would drop instantly to the neighbourhood of zero. With the fall in temperature the cold air began to move downward toward the valleys, causing savage "glacier winds," which fact probably accounts for the coldest temperatures on the high glaciers occurring in the evening, whereas in the valleys the coldest time is early in the morning.

On the 3d of April we pushed our main camp to a height of 6000 feet. We could stand by our tent and see our trail winding away down the steep slopes of snow like a silver wire until it was lost to view on the lower glacier. When Aten and La Voy would start on the down trail for a load of freight, the dogs would take the steep grades on the gallop, with the heavy sleds in pursuit.

The temperature in this camp stayed close to zero when the sun was not shining. A gale struck us the first night and our tents could not have stood the strain had it not been for our having dug a deep shelter into the mountainside.

The tents were covered with frost and we suffered much inconvenience as it stuck to our clothes and then melted when we got into our sleeping-bags.

After the storm had subsided I prospected a good route across the summit and down over the steep pitch on the arête, chopping deep steps to facilitate the carrying of heavy loads. To save back-packing our entire outfit down the arête we decided to slide some of our freight down a steep 1000-foot snow slope that forms one wall of the glacier basin, and while Aten and La Voy were bringing up our remaining freight I packed 400

17

pounds of equipment across the pass. Later Aten went back for the last load and La Voy and I soon had the bulk of our belongings on top.

The "big day" of our crossing was set for April 5th, but another blizzard hit us and for twenty-four hours the wind shrieked about our tents. With the coming of the storm I was attacked by a severe case of snow-blindness which—as is often the case—affected my stomach so that I could not eat. It was bitterly cold. Our rubber shoe-packs froze solid and our alarm clock refused to work.

In the evening of our last day on the summit we had a party. Aten broke up an empty pemmican case, which, helped out with a bundle of willows that we had used for marking our trail, gave us enough wood for a fire. After they had set up the camp stove in the big tent they invited Professor Parker and me to "come in and get warm." It certainly was a weird picture! Four men and a pack of wolf-dogs, in a storm battered tent, slung on two sleds 6000 feet up on an icy ridge! The red hot stove cast a crimson glow on the strange gathering. Our party progressed splendidly, until "Laddie," Aten's "leader," backed into the red hot stove! In an instant the tent was filled with a choking, blinding cloud of smoke from the burned hair. A deep growl of disapproval came from the pack of dogs, and Professor Parker went head first through the tent door, and showed good judgment by refusing to come back, although we urged and beseeched him between our fits of laughter and coughing. So ended our only entertainment in the Alaskan Range.

The morning for the crossing of the divide dawned clear and cold. We broke camp early, and soon had all our duffle on the summit. Later on it began to

THE WHITE SHEEP OF THE ALASKAN RANGE.
(OVIS DALLI.)
THE MEAT AND SKINS OF THESE ANIMALS WERE A GREAT HELP TO US IN OUR
EXPLORATIONS AT THE BASE OF MOUNT McKINLEY.
From a painting by Belmore Browne.

storm, and all day long we worked in clouds of blinding, wind-driven snow.

The question of the day was whether or not our belongings would stand the strain of shooting down over the 1000-foot drop into the glacial hollow. After due deliberation I took a can of hardtack and pushed it over the edge. Away the can sped—slowly at first—but as the slope grew steeper the can gained momentum in leaps and bounds, until, spinning like a pin-wheel, it dropped from sight over the steep slope. Anxiously we waited until after what seemed hours had passed we saw a dark spot shoot out over the white floor of the basin far below us, and a whirring noise came up through the cold air. Slower and more slowly the tiny spot moved until finally it came to rest at the end of the long white line that marked its course. Our experiment was a success!

Emboldened by our first venture, we decided to send over La Voy's broken sled with a load on it. To keep it from travelling too fast and to hold it straight on its course, I tied two fifty-pound packages of pemmican to a rope and made the drag fast to the rear of the sled as a rudder. With considerable apprehension we pushed the sled down to the top of the steep pitch and "let 'er go!" The old sled shot downward like a live thing and dropped out of sight. Anxiously we craned our necks to see it slide out on the glacier far below, but we waited in vain. Professor Parker and Aten had descended the arête by the steps I had chopped that morning and they yelled to us that the sled had buried itself under an ice cliff, but that it seemed to be intact.

After that we were more cautious. We rolled down the solid stuff piece by piece, and then loading our alcohol and fragile dunnage on a sled we began the most

difficult part of our task. We had 300 feet of good
rope which included 200 feet of Swiss Alpine rope. Sinking a gee-pole deep in the snow, we lowered the sled
as far as it would go. I then went down backwards on
the rope, hand over hand, until I reached the sled. As
our first sled had upset about one-third of the way
down, I decided to cut the second sled loose. Aten
had by this time gathered our duffle into a pile—and
straight for this cache the sled sped! It must have
travelled at the rate of a mile a minute, for from where
we were standing, 800 feet above, we could hear it hissing
through the air like a one-pound shell. If it had hit
the cache it would have smashed everything to bits,
but it swerved just in time, the gee-pole ring just touching the edge of the cache, and onward it sped down the
valley until the soft snow brought it to rest.

After the excitement was over La Voy and I chuckled
as Aten's remarks reached our ears. Their long journey
through the cold air had not cooled them one whit!
So partly out of deviltry we cut the second sled loose.
We had not the slightest idea that it would go anywhere
near the cache—although Aten, to this day, says
differently—but the fact remains that the perverse
sled did shoot straight for the cache. Aten had just
started to put up the mountain tent and was inside
arranging the pole when he heard our frantic shouts,
and he escaped in the nick of time, for the leaping sled
dashed across the tent and crashed into some soft roll
of bedding at the end of the cache!

That was the last exciting event in a great day, and
we were lucky to get across the pass, for that night
another shrieking blizzard struck us and we were held
storm-bound for thirty-six hours. During the first night
a mighty gust of wind tore the wall tent down and La

Voy and Aten, rather than leave their robes in the storm "lay dogo" while the wind drifted them deep in snow.

To our joy we were now through for the present with up-hill work—at least our path lay downwards until we reached the big glacier. The small glacier we were on was only a feeder and it rolled downward so steeply that we were forced to go slowly. On the steep pitches we unhooked the dogs and one man rode the gee-pole while a second braked with a shovel handle. We advanced slowly, now toiling across a level flat and then plunging down some great hill while the snow flew up in clouds. It would have been fine sport with empty sleds; as it was it was hard work. We camped on the edge of the big new glacier that ran east and west. Five minutes' walk below our camp was a snow dome from where we could get a good look down the glacier, which ran eastward, and at its lower end we could see timber—solid black lines of spruce that called to us with promises of game and warm fires. But it was not in the right direction, as our course was westward toward Mount McKinley, and we realised sadly that we would have to climb again and follow the big glacier westward—if such a thing were possible.

To make sure I made a reconnaissance up the glacier and saw a low pass at its head. According to my observations this pass would lead us to the Muldrow glacier whose snout was mapped by Brooks in 1902. Overjoyed at our good prospects I started homeward, when suddenly the snow broke under my snowshoes and down I dropped. My long Susitna shoe (bless the Indian who made it!) caught on the side of the crevasse and threw me across it, and then the downward pressure forced my foot out of the "siwash hitch" and I jammed it into a crack in the ice; but had the crevasse been a few inches wider I might have had a serious accident. This was the first crevasse that I had broken into since the beginning of our glacier travel, and I made up my mind that henceforward no man should travel over untested snow alone.

The following morning Professor Parker and I started out for the pass that lay about seven miles east of our camp. We were roped in case we found another crevasse. On our way eastward we passed·four large ice-feeders that came into our glacier from the south, and on reaching the pass all our worries were swept away, for there below us lay the Muldrow glacier. We knew it by its size and also by its course, as it swept in a great curve to the foothills of Mount McKinley that rose like a great white cloud against the south-west sky.

Our success in crossing the range reminded me of Coffee whom we had met beyond Talkeetna. As he had not reached the Muldrow glacier I am to this day uncertain as to what river he followed, and as he crossed the range in one long day (as Doctor Cook did) the most probable supposition is that he crossed farther to the eastward and came out on one of the tributaries of the Toklat River.

Finding Muldrow glacier meant a lot to us. It made the first part of our journey a success, from the point of view of an exploration. And it also insured our reaching Mount McKinley in fighting trim.

We attacked the big glacier with renewed enthusiasm, and three days later found us pitching our tent on the wind-swept moraine of Muldrow glacier. We were a wild-looking crew, for we had fought our way across the pass in the face of a blizzard. The savage wind drove a solid cloud of ice-dust across the snow and at times we could not see one foot ahead.

Aten and I were delayed on the pass by a top-heavy sled. We had attempted to carry too much as we expected good weather and a down-hill pull. The wind finally reached such terrific force that we had to hold the heavy sled *to keep it from being blown over!* Several times we had to stop and relash our loads and each time the dogs rebelled at facing the storm.

While lashing the sled we had to yell to be heard, and Aten's face through the flying drift looked like a solid piece of ice. Once when we were hauling shoulder to shoulder on a frozen rope he turned and grinned at me and I saw the ice on his face crack open. I had shaved the day before and the ice-dust did n't stick to my face much. We were coated with ice from head to foot when we reached the protection of the moraine of Muldrow glacier and were lucky to pull through with nothing more severe than frozen ears and a few frost bites. We were forced, however, to leave a large cache behind on the summit of the pass.

But these details were instantly forgotten the moment we reached the moraine, for the dream of years had come to pass,—*we were on the northern side of "the range"!*

CHAPTER XXII

"THE HAPPY HUNTING-GROUND"

FOR years during my wanderings in Alaska I had listened eagerly to the tales told about the northern side of the Alaskan Range. Few men had seen this country, but now and then I met one who had, and always these men spoke of it as a land trampled flat by game! A land where bands of white sheep dotted the upland pastures, where caribou herds drifted across the foothills, and moose browsed in every timber-line valley!

As time went on and I attempted to reach this country something always occurred to keep me from my heart's desire.

First, in 1906 Ed. Barrill and I had to turn back from the Kuskoquim side after having actually feasted our eyes on the sheep pastures of the northern slope.

It was during our retreat, around our foodless campfires in that hungry land that partly on account of its inaccessibility, and partly on account of the longed-for game it harboured, we first spoke of the northern side as "the happy hunting-ground."

In 1910 we were again turned back from swinging Mount McKinley's flank, by the great serac. Here

THE AUTHOR SKINNING ONE OF THE WHITE SHEEP KILLED IN THE STORM.
THE DOGS WERE GREATLY INTERESTED IN THE OPERATION.

Photo by Merl La Voy.

OUR CAMP AFTER A THREE DAYS' BLIZZARD. DRYING OUT AND WAITING FOR
THE AVALANCHES TO FALL BEFORE WE GO UNDER THE CLIFFS.

Photo by H. C. Parker.

again we reached "bed-rock" with our food, and once more our one topic of conversation was meat, and how we would eat if we could reach "the happy hunting-ground."

They say "the third time never fails," and, with us at least, it was true to its reputation, for it was on the 12th day of April that somewhat battered from our struggle with the storm we pitched our tent beside the Muldrow glacier.

In crossing the range we were seventeen days on the ice without seeing a sign of vegetation and over our pemmican we again talked of the northern game herds.

Now, as we looked northward from the glacier the blizzard was lashing the mountainsides, it was impossible to hunt! I knew the game was there, for from the top of the second pass we had already seen the change that told us game was at hand. The mountains were no longer covered with dense carpets of soft snow, but here and there on the northern slopes were bare patches of brown grass where the winter winds had swept the snow away—and those brown patches meant mountain sheep bands which to us in turn spelled warm white skins to sleep on and juicy steaks and rich stews for the inner man.

The following lines are the entries from my diary made during our first day on the northern side of the range:

"Camp 22, April 13th—Just awake and breakfast is melting. (We had to make our tea from melted snow and ice.) The blizzard is still raging and all night long the tent rattled and heaved. Aten slept with Parker and me in the mountain tent. Merl rolled up in the wall tent outside, and a mournful picture he made when I awakened him. All you could see was a round form under the snow-drifted canvas and all about;

over and under were sleeping dogs covered with snow and ice. I cannot hunt in this weather. *Eight hours later*—grand, big day! This morning (as I said before) we awoke to the roar and thunder of the gale, and the hiss of blizzard-driven sleet.

"After breakfast we sat in our corners and played 'hearts'—for tobacco. About 9.30 A.M. Cliff bundled up and went out to get a report on the weather. He returned in about half an hour blinded by the snow and said that the weather was awful. As he entered the tent door I caught a glimpse of distant mountain-sides that looked clear enough to hunt on, so I started to dress although he advised me not to go. But I became desperate and getting into my parka and mittens I went out into the storm. On my left lay the jagged morainal hills of the Muldrow glacier and on my right rose the blizzard-swept flanks of the Alaskan Range. Before long I found sheep sign that had been blown off the mountainsides above me, and as I advanced before the wind I studied the hills above as well as the flying snow clouds would permit. My eyes were weak from an attack of snow-blindness and my smoked glasses were frost covered, and when I finally saw what appeared to be a band of sheep above me I laughed at myself for being deceived by what I thought was an optical illusion. To advance I had to descend into an ice-filled cañon where the wind blew with such fury that I was unable to see, but I soon reached the smooth, frozen surface of an open flat where the gale swept me along as if I was sail-skating. When I came to a stop I glanced up the mountain, and *there, two hundred yards away, was a big band of white sheep just breaking into a run!*

"I had not a second to spare as the band was making

around a shoulder of the mountain, but I began to shoot in fear and trembling as I still had a touch of snow-blindness and I could not trust my eyes. After my first shot, however, my coolness came back for I saw a spout of snow just under the band where my bullet had struck.

"Throwing off my snow glasses I fired again and saw the sheep turn and leave the band. I will never again (I fear) feel such a surge of savage triumph as I did when I saw that the sheep was hit. No man who has not felt the cruel hunger that we have felt in this hard land; who has not felt the revolt of living on ice-cold canned things day after day can appreciate the longing with which we looked forward to juicy, steaming, sizzling steaks! Add to this hunger the fact that mountain-sheep meat is the finest meat in the world, and you will understand how I felt."

But fully as great as the desire for flesh is the joy of the successful hunter's return to a "hungry camp,"— the triumph of staggering camp-wards under a heavy load of meat. I have often walked buoyantly mile after mile with a heavy meat pack, when without the stimulation of the joyous reception that I knew was awaiting me I would have had to rest many times along the way.

After the wounded sheep turned aside the band swerved away from the ridge and as their white bodies came against the sky I secured two more. Running up the frozen slope I finished the wounded animal and after marking down the others I started on the run for camp.

As I ran I thought of how I could best surprise my companions, as I knew that the sound of my rifle shots had been drowned by the wind. On entering our little tent I began by calling the weather names and grumbling about the difficulties of hunting under such conditions. Then I added that although the weather was bad we really ought to bestir ourselves and get our freight off the mountain. My comrades thought I referred to our dunnage on the pass and as a thick wall of snow was roaring down the pass beyond our protecting mountain-side, my remarks were met with contemptuous silence. I then bantered them by saying that they need not go, but that I thought I would take a dog team and try it myself. The atmosphere had by this time reached a point where fireworks were about to begin, so I played my trump card. "If we don't go now, "I said," our freight will spoil."

"What will spoil?" Aten and La Voy asked together.

"The sheep meat I 've got up on the hill, " I answered slowly.

For a minute they looked at me wildly and then they decided I was fooling, but they finally hitched up a team and followed me doubtfully down the mountain side; but when we reached the sheep our spirits broke loose and we executed a "Wakamba meat dance" around the bodies.

In cold weather one has a craving for fat, and in the wilderness one is less particular about the way meat is cooked. Our desire for fat was so intense that we tried eating the raw meat, and finding it good beyond words we ate freely of the fresh mutton. I can easily understand now why savage tribes make a practice of eating uncooked flesh. We slid the sheep down a snow chute to the base of the mountain and after making the tug-line fast to their horns, the happy dogs pulled them to the sled and we were soon in camp. For hours afterwards we fried meat over our alcohol lamp, and ate—

each man taking turns at the cooking when his hunger was temporarily satisfied.

I found that the sheep, as far as outward signs were concerned, were in no way different from the sheep of the Chugach or Kenai Mountains. They were (or had been) snow-white all over, but the long winter had left its mark on them and they were badly scarred and weather-beaten.

Their brittle hair had been torn and broken until they had a shaggy or rough appearance, and their pelage was stained to a yellow and brown colour by contact with rocks and gravel.

None of the sheep were fat, but they were in good condition, and at the time that I surprised them they were feeding in the driving snow on a wind-swept patch of winter-cured grass. Their stomachs were well filled with grass, and I found that they had eaten caribou-moss, or lichens, as well.

I found, by back-tracking the band, that they had been down in the flat at the base of the mountain before my arrival, and the experience that I gained in that locality shows that the sheep in the winter time range very low.

At the time that I hunted, the sheep had begun to move upward towards the high mountains, and yet I saw quantities of sheep tracks at an altitude of only 3000 feet. From my own observations I feel sure that in localities where sheep have never been hunted they range much lower than they are supposed to. Even in little hunted regions, they have learned to fear the lowlands.

The next morning the wind had moderated to half a gale so we decided to bring our duffle down from the pass,

When we started to hitch up after breakfast there were only a few dogs around camp. Losing patience over the threatened delay I went down to where we had butchered the sheep, knowing that the dogs would gather there for scraps.

I found two of them and brought them back to camp and started up the glacier on a hunt for the rest, but I returned unsuccessful to find that Aten and La Voy had left camp on the same quest. About half an hour later they returned and I heard Aten calling to me to come out of the tent. His voice had an unfamiliar sound and I decided that the dogs had killed some wild beast.

As I emerged from the tent a sad sight met my gaze. Muckluck, Aten's left-wheel dog and the best animal we owned, lay dead on the gravel and by his side kneeled Aten with tears coursing down his weather-beaten face. Muckluck was a clean strain malamute, courageous to the point of madness, and willing to fight any number of dogs up to a whole sled team. He had gone down alone to the sheep grounds. There he had encountered La Voy's team of five dogs, and in the fight that followed he had fallen before a superior number.

It was a great loss to us and after trying to cheer Aten up we started up the pass. As usual we encountered a stinging snow-laden gale, but we forced our way upward through a narrow gully. On the way home I followed the course of our first descent and found a ten-pound box of chocolate, that we had lost during the blizzard. I reached camp ahead of the teams, and by the time Aten had arrived I had buried Muckluck under a great cairn of boulders and placed a sharp shaft of granite at his head.

MOUNT McKINLEY CARIBOU.

FROM DRAWINGS MADE FROM AN ADULT MALE KILLED BY THE AUTHOR
ON THE 27TH OF MAY.

From a painting by Belmore Browne.

Aten soon joined me and thanked me with a grip of his hand and we stood over the old dog's grave crying like children. In that savage life so little tenderness or affection enters into the daily grind that a man loves his dogs passionately—and it is well that he does. We named the pass at the base of which the grave lies "Muckluck Pass," in memory of our faithful friend.

After rescuing our cache we turned all our energies to reaching timber. As the snow in the vicinity of the Muldrow glacier had been blown down into the lowlands by the fury of the winds we had difficulty in finding a good sled route.

The Muldrow glacier acted as a huge wind funnel; I have never seen the wind blow with more regularity and fury than it did at our first camp on the northern side of the range. In order to save our tent we were forced to build wind-breaks out of our freight.

Between the moraines and the mountains there were deep hollows in which during the summer time rushing streams led to the lowlands. In the bottom of these miniature cañons we found enough ice and snow to allow us to pull our sleds.

We moved our camp outfit first and after a long day we pitched our camp at the base of the last range of foothills. Along the glacier moraines I saw caribou and bear sign, but it had all been made in the summer time. At this time I knew nothing about the movements of the caribou on the northern side of the range. I had heard from Fred Printz, who was chief packer for Brooks, that caribou were to be found along timberline in August, but it did not follow that we would find them in the same place in April. I therefore decided to shoot one more sheep before we left the mountains behind us in order that we would have enough meat to last us until we reached moose country. I had no time to spare, as we were camped in the last range of foothills. The mountains about us were beautiful in the extreme and showed variations in form and colouring that I have never seen equalled. To the east of our camp rose a majestic range of a leaden blue colour. It was capped with rugged pinnacles of broken rock and its sides were formed of huge slopes of scree. The pile formed a shoulder or turning point of the main mountain system, and at a distance of two miles I could see through my binoculars trails made by the countless feet of wild sheep during their short migrations or journeys along the range. Surrounding the blue mountains were the typical "sheep-mountains" dear to a hunter's heart.

When, in the north, you see high, eroded mountains splashed here and there with snow-fields between the dead-brown of the mountain pastures, and broken now and then by more rugged peaks that rise still higher into the blue, you can rest assured that sheep are near at hand. I, however, did not need these signs to cheer me, for in the little valley where our tent stood, a broad rut in the snow showed where a band of sheep had passed by.

Leaving camp I climbed a low hill that rose near the centre of a wide valley. From this strategic point I could sweep many miles of mountain pastures with my binoculars. Lying on my stomach with a convenient rock for an elbow rest, I began one of the most interesting operations enjoyed by man—the search for wild game with powerful binoculars on rugged mountain-sides. Ranges miles away are brought close to the eye and, fascinated by the secrets of nature that are unfolding before you, you forget everything except

the wonderful details that your eyes are drinking in;
in imagination you are climbing rugged peaks as you
study their ridges and snow-filled couloirs; now you
join a great eagle as he soars above some blue void and
in imagination you hear the hiss of wind through his
broad pinions; or you follow the marmot on his morning
constitutional along the talus slopes, and whirr onward
with a cock ptarmigan to the side of the demure hen
whose love song has lured him. Through it all you
have an amusing, guilty feeling of taking advantage
of your wild neighbours.

I had been lying thus for probably ten minutes when
I saw a sheep. The animal was about two miles
away, and I settled myself for the serious work in
hand. I had determined that under no consideration
would I kill a ewe, so the first fact to settle was whether
or not the sheep was a ram. As I looked the ground
over I located six more sheep, or seven in all. This was
encouraging, for rams often travel in bands of this
number, and they all appeared to be of the same size.
They were feeding lazily in the shadow of a grassy
mountain, and the blue morning haze prevented me
from ascertaining how large their horns were.

From their actions and size I finally came to the conclusion that they were rams, and once decided I began
the solving of an interesting problem. The sheep were
moving slowly, and they were about two miles away
and 1500 feet above me. The question was how long
it would take me to reach a point ahead of and above
the moving band.

It is in the solving of these hunting problems that
experience is necessary, for to be able to judge successfully where a certain band of sheep will be after an
hour has elapsed, requires an intimate knowledge of

their habits, and more hunters have failed by forgetting to study the problem before them than from any other cause. After deciding on the details of the stalk I saw that it would of necessity be a blind approach (that is, that the sheep would be out of sight during the entire stalk), and I was forced to study every distant landmark on the mountain, so that after reaching my desired position I could recognise each rock and gully, although my point of view had changed. This precaution is most necessary in hunting, for the hunter often forgets that the particular rock that he desires to reach will look entirely different to him when he has changed his position, and success often depends on these minute precautions.

As it was early in the morning I knew that the sheep would continue to feed for some time and that in all probability they would feed downward, as they were then near the summit of the mountain.

There were several gullies lying in the path of the band, and after choosing the one which I thought would lead me to a point near my quarry, I started on a trot across the valley. At the base of the mountain I shed all my useless clothing and impedimenta, and began the climb with nothing to bother me but my rifle, knife, camera, and pack-strap. About an hour had passed before I reached a rock that I had chosen as a point of vantage when I planned the stalk, and as I raised my head slowly, watching every point about me, I saw a sheep's horns sticking up above a little knoll thirty yards away. With the thrill of exultation that swept over me came a note of disappointment, for the horns were those of a ewe, and I felt pretty sure that there would be no large rams in the band. Another circumstance that vexed me greatly was, that although the sheep were unaware of my presence, and feeding towards me, the sun was directly behind them and I could not photograph them. Had it not been for this fact I could have secured at least one clear picture of a band of seven sheep less than twenty-five yards away, with Mount McKinley and a large sweep of the Alaskan Range for a background. Although I knew it was hopeless, I waited in the hope that the band might pass me and give me a chance to photograph them. They advanced slowly, eating greedily of the short wind-cured grass, but, unfortunately, they came directly towards me. Several times different sheep raised their heads and stared fixedly at me, but I gave them as good as they sent and held my breath into the bargain, and eventually they would go to feeding again. They finally came so close that I could hear them feeding. · If I had been armed with a bow and arrow I could have killed one easily enough. At last an old ewe fixed her eyes on me, and although I lay motionless with my chin in the dirt, I saw her body begin to stiffen with suspicion. When I saw that I was discovered I slowly brought my rifle to my shoulder, and, aiming behind the ear of a young ram, fired. The force of the bullet nearly turned him over, and he almost fell on his back, and so far as I could see, he never moved again. Death was instantaneous and he never knew what had happened to him.

At the report of my rifle the sheep nearly fell over backwards from fright, and then, following the old ewe, they dashed madly up the mountain.

Dropping my rifle I grabbed my camera, and as the sheep turned by a point of rock, I made my first exposure. I had remained in the same position, and as they saw nothing to frighten them, they began to slow down, and I secured several more pictures, the last of which shows the band feeding peacefully out of sight over the top of the mountain.

My victim was a yearling ram. He was in good condition, but had little or no fat on his ribs, although there was enough around the kidneys to fry a few pans full of steak. He weighed close to ninety pounds, and after I had cleaned him I packed him entire to camp, which I reached at 11 A.M. Had I wanted more meat I could have killed the entire band, but during our stay in that country we used the most rigid economy in the use of meat, and we often went without when we were surrounded with game, rather than kill immature animals or females.

Every scrap of meat was used, as well as the bones and hides, as rawhide with the hair on is good for the dogs and we fed it to them regularly after cutting it in strips. We saved the best skins and staked them out to dry, and used them to sleep on. These untanned skins were splendid for mountain work, because the fat remaining on the skin kept them from absorbing moisture when laid on the tent floor next to snow or ice, and we carried them to our highest camp on Mount McKinley at 16,615 feet. Aten was the inventor of a method of shortening the hair on the hides so that we could make insoles for use on the mountain. He would first cut the hide into the necessary shape and then singe it on the side of our camp stove until the hair was even and about one-half inch in length. The insoles were a great success, as they were light and easily dried when damp.

As we now had plenty of meat to last us until we reached timber-line, we broke camp the following morning and headed towards the lowlands. As we

ICE FORMATION ON THE NORTH FACE OF THE CENTRAL NORTH-EASTERN
RIDGE. THE RIDGE IN PLACES RISES 4000 FEET ABOVE THE GLACIER.

Photo by Belmore Browne.

CLIMBING THE BIG SERAC. THE SMALL SIZE OF THE FIGURES GIVES AN
ACCURATE IDEA OF THE SIZE OF THE AVALANCHE DEBRIS.

Photo by H. C. Parker.

were leaving camp two cow caribou came around a low
point in the stream bed and looked our outfit over
thoroughly before breaking into their long, smooth
trot. La Voy ran to the top of a little knoll and brought
back word that they had joined a small band of seven
and had left the valley. This was my first view of the
caribou of the Mount McKinley region, and during
the days I spent in their country I studied them carefully and learned their habits well. This small band
of cows was the forerunner of the many bands of females
that work their way far into the mountains in the spring
to drop their young.

We were now in a wilderness paradise. The mountains had a wild picturesque look due to their bare rock
summits, and big game was abundant. We were wild
with enthusiasm over the beauty of it all, and every
few minutes as we jogged along some one would gaze
fondly on the surrounding mountains and ejaculate,
"This is sure a white man's country!"

In one of these camps we were awakened by the
short excited barks of our dogs, and then we heard a
pitiful scream that rose in a shrill crescendo. Aten
rushed out of the tent in time to see "Laddie" leap in
the air and snap up an Arctic hare that had blundered
into camp before discovering its danger.

From the high mountain where I had killed the last
sheep I had secured a wonderful view of the great
expanse of country below us. I could see a hollow
following the eastern wall of the rugged terminal moraine of the Muldrow glacier. One glance at Brooks's
map confirmed my opinion that it was the headwaters
of the McKinley Fork of the Kantishna. The little
stream on which we were camped joined the main
gulch about two miles below. Beyond the end of the

great moraine began a mile-wide glacier flat which was covered evenly with the snow which the winter winds had blown downward from the mountains. Far beyond were thin dark lines that made my heart leap with expectation, for they were groves of spruce, and after the frigid days among the ice-fields we longed for the crackle and warmth of leaping flames, as a starving man longs for food.

The sight of timber was enough in itself to draw us aside in our advance on Mount McKinley, but we were forced to travel to timber as the nearer foothills were bare of snow. By following timber-line to the next river on the west, the Clearwater, we would find ice which we could follow with our sleds to the very base of Mount McKinley. All this I could see through my binoculars from the mountainside, and as Aten and La Voy brought up the remainder of our freight during the day, we lost no time in pushing forward.

At first we found rough travel. Boulders choked the cañon bed, and over-flows had frozen into steep cascades of ice where we donned "ice-creepers" and "rough-locked" our sleds. But when we entered the main bed of the McKinley Fork we found broad expanses of crusted snow and changing our ice-creepers for snowshoes we made fast time. But the surprise of the day came when we entered the gulch on the edge of the great moraine, for instead of the rough travelling we expected we began to encounter glassy over-flows down which we sped behind the galloping dogs. At first we accepted the new conditions stoically—they seemed too good to last—but as point after point flew by and the ice-fields increased in size instead of diminishing we gave way to the exhilaration of the wild ride and urged our flying dogs into a mad race downward.

Had we relayed all our freight two miles farther we would have been able to load it all on our sleds and pull it easily, for the dogs were running hard to keep ahead of our leaping runners and our brakes were throwing up clouds of ice-dust. The splendid speed and the proximity of timber after the stern struggle through the mountains intoxicated us and we yelled with excitement.

As we "boomed along" we at last began to pass patches of stunted willows, and finally a wild cry from Aten drew our eyes to a small clump of dead brush. "Almost enough for a fire!" he shouted and smiles creased our faces from ear to ear. The patches of dead brush increased in number, and as we neared the end of the cañon on the edge of the glacier flat the ice gave way to soft snow and we came to rest beside a small thicket of stunted cottonwoods. To men used to camping in a timbered country it would have been a desolate spot, but the following entry in my diary will show the childish and extravagant delight with which we welcomed our first sight of real wood.

"Camp 25, April 17th—Timber! By all the Red Gods! Timber!! If any one ever reads these scrawled lines I wonder if they will realise what it means to us. First it means success, for we have crossed the Alaskan Range 'from wood to wood.' Secondly, it means that we have added slightly to the world's geographical knowledge—not an easy thing to do in these days —for we have added two new glacier systems to the map. Then comes the delight of warmth and cooked food after seventeen consecutive days' travel through snow and ice smothered mountains. But greater than this is the triumphant feeling of having at last beaten the old mountains themselves; of having withstood their piercing cold, and weathered their savage blizzards; of having dragged our sleds across the faces of their virgin snow-fields and glaciers; and, lastly, of having untangled the route through their twisting cañons and passes."

Besides we are in "God's Country," with the whole majestic sweep of the Alaskan Range towering over us, and culminating in the great, snowy king of mountains —McKinley. Caribou tracks roughen the sand-bars. The air is pulsating with the cackling of unnumbered billions of ptarmigans, and a bushy-tailed old fox is watching our camp from the river bluff.

We are now on the McKinley Fork of the Kantishna River; our struggle with the Alaskan Range is a thing of the past, and five miles below us are dark lines of spruce—real timber—awaiting our arrival!

CHAPTER XXIII

TO THE BASE OF MOUNT McKINLEY

Ptarmigan—We reach spruce timber—We find a deserted camp—We find magazines and newspapers—News of another Mount McKinley expedition—I find a spot for a base camp—Professor Parker and Aten go in search of food—Hunting moose—I find a possible pass to the base of Mount McKinley—Professor Parker and Aten successful—We advance to "Base Camp"—Among the caribou herds—Successful reconnaissances.

AS we worked our way into the lowlands, and left the frozen snow-covered ranges behind, we came into the country of the ptarmigan. Words fail me when I try to sing the praises of this noble bird. Without him the barren mountainsides would be as silent as the tomb, for wherever there is a patch of moss or a wind-stunted willow, there you will find the ptarmigan. In the winter time they gather into flocks of from a few birds to several thousands, and when they are found together in large numbers they are difficult to approach. This was the condition of affairs when we entered the Alaskan Range, but when we reached the northern timber-line the mating season was commencing and they were very tame. One of the most impressive experiences of my sojourn on the north side of Mount McKinley had to do with these birds. I had gone down towards the great glacier flat below the moraine to study out the best sledding route through the maze of frozen river channels. It was the first time in months that I found warm, dry grass to lie on. The country about me was still covered with snow, but the sunshine had a hint of spring warmth as I sat on the little hill. There were thousands of ptarmigans about me, and wherever my binoculars rested I could see the white forms of these beautiful birds. When I first sat down I could hear them cackling on every hand, but as I lay in the sunshine with the whole majestic sweep of the Alaskan Range shining through the spring haze, my ears became attuned to the sounds of the great wilderness about me, and I sat unconscious of all else except the mighty ptarmigan chorus that filled the air. From every knoll and willow, glacier flat and hillside, came the distinctive love song of this bird, and as I listened I became aware of a deep pulsating undertone of sound that filled the whole world about me, and I knew that winter was dead and spring had come. The call of the ptarmigan is not beautiful by itself, but it is so distinctive that once heard it is never forgotten.

A pleasing side of their mating is the habit of the males of uttering their call while they are on the wing. They commence with a guttural cackle which they utter faster and faster until they alight, when they end their song by repeating slowly a call that sounds like *ged-up, ged-up, ged-up, ged-up,* or, *parler vous? parler vous? parler vous?* as they strut proudly about. The males fight constantly and the hens seem to enjoy these battles and sit about clucking among themselves. But once a hen has decided on a mate she comes into her own share of trouble, and is beaten and bullied by the bird she has promised to love and obey. A striking illustration of the cruelty of the males occurred one day when by accident I had shot a female thinking it was a male. As I advanced to pick the hen up a cock

MALE ALASKAN WHITE SHEEP (OVIS DALLI), KILLED BY THE AUTHOR ON
THE FOOTHILLS OF MOUNT McKINLEY.
Photo by Merl La Voy.

HOW WE DID OUR "MARKETING." ATEN WITH YOUNG CARIBOU.
Photo by Belmore Browne.

rushed out of a clump of willows and pecked and struck
the dying hen viciously with his wings, and he had
actually dragged her about before I drove him off.
The ptarmigan makes delicious eating, and although
we seldom killed them we enjoyed the addition they
made to our rather restricted menu.

From the mossy hill I decided on a route through the
flat valley, to where, five miles away on the northern
horizon, I could see a dark line of spruce sentinelling
the distant timber-line.

Aten and La Voy came into camp later with all our
freight and enthusiastic over their rapid journey down
the frozen river, and the following morning we "hit
for the timber." The journey across the blazing snow
flats was uneventful.

We pulled our sleds through the broken ice of brittle
over-flows but we laughed at the wetting, for the dry
spruce grove was drawing nearer. Once in a clear unfrozen pool I saw trout, or grayling darting by, and
every exposed bit of river gravel was dotted with
mating ptarmigan.

As we neared the timber the dogs broke into a run
and with our sleds rocking and leaping over the frozen
crust we came to rest among the trees.

A reaction from the weeks of toil came over us and
we sat aimlessly on our sleds, laughing and smoking.
Aten walked over to a large dead spruce and patted it
affectionately, calling it endearing names the while,
and we grinned appreciatively at each other and the
world in general—we were supremely happy.

After we had become used to our new surroundings
we began to think of our duties in camp building, and
we were looking about us for a suitable camp site when
Arthur Aten gave a wild whoop and started on a mad

run down the bank. We were after him in an instant, for a gleam of white that was different from the surrounding snow had caught our eyes, and as we dashed into a little clearing an old battered tent stood before us. As I ran I noticed also two meat caches, from one of which a great black moose skin hung, swinging in the wind. Nothing stirred nor were our hails answered as we approached, and when Aten looked in he turned to us and said, "No one at home."

The camp was an old hunting camp used occasionally by the miners from the creeks on the lower Kantishna, and a pile of beautiful caribou antlers bore witness to successful hunts in bygone days. The tent was an old 12 x 14 patched in one corner where a conflagration had occurred. There was a raised sleeping platform in the end with plenty of dried caribou skins for mattresses, and an old stove burned through on top and a "grub-box" stood in the corner. The invariable pile of dry shavings demanded by the unwritten law of the trail had been placed before the stove by the last occupant before his departure. But the greatest "find" we made was a number of old magazines and newspapers. The latter included some copies of the *Fairbanks Times* wherein we discovered some articles about our own movements that amused us greatly. One of these stated that Tom Lloyd and a party were coming with dog teams to the foothills "to watch us climb the mountain." As I knew Lloyd personally I could picture his facial expression on reading the item!

After we were settled we held a council of war. Even the crossing of the Alaskan Range had been easy compared with the task that now confronted us. The first thing to accomplish was the location of the best spot for the camp that was to be our base while climbing "the big hill." As Mount McKinley towered above a low range of "caribou-hills" only twenty-five miles away in an air line, this task would not be difficult; but the finding of the best route for scaling the great peak was a serious matter, and I determined to devote all my time and energy to solving it. Since reaching the Muldrow glacier we had had many clear views of the big mountain, and on every occasion I had studied every foot of the north-eastern approach through my powerful binoculars. The views from the end of the Muldrow glacier and the headwaters of the Kantishna showed clearly, in every detail, the contours of the three north-eastern ridges. At the first glance that I secured away back on my moose hunt on the Chulitna the Central North-Eastern Ridge had seemed to promise the best route, and every view that we got as we approached nearer and nearer to the mountain confirmed my first opinion.

From Muckluck Pass we had been able to see distinctly a great glacier running up to a high altitude between the Central and Northern North-East ridges. On this glacier we hung our hopes, for the present, and my base camp and climbing-route reconnaissances were made with this glacier as an objective.

Now the *Fairbanks Times* copies that we found in the tent were dated January, and an old trail apparently more than two weeks old led towards Mount McKinley in one direction, and towards Fairbanks via Moose Creek—a river to the eastward—in the other direction. A careful study of the trail convinced me that the men that made it were travelling from, and not towards, Mount McKinley.

Early the next day I followed the trail towards the mountain. It led me across the low caribou-hills from which I obtained a magnificent view of the whole Alaskan Range sweeping in a great arc from the far east or Tanana River side to the western or Peter's glacier side of McKinley. From this point too I saw that a comparatively low range of eroded mountains separated the headwaters of the Clearwater River from the big glacier that separated the Central and Northern North-East ridges. These rounded mountains were the continuation of the Northern North-Eastern Ridge that led to the northern summit of the mountain. The eroded range was gashed by deep valleys drained by the numerous feeders of the Clearwater River, and it was obvious that the best place for a base camp would be at the highest growth of firewood in one of these valleys. Without going farther I was able with my binoculars to locate the last grove of cottonwoods on the central main branch of the Clearwater. From this branch a deep valley ran upward through the eroded mountains towards our promising glacier, and I realised at once that it was my duty to explore this valley at the earliest opportunity. I dismissed the old trail without another thought, for instead of leading towards the promising north-eastern approach at the head of the Clearwater, it continued to spruce timber on the Clearwater on a parallel line with the foothills, and I decided that no party trying to climb the mountain would have passed the north-eastern approach by.

Returning to camp I reported my discoveries, and we began our preparations for an advance to the head of the Clearwater.

While studying our maps at the old tent, we saw two dots on the map that were marked Glacier City and Diamond City. They were a small matter of about forty miles away—a day's run with an empty sled, under good travelling conditions. Not knowing that these towns were deserted we figured that the inhabitants would have broken trails to the heads of Moose Creek and other tributaries during their winter moose hunts. We were badly in need of oatmeal, and we longed for a few simple luxuries such as canned butter and milk. Thinking that Glacier City or its neighbour would certainly boast a store of some kind, it was decided that Professor Parker and Aten would go on a hunt for groceries, while La Voy and I pushed our freight towards the Clearwater and prospected for a pass to the promising glacier.

But first of all we needed meat and I decided to put in the following day in an effort to kill something.

On our arrival at timber-line we entered the home of the Alaskan moose. Moose, however, range over such a variety of country that one is never quite sure as to what kind of country they are to be found in. Sheep are always near the snow-line, caribou range from the snow-line to timber-line, generally speaking, but moose may be found anywhere, or, as it sometimes seems, *nowhere*. I spent the following day in trying to find a moose, and while I was unsuccessful in securing meat I had a novel experience. For years I had listened to discussions between Alaskan hunters as to whether or not the Alaskan moose utters a call. I have been asked a hundred times for my opinion on this matter and could only answer that, while I had never heard·an Alaskan moose call, I believed that they did.

On this occasion I was returning to camp and stopped to leeward of a storm-stunted spruce to take a last look over the country.

Timber-line lay about three hundred feet below me and consisted of two great groves of spruce joined by a narrow line of the same tree. Suddenly, as I stood sweeping the country, I heard a moose call from the narrow connecting line of spruce. I knew it was a cow moose from having heard New Brunswick moose hunters utter the call on a birch-bark horn. The call was loud and reached my ears distinctly; it was a single note. After a wait of about five minutes I heard it again, but this time the sound came from the centre of the large group of spruce. To make sure of the animal's sex, I snowshoed down to the narrow connecting line of timber and there I found the fresh track of the cow leading towards the large grove. The snow was in the condition when the surface for ten feet about me would settle with a loud noise, and as a stalk through the timber was out of the question, and as I would have under no circumstances killed a cow at that time of the year, I returned to camp.

La Voy had done a good day's work, and after talking of the probable success of our companions' search for food we made plans for the morrow. La Voy was to continue advancing freight to the top of the range of caribou-hills, while I was to prospect a route to the grove of timber where we were to locate our base camp and, if possible, proceed on a search for a pass to the glacier.

Early on the following day I started out. Leaving the old tent I made good time on the crusted snow across the rolling hills that divide the McKinley Fork from the Clearwater.

As the sun rose the travelling conditions grew worse, for the snow that overlay the willow thickets kept breaking through, and until nightfall I was forced to plough along through heavy water-soaked slush.

Entering the valley that I had chosen as the most promising road to the North-Eastern Ridge, I located a

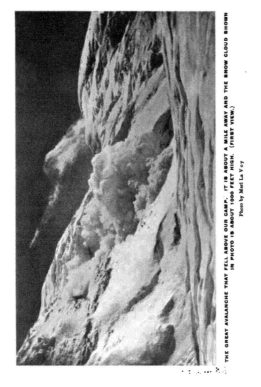

THE GREAT AVALANCHE THAT FELL ABOVE OUR CAMP. IT IS ABOUT A MILE AWAY AND THE SNOW CLOUD SHOWN
IN PHOTO IS ABOUT 1000 FEET HIGH. (FIRST VIEW.)

Photo by Meri La Voy

fine grove of alders with a few stunted cottonwoods scattered through it and saw that it would make a splendid camping place. Noon found me well up toward the head of the valley and directly under the snow-covered mountain range that barred our path to the North-Eastern Ridge. Tracks of caribou were abundant, and I also saw a few sheep tracks, but I was moving at top speed and I did not look for game.

The sun was burning down through a clear sky, and as I jogged along on my long shoes I had to keep removing my clothes or night would have found me wet with perspiration. My clothing was finally reduced to first principles and I climbed upward through the snow-buried mountains naked to the waist.

It was a great relief later, when the long, blue shadows began to creep along the mountainsides, to have dry clothes to temper the chill air. At the base of the mountains my valley split into three forks and I chose the left or eastern fork as the most promising. Following an ice-filled gorge where I had to remove my slippery snowshoes, I came up into a desolate mountain amphitheatre, where cast antlers of caribou lay in the snow.

Crossing this silent valley, I climbed the southern wall and suddenly found myself looking down on a huge gleaming glacier, while directly in front of me rose the ice-encrusted flanks of Mount McKinley's Central North-Eastern Ridge.

After one glance, I saw that the glacier was the Muldrow and that it was split by the Central North-Eastern Ridge and flowed in two great streams from the stupendous ice cliffs of Mount McKinley! This was an important discovery, for it filled in a large blank on the map and tied on the snout of the Muldrow Glacier mapped

19

by Brooks, with one of the largest glaciers of the Mount
McKinley region. But I was delighted particularly
by a second discovery namely, that the northern branch
of the Muldrow made a roadway to the very base of
Mount McKinley, and with my binoculars I got a view
of the North-Eastern Ridge that was more promising
even than our previous views.

I was overjoyed, as in one day's travel from the Mc-
Kinley Fork of the Kantishna River I had actually
prospected a route to an altitude of 12,000 feet on the
big mountain, and the impressions I got from studying
the ridge from 12,000 feet to the summit proved to
be correct, as we eventually followed the course that
looked most promising to us from this point.

With a light heart I started down from the pass,
which was 6000 feet in altitude, and as the sun grew
lower I made fast time downward over the long, blue
snow slopes. On the way home, I followed a new route
to facilitate our freighting. Including side trips I had
climbed 6000 feet and covered about thirty-five miles.
Due to the soft snow, and my observations, it required
fourteen and a half hours, but, except for a pretty keen
appetite, I was as fresh as when I left camp.

On reaching home I heard voices and found that
Professor Parker and Aten had also been successful
on their quest and had purchased some provisions from
two generous miners named Clark and Fink who were
camped about twenty miles below us. Finding Clark
and Fink was a piece of good luck, for Glacier, and Diamond City had long been abandoned. From these
men they heard that the sled trail we had seen was made
by a party sent out by a Fairbanks newspaper to climb
Mount McKinley. This party failed to find a climbable route and returned to Fairbanks before our arrival.

With ample food, plentiful signs of big game, and our route to Mount McKinley decided on, we lost no time in pushing forward. We camped the first day near a little lake in the caribou-hills and pitched our tent on a moss-carpeted hill where the sun had melted the snow.

The following day we reached our base camp on a little stream that ran into one of the four main forks of the Clearwater River.

Seventeen caribou trotted across our line of march and gathered in a picturesque band on a bluff to survey our party. Ptarmigans were about us in millions and rabbits hopped about through the willows, while our eager dogs strained vainly in their attempts to give chase; but it made the sleds go faster, and Aten suggested that "if we could get a rabbit for a 'leader' we would have the fastest dog team on the Kantishna." While we were pitching our tents we saw fourteen caribou feeding up the valley beyond our camp, and the snow was punched through with moose tracks—we were in a big game paradise.

Immediately after our arrival I began a series of long reconnaissance trips among the snow-covered mountains that lay between us and the glacier that we had chosen as a roadway to the base of Mount McKinley. My object was to discover if the left-hand valley that I had explored on my long reconnaissance trip from the McKinley Fork was in reality the best pass. There were several valleys lying west of the one I had seen that might offer a better route for freighting.   •

On the first day I chose the highest and most westerly valley and it was during these long days spent among the desolate mountains that I became acquainted with the caribou of the region. At this particular time of year (April) most of the bulls were in the lowlands, but almost every high mountain valley sheltered a band of cows. On one occasion I was snowshoeing up a high snow-filled valley when I saw a cow caribou about a mile away. As I advanced I began to see others—some feeding, but most of them lying down, and I used great caution as I thought that there would be some bulls among so large a band.

I spent at least an hour in making the stalk, and finally I reached a point among some boulders where there were caribou all about me except to leeward. Seeing that I could go no farther without being seen, I lay still enjoying my wild surroundings. I have always, when watching wild animals at home, been struck with the seeming peacefulness of their lives. I thought of the years that the animals about me had spent in feeding, lying down, getting up, and feeding again, just as they were doing then. Once in a great while a tragedy happens; a snow slide, a rock slide, a bear, a wolf, or a man takes one of their number, and then come more days of absolute quiet and rest. As I lay there watching I sympathised with that curiosity which leads so often to their undoing, and I felt that if I were a caribou I would investigate every interesting or unusual thing that came within my vision. My thoughts were interrupted by the approach of a meddlesome old cow. She must have been a great-great-grandmother at least, for, with her extreme age, she carried herself with a stiff dignity that was amusing.

When she was only twenty feet away and I saw that there was no longer a chance of remaining unseen, I rose slowly to my knees and in the most polite manner of which I was capable, said: "Hello, Carrie, where are all the bulls?" I have never seen an animal assume so ludicrous a look of surprise, combined with outraged dignity, and for a moment she stood stiffened in her track, and then, with a deep grunt of disapproval, she turned and trotted stiffly down the valley. The other caribou that had been lying or feeding all about me took a keen interest in the old cow's actions. They evidently thought that anything that could make the old cow run so fast must be terrifying in the extreme, and so in a moment they were all under way. The old cow stopped at times to gather others about her, and at regular intervals the band would stop, as caribou always do, stare indignantly in my direction, and then run on to another band. In this way the individuals gathered into small bands, and these in turn amalgamated until they had formed a large herd that contained twenty-four cows, and after a last long look the herd wound like a great brown snake across a snowy ridge and left me alone to resume my reconnaissance.

On the following day I explored the central valley, and as I snowshoed upward through a narrow cañon, I saw nine caribou lying on a moraine below me.

On returning from the head of the cañon I wormed my way between the rocks until I was within rifle shot of the band, and, getting out my binoculars, settled down for an interesting half-hour.

Through my powerful glasses I could see every detail and movement of these interesting animals. The thing that interested me most was that they were in a place where in all probability no man had ever been, and in a country that is seldom hunted, and yet they were always on the alert. They were lying on gravel or snow, and their siesta time at this time of year seems to be between 11 A.M. and 4 P.M.

They sometimes lie as horses do, with their heads flat on the ground, and I have seen them yawning, as horses do, when the sun was hot. At this time of the year (April 27th) every cow, with the exception of a few very old animals, carried antlers.

Alfred Brooks, in his account of his trip along the range, speaks with surprise of finding a caribou high up among the snow-fields, but after studying these animals I have found that most of the caribou spend the summer among the ruggedest snow-capped mountains; stranger still, were I to take my experiences in the Alaskan Range as representing the usual conditions of affairs, I would be forced to say that the caribou of the region ranged higher than the mountain sheep, for *it so happened* that I saw caribou higher up than I saw sheep, and I likewise saw quantities of caribou tracks higher up than I did those of sheep. But while it is true that the sheep in general range higher on an average than do the caribou, the fact remains that in the Alaskan Range caribou frequently range as high as the mountain sheep. This fact holds good at all seasons and does not depend on their migratory instinct leading them across high passes, as the large quantities of cast antlers and the deep worn caribou trails among the high snow-fields bare witness. In fact, the only accurate descriptive title for these animals is that of *Mountain Caribou*. One must be very careful in studying the habits of animals not to take the actions or habits of one animal as representing its kind, and it is on this account that the value of a statement depends on the experience of the observer. In studying these caribou I had the advantage of an intimate knowledge of other caribou in different ranges, and while I saw many interesting occurrences among these animals, I put them down to individuality unless their frequent re-occurrence warranted their being classed as habits of this species.

AN AVALANCHE FALLING 3000 FEET ON THE
NORTH-EAST RIDGE OF MOUNT McKINLEY.
(2ND VIEW.)

Photo by Belmore Browne.

AN AVALANCHE FALLING 3000 FEET FROM THE CENTRAL NORTH-EAST
RIDGE OF MOUNT McKINLEY.
(3RD VIEW.)

Photo by H. C. Parker.

While my scouting trips did not swell our larder as
I saw nothing but cow caribou, they resulted in the
discovery of three passes by which we could reach
the glacier.   Of these three, the central pass, which
we called "Glacier Pass" for purposes of identification,
was the best.

CHAPTER XXIV

TO 11,000 FEET WITH A DOG TEAM

We decide to use dogs in our first advance—Aten remains at base camp—Night travel—The first serac—Crevasses—Snow-storms—The big serac—La Voy falls down a crevasse—We find a snow bridge over a large bergschrund on the big serac—We reach the top of the big serac—Cold—Earthquakes—Avalanches—We reach 11,000 feet—We see the Central North-Eastern Ridge—Our outlook hopeful—We cache our provisions—Return to Glacier Pass—Return to base camp.

WE reached our base camp on the evening of the 24th of April and just four days later our advance on Mount McKinley began. Our idea was to make a reconnaissance in force with a dog team. What we would accomplish would depend entirely on the kind of "going" we found, but we figured that the dogs would be a help in pulling our freight up the glacier.

Our mountain food consisted of:

    Pemmican (man)..............102 lbs.
    Hardtack....................3–32 lb. cans
    Sugar.......................30 lbs.
    Raisins.....................30 lbs.
    Chocolate...................7½ lbs.
    Alcohol.....................15 gals.
    Pemmican (dog)..............75 lbs.

In equipment, we carried one mountain tent, mountain rope, ice-axes, ice-creepers, alcohol lamps, aneroid barometers, hypsometers, thermometers (mercurial and spirit), anemometer, binoculars, prismatic compass, etc. Our outfit complete weighed in the neighbourhood of six hundred pounds. Aten remained at base camp, to feed the extra dogs and look out for things. He also read the thermometer and barometer twice daily.

On reaching the head of "Glacier Pass" we decided to lie over until night came and to do our travelling then as the snow would be firmer. We had our fill of pemmican and tea at 10 P.M., and then we struck out over the frosted surface of the great glacier, which we called the McKinley Glacier. A more appropriate name for this fork of the Muldrow, as well as its sister on the East, would be the Tennally Glacier, as they come directly from the ice-falls of the big mountain, and feed the country of the Kantishna's, whose name for the mountain, as I have stated before, was Tennally. The night travel was picturesque and beautiful in the extreme and as I looked back our procession made a weird picture. We had donned the mountain rope for good as the glacier was badly crevassed. I broke trail, followed by Professor Parker, who was in front of the dogs. La Voy was at the gee-pole of the sled.

Professor Parker was roped to La Voy, but we took care to keep the rope free from the sled as its weight was sufficient to carry us with it had it broken through the crust into a crevasse. About 11.30 the moon rose and its light looked almost golden against the deep blue shadows instead of silvery as it does in the Southland.

We crossed tracks of grizzly bears that were leaving their winter dens high up among the ice-falls of the upper glacier. We reached the base of the first serac at 3 A.M and we were glad to rest as it was bitterly

cold and we had made good progress. After a cat-nap
La Voy and I made a trip to the top of the serac. We
told Professor Parker that we would return in an hour,
but we had not yet begun to appreciate the difficulties
of travelling on the McKinley Glacier. There were
countless crevasses and I was forced to sound every foot
of our trail with my ice-axe, and although I used the
greatest caution, I broke through into several ice
caverns, but was saved by the rope from any serious
accident. After we had been absent from camp for
two hours, Professor Parker became worried, and thinking that the trail that La Voy and I had made would
be perfectly safe, he started after us. He had only gone
a short distance, however, when the trail itself caved in.
Luckily, he caught himself with his hands as the crevasse was not wide, or he might have suffered a dangerous injury, or, probably, come to an end of his climbing
career.

   In the afternoon La Voy and I took the dogs and
hauled a good load to the summit of the serac. Near
the head of the ice-fall we were forced directly under the
avalanche-polished walls of the Central North-Eastern
Ridge, but when we had to cross areas that were swept
by snow-slides we studied our chances carefully and
crossed at the most favourable time.

   The McKinley Glacier rises in steps, like a giant
stairway. We rose about 1000 feet while climbing
the first serac and then an almost level plain of snow
lay before us. Crossing this blinding ice-field, we pitched
our camp at the base of a tremendous serac that rose
in two great cliffs with a narrow platform between.
It was a wild-looking spot! Great blue cliffs of solid
ice, scarred here and there by black rock, rose 4000
feet above us, and while we staked down our tent a

snow-storm whirled down from the upper peaks, blotting
everything from view and wrapping us in a white mantle.
Moving cautiously in the storm, La Voy and I felt our
way to the top of the first bench of the "great serac."

The western walls of this ice-fall were fed by the
snow from the north peak of Mount McKinley, and we
were thrilled by catching a glimpse of the main wall of
the mountain hanging high above us. On May 3d,
we advanced to the top of this first bench and brought
up all our belongings. We had now reached an altitude
of 8500 feet. We had a hellish morning; our tent was
in an accursed spot and we feared to move a step without being tied to the rope.

La Voy fell into a crevasse when we were about to
make camp. I made it a rule to lead as I was used to
the treachery of the ice and being light of weight was
less of a burden to handle if I broke into a crevasse.
That morning, however, I felt an attack of snow-
blindness coming on and asked La Voy to lead. He
was very careful at first, but on reaching a level bench
he became over-confident and swung rapidly along without sounding with his axe. Suddenly the snow broke
through and the fact that he had reached the centre of
the crevasse before he fell resulted in his dropping a
good distance before the rope became taut. When his
weight came on the rope, it did so with crushing force.
I was in the middle of the rope and was unable to hold
my feet, as my snowshoes slid on the crust. At the time
of the shock on the rope Professor Parker was carrying
a large coil in his left hand. This hand had been
weakened by a gunshot wound on one of our former
trips and when the rope came taut with a snap the
loose coil was snatched from his hand and he was unable
to help. I will never forget the few seconds that

followed while La Voy's weight was pulling me towards the crevasse. I remember straining until my tendons cracked, and jabbing my ice-axe again and again into the hard crust. Just below we had had soft snow, but now, when soft snow would have been a boon, the crust had hardened so that I could not drive my axe home. I then braked with the head of my axe and when only six feet from the edge of the chasm I came to a stop. La Voy was almost at a standstill at the time and I thought that *I* had stopped him, but after calling several times, he finally answered and told me to give him more rope, as he was on a ledge of ice that protruded from the ice wall. I will always wonder whether I would have stopped him *without the aid of that ledge!* After anchoring myself firmly I had a talk with La Voy and he told me that he could follow the ledge upward to a point where he saw light coming through the snow. And while I paid out the rope he made the ascent and it was a welcome sight when he pushed his head through the snow some thirty feet to my left. I examined the crevasse as soon as he joined us; it was about six feet wide and as far as I could tell it extended to China.

This experience did not tend to make us enjoy the glacier work, for we now knew that even with the rope on we were in danger and that a large party would be required to make exploration of this glacier safe. I have heard many men speak of the thoughts that come to one when sudden death is imminent, and there is a popular idea that childhood scenes, or other happy moments, return and fill the mind. I can assure my reader that this is an idle theory for while we were sliding towards "kingdom come" La Voy was wondering how deep the crevasse was and I was cursing the hard snow that would not grip my axe.

AVALANCHE. 4TH VIEW. THE SNOW CLOUD IS SWEEPING
DOWN WITH TERRIFIC SPEED. AFTER THIS PHOTO
WAS TAKEN WE HURRIEDLY TOOK OUR TENT DOWN
AND LAY ON IT TO PROTECT IT FROM THE
WIND AND FLYING ICE PARTICLES.

Photo by Belmore Browne.

SHOVELLING OUT OUR CAMP AFTER A THREE DAYS' BLIZZARD.
THE BASE OF THE "1ST SERAC" WHERE THE BIG AVALANCHE FELL.

Photo by Merl La Voy.

After La Voy appeared, I took a photograph that shows him emerging from the crevasse, and we advanced thereafter with redoubled caution. We relayed our last load through driving snow and when nightfall came we were happy, for our altitude was now 8500 feet.

The day following was a "big day." The night before we had camped in driving snow and howling wind, surrounded by crevasses and a huge menacing serac rising one thousand feet sheer above us. Our chances of getting our dogs up the avalanche-scarred slopes looked slim indeed. The following day we made a reconnaissance in force and after I had broken into two crevasses we found a snow bridge across a yawning bergschrund, and after making sure that our dogs could cross, we reached the top. Then the sun came out. Our outside shirts were discarded, mitts thrown aside, and our benumbed feet came back to life under the blissful warmth. In the afternoon La Voy and I hauled two sled-loads to the top of the worst pitch and back-packed three hundred pounds over the bridge that spanned the bergschrund. While climbing the serac, Dewey and Fritz, our two "wheel-dogs," fell into a crevasse and they were unconscious by the time we pulled them out, although they recovered quickly when we loosened their collars. Strange as it may seem, the heat of the sun had little effect on the air temperature. On this day, when our faces were blistering and the glacier was a blinding glare of white, the temperature was 33°, *or only one degree above freezing!*

We were welcomed by another snow-storm when we camped at the summit of the "great serac." We did not know it then, as the driving snow shut out all sight of the surrounding mountains, but our labours to reach the head of the glacier were nearly over. When the clouds broke away on the following morning, we could see the grim walls of Mount McKinley high above our heads, and it was only about three miles to the end of the great amphitheatre where our glacier had its birth.   We had risen 1175 feet in climbing the second step of the "great serac" and our camp was now at an altitude of 9675 feet, or nearly half-way up Mount McKinley.

We were not to have everything our own way, however, as a second snow-storm swept down the glacier and the new snow banked up by the ton on the mountain-side made our returning under the great cliffs for our equipment a dangerous enterprise.   Later, we were glad indeed that we had chosen the wiser course.

To understand the unpleasant side of what happened, one must have gone through the days of anxiety that we had known; we had fallen through treacherous snow into blue-black crevasses and edged breathlessly over precarious snow bridges, until we came to feel that we were never safe and that at any moment the snow might give beneath our feet with the familiar sickening feeling of a dropping elevator.   Our position on the edge of the ice cliffs that fall away for more than a thousand feet added also to the terror of what happened.

It was after lunch; Professor Parker was sleeping and La Voy and I were talking in whispers while we listened to the rattle of storm-driven snow across the sides of our frail shelter.   Suddenly we felt the glacier under us give a sickening heave and the nearby mountain thundered with avalanches. For an instant I thought that an ice cave had broken in with us, or that the serac was falling and taking us with it! But in a moment we were undeceived for another shock came, and as the thought *earthquake* flashed through my mind the air thundered and pulsated under the force of the countless avalanches. It was an awful and terrifying sound, and we were glad when the echoes ceased and we once more heard the dreary sound of wind and snow.

The following morning we awoke in a cloudy world, but it was clear enough for La Voy and myself to go down the back trail for our freight. The tent was thick with frost when we awoke, but we thought little of the cold until we began to travel and then our rubber shoe-packs froze. When we returned to camp an hour later the temperature had risen considerably but the thermometer still registered 10° below zero. We advanced immediately through a heavy snow-storm and broke a trail well up into the great gathering basin, and in the afternoon we hitched up the dogs and relayed a good load forward.

It cleared a little between snow flurries and on reaching the end of our morning's trail we left the dogs and broke forward to the top of the last serac on the McKinley Glacier.

We finally reached a point where we could study the whole sweep of the great North-Eastern Ridge and to our delight we saw a low col, or break in the ridge, that could be reached easily from our glacier and the ridge itself looked climbable all the way to the big basin between the two highest peaks of the big mountain.

We drew the following conclusions: As we had now attained an altitude of 11,000 feet, our camp on the col, or lowest portion of the ridge, would be close to 12,000 feet, which would leave us between three and five thousand feet of climbing before we reached the big basin between the north and south peaks. This meant that we would have to return to our base camp with the dogs. They had been good and faithful servants, but they were already showing the effect of the altitude and we could not risk leaving them on the ice while we were climbing, for if we were held by a storm they would perish.

We were highly elated by the promising appearance of the great ridge, and although we would lose some time in returning with the dogs, our chances were improving as the days were growing longer. Indeed, for the first time we felt confident of conquering the mountain. We were not so foolish as to belittle the task ahead of us, although we could see no natural climbing difficulties that we did not feel able to overcome. It was the "unknown dangers" that filled our minds with vague forebodings of hardships and difficulties. An altitude of 20,000 feet had never been attained so close to the Arctic circle, and we knew from previous experience that the hardships to be undergone at an altitude of only 10,000 feet on this northern giant were far more severe than those encountered in climbing a 20,000-foot peak in the Andes of South America. We knew that the severest weather conditions ever recorded occurred on Mount Washington only 6000 feet above the sea, when a wind of 180 miles an hour was noted with an accompanying temperature of 40° below zero! If these conditions could exist at 6000 feet, what might we not expect 20,000 feet up in the sky within 250 miles of the Arctic circle? It was this feeling of uncertainty as to what might happen that made our attempt on Mount McKinley as exciting a sporting proposition as the heart could desire.

On May 7th we awoke to another day of bitter cold, and snow squalls were sweeping across the glacier. La Voy and I drove the dogs to 11,000 feet through the storm and there we cached our trail sled, heavily loaded with food and mountain equipment, and securely lashed with ropes tautened over protecting caribou and mountain-sheep skins. As an added precaution I anchored the sled by driving an extra ice-axe between the forward braces deep into the snow.

The weather showed no signs of improving and as we would be unable to advance much farther with the dogs, and as every day of inaction meant just so many more rations of mountain food wasted, we decided to return to base camp at once. After a hasty lunch we packed up our belongings and started down the glacier.

For a short distance we had a faint trail to follow, but it disappeared at the base of the big serac. At first the dogs were able to follow it by scent, but they, too, were soon at fault.

Between the two cliffs of the great serac I had to begin sounding and trail-breaking and for seven hours we struggled against the worst glacier conditions that I have ever experienced. In the seven hours we crept down over six miles of ice and over the whole distance I sounded every foot that we advanced. On the middle serac the clouds closed down on us and then the snow fell, wrapping us in a chilling shroud and blotting out every mountainside and landmark. Crevasses were the least of our troubles. On the edges of the seracs the ice had formed great caverns, and avalanches had covered these caverns with a treacherous layer of rotten snow.

When I had located a crack I would make a hole with my ice-axe large enough for me to see which way the crevasse ran and at which point it "pinched out." The caverns, on the other hand, ran in no definite direction and as La Voy was following with the sled and dog team, my responsibility was a great one. The last serac we crept over in darkness. We were six miles from Glacier Pass, night had fallen, and the driving snow had turned us—men and dogs alike—to dim, white forms, so we decided to camp. We had only two hardtack and one-eighth pound of pemmican between us. Luckily I had a piece of candle over which I melted a cup of snow water. After dividing our food scraps we rolled into our fur robes.

The next morning was brighter, and as our trail was downhill Professor Parker rode the sled and we jogged down to Glacier Pass in fine style. There we broached our cache and filled up on hardtack, tea, and sugar, and after a nap we struck out for base camp, which we reached in the evening of May 8th.

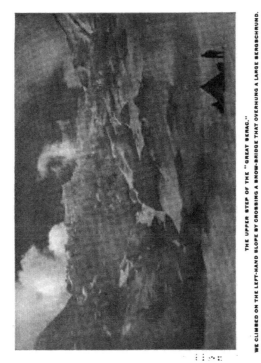

THE UPPER STEP OF THE "GREAT SERAC."

WE CLIMBED ON THE LEFT-HAND SLOPE BY CROSSING A SNOW-BRIDGE THAT OVERHUNG A LARGE BERGSCHRUND.

CHAPTER XXV

DAYS AT "BASE CAMP"

EVERYTHING had gone finely with Aten. He had killed one caribou and had fixed up our camp until it was positively luxurious.

After our return to Base Camp the time went by in a succession of delightful days.

It was our first sight of grass and flowers and running water in many months, as the lowlands had still been in the grip of winter when we started up the mountain. We took the most extravagant delight in our new life, for living on the ice is an unnatural and trying ordeal, and experience does not bring immunity from the dislike of it, as a man must steel himself to every new experience.

Judged by civilised standards, our life was anything but lazy; but after our ceaseless struggle against the blizzards and cold of the high snowbound ice-fields everything seemed easy.

We lived largely "off the country" and my days were filled with hunting big game or studying the topographical features of the magnificent mountain country that encircled McKinley. From the first

307

we had been in no hurry to begin our final attack on Mount McKinley. Our early arrival had been due to the necessity of crossing the Alaskan Range while the snow was still in good condition for dog-sledding, but now, with a cache of 300 pounds of mountain provisions at 11,000 feet, we could take our time and wait for the days to lengthen as our chances would be better then.

While we were coming into the main valley on our return from Glacier Pass we were forcibly reminded that the caribou were still living in the vicinity. We had been having a hard time with our sled as most of the snow was gone, and we frequently came to large patches of bare stones where we had to put our shoulders to the sled to help the panting dogs. Suddenly they broke into shrill howls and dashed madly across the valley and as we sprang after them we saw three caribou trotting along the mountainside above us. The dogs' fatigue had disappeared, however, and they continued on their wild stampede until the sled jammed between two large boulders and brought them to a sudden stop. Our sled load was scattered "all over the scenery." Their strength in these moments of excitement was marvellous and they would pull a heavily loaded sled over rough ground and boulders, as if it weighed nothing. This method of "following the hounds" was exciting, but it had its drawbacks.

By the 10th of May, a few caribou cows had dropped their antlers, and the antlers of the bulls were beginning to form. The bulls moved but little while their horns were growing, and my experience leads me to believe that they usually fed at night or very early in the morning.

The caribou cows seemed less regular than the Behring Sea species (*Rangifer granti*) in dropping their antlers, for I saw individuals carrying apparently strong heads as late as the 4th of July. On the 26th of April, Professor Parker climbed one of the mountains near camp, and on his return he told us that high up on the snow-swept ridges he had encountered a cow caribou with a young calf, and photographed them at close quarters. We were greatly interested in the outcome of these photographs, and great was our delight after our return to civilisation to find that the photographs were a success.

On the following day Aten and I had an amusing adventure. We had made it a rule to have only one man hunting for meat, for if two men were hunting and both were successful, we would have a great store of meat in camp at one time and the chances of wasting it would be greater. But on this day we needed meat badly and as Aten and I had hollowed out an elaborate smoke house under the hill we knew that we could take care of an extra animal.

Aten started up the valley and I laid my course along the foothills of the range in a north-easterly direction. I saw no game until I was several miles from camp, and then I located three caribou above me on a steep mountainside. They were too far from camp and in too rough a place to make shooting worth while, and as I had nothing better to do, I began the stalk in the hope of getting a photograph. The animals were moving slowly along in the direction of our base camp, and they crossed in front of my last bit of cover within easy rifle range, and climbed a snow-field where I secured a long range photograph which shows their surroundings well. As they continued to travel towards camp I followed them, taking care that they did not see me. While they were climbing a hill I would lie flat behind a rock or bush, and when they disappeared over the skyline I would trot along in their tracks until I could see them again. We had covered a mile or more playing this exciting game of hide-and-seek when we reached the large valley where our camp lay. The caribou trotted down the long hillside, crossed the rushing stream, and stopped to feed by a little hill within one hundred yards of our tent. The chance was too good to lose, and I ran downward, forded the ice-cold stream, and began to crawl through the low willow brush. I was afraid that the caribou might smell our camp, but the wind held true, and in a short time I was in easy rifle range. Rising to my knees I aimed at the fattest and shot. The animals were standing in thick brush that hid the lower portions of their bodies, and left me only a narrow strip of their backs to aim at, and in consequence I fired several shots before I secured my quarry.

As I stopped shooting I heard a slight noise behind me and turning around, I was surprised to see Arthur Aten. He was standing as I was with his rifle at "the ready" and a disappointed look in his face, which soon turned to one of amusement. He was walking towards camp when he caught sight of the caribou, and as they were crossing the valley and moving in his direction, he hid himself in the brush ahead of their line of march, and was on the point of shooting when I arose from the brush ahead of him and "turned my artillery loose."

We often saw caribou feeding near our camp, and in the evening after the day's labours were done we loved to lie full length in the soft moss on some hilltop and smoke our pipes and watch for game. One day towards the end of our stay a great bull caribou, with his horns in the velvet, walked slowly past our camp in broad daylight, and strangely enough, he paid no attention to us although he was only one hundred yards away, and the wind was blowing towards him. He knew perfectly well that we were there, for he raised his head several times and looked the camp over, but instead of breaking into a run, as we expected him to, he would lower his head and stalk onward at the fast, swinging walk peculiar to caribou.

Although we shot as few animals as possible, I spent all my time wandering through the mountains with my gun and camera. The mountain country at the northern base of Mount McKinley is the most beautiful stretch of wilderness that I have ever seen, and I will never forget those wonderful days when I followed up the velvety valleys or clambered among the high rocky peaks as my fancy led me. In the late evening I have trotted downward through valleys that were so beautiful that I was forced against my will to lie down in the soft grass and drink in the wild beauty of the spot, although I knew that I would be late to supper, and that the stove would be cold.

The mountains were bare of vegetation, with the exception of velvety carpets of green grass that swept downward from the snow-fields; in the centres of the cup-shaped hollows ran streams of crystal clear water; as the sun sank lower and lower the hills would turn a darker blue, until the cold, clean air from the snow-fields would remind you that night was come and that camp was far away.

During my wanderings I travelled or studied through my glasses every vale and mountain between the tongues of Peters and the Muldrow glaciers. I know of no joy comparable to that of wandering aimlessly among the mountains. You may lie for an hour watching a ground squirrel trying to build a bear proof burrow, and move off at last filled with amusement at his fright on discovering you, and the abuse that he chatters from the protection of his hole.

As you walk along you may be attracted by the antics of a willow ptarmigan who tries to entice you from the vicinity of his nest. Knowing that his brown mate is setting near by, you allow him to lead you until he flies away with derisive cackles. Then is the time to double back quickly, using your ears and field-glasses, until you hear the happy pair talking over the ease with which you were duped, and if your ears are sharp and you have located the sound aright, you may creep up and see the rare sight of a ptarmigan sitting on her eggs.

I found two nests which I was careful not to disturb, and later La Voy and I returned and photographed them. Even about camp there was always some wild bird or animal to watch. During our first trip on Mount McKinley, Aten had succeeded in taming a Gambel's sparrow. The little bird formed the habit of flying into our tent at all hours, and he became so bold that Aten named him "Nervy Nat." We always kept a few crumbs on hand, and he would alight on our knees or feet, and make himself at home generally. On one occasion he had a severe lesson, for he made the mistake of *alighting on the hot stove!* Several days went past before he would venture inside the tent, and when he did begin to visit us again, he always gave the stove a wide berth! In time the rabbits grew accustomed to our presence and grew so bold that we had to see that nothing that they would eat was left lying about the camp. We paid a price in learning what they would eat, for we finally came to the conclusion that they would eat anything. Our axe handles were decorated with their

THE HEAD OF THE McKINLEY GLACIER. THE CENTRAL NORTH-EASTERN RIDGE
IS SHOWN ON THE LEFT.

Photo by Merl La Voy.

THE "COL CAMP." ALTITUDE 11,800 FEET. WE DUG A DEEP HOLE FAR INTO
. THE SNOW TO PROTECT OUR FRAIL SHELTER FROM THE STORMS.

Photo by Merl La Voy.

tooth-marks, they ate the soap we left by the brook, and on one occasion one of my undershirts which I had just washed and hung on a low willow bush to dry was destroyed during the night.

One day we were all lying in the sun on our little hilltop when a rabbit hopped out into the gravel bar looking for a place to cross the creek. He studied one place critically, and we watched him hopefully, for it was a broad part of the brook and would have made a difficult jump. Odds were offered that he could jump it, when he changed his mind, and choosing another place, gave a tremendous leap and—landed in the water. He went off shaking his wet feet, followed by our laughter. On the same day three big bull caribou and a cow paid us a visit. We saw the first caribou calf on May 16th, and I found that these caribou were not nearly as regular in dropping their young as are the Grant's caribou of the Behring Sea coast, for we saw very young caribou a month or more later; whereas on the coast of Behring Sea the young are usually dropped within a period of two weeks. It is probable, however, that no two seasons are necessarily alike in this respect.

The migrations of this caribou were a matter of great interest to me, and I lost no opportunity to learn what I could on this subject. The results of my observations have convinced me that during the months of April, May, June, and July the caribou of that region do not migrate in any particular direction. Whether some of the bands do or do not later in the year can only be decided by careful observations at some future time, altho' the indications I saw again led me to believe that no general migration occurs. The animals I know, are found all along the northern side of the Alaskan Range during the rut. This would mean that they remain in

the vicinity between the month of July, when my observations ceased, and October. In addition to this
knowledge I found quantities of bull caribou antlers
both at high and low altitudes along the range. While
I do not know at just what time the males of this species
shed their antlers, they cannot differ greatly in this
respect from other caribou, which fact would place this
shedding period well on towards the middle of the
winter, or later than the time chosen by other caribou
for making their general migrations.

On the first day of my arrival in the foothills of
Mount McKinley, I found plentiful indications that
there had been bears about, and during all my hunting
I was constantly on the lookout for bruin. But while
they were very scarce during our stay on the Clearwater River, I feel sure that at certain times in the year,
probably when the blue-berries are ripe, they are quite
plentiful. Our only experience with a bear occurred in
camp.

I was washing the breakfast dishes one morning
when Aten said: "Hand me the binoculars; I think
there is something moving on the mountainside." I
did so, and in a moment he added: "Big grizzly!
coming this way!"

Excitement reigned and the dishes were forgotten.
Aten generously told me to go after the bear, and I
refused on the ground that the bear belonged to him,
as he had seen it first. He answered that he had no
use for a bear skin, and that he wanted me to get the
bear. After we had talked it over some more I grabbed
up my rifle and, after thanking Aten, started on the run
for a little hill that lay in the bear's course. But it
proved to be a case of "he who hesitates is lost," for
the bear smelled our camp just before he was within

good rifle range, and galloped up the mountainside.
Now, the bear was very fat, and although I might
have been able to hit him, I thought that I would get
a better chance by following him. The country was
open as far as the west branch of the Clearwater, and
having moccasins on my feet I knew that I could make
fast time, and I also knew, from two experiences, that
I had had on the coast of Behring Sea, that a big bear
would not travel very far without resting.

I waited until he had crossed the skyline and then
I followed him. There were patches of snow lying over
the uplands and the bear's tracks were as easy to follow
as the white paper in a game of "hare and hounds."

Every time I crossed a valley I would climb the sky-
line slowly and scan the country ahead, but always the
tracks lay before me, and, finally, by the west fork of the
Clearwater River, the tracks led downward into dense
alder thickets and the chase "was up." This bear and
the tracks of two grizzlies that we found on the upper
glaciers were the only indications that we saw of the
presence of these animals in the spring time on the
northern face of Mount McKinley.

The white sheep ranged everywhere on the northern
face of the Alaskan Range. We even found them on the
most northern of the north-eastern ridges of Mount
McKinley, and on our return from the summit two ewes
walked up to our last glacier camp and moved off slowly
after satisfying their curiosity. They range low at all
times of the year on the mountains near Mount McKinley, as the snow line is lower than it is to the east -
west of the great mountain.

My diary for May 19th says: "May 17th was a
hazy day, in fact for days past the haze has been growing
deeper and deeper, till the mountains have hung like

mirages in the sky, with nothing to suggest their rugged
frameworks of rock and ice. In the evenings the skies
have been the palest of greenish blues, almost grey,
and the mountains have stood out very softly in their
sunset colours. I started out early in the morning to
try to find a bear, and carelessly left my binoculars in
camp.

"About two miles from camp I saw some spots on a
mountainside. The sun shining through the haze made
it difficult for me to make out what kind of animals
they were, as the band was a mile distant. Something,
a 'hunch' may be, told me that the spots were mountain sheep, but my pessimistic, every day common sense
said that they were caribou, for I had frequently seen
caribou at a higher elevation on the same mountain.

"From force of habit I was taking in unconsciously
every detail of the stalk, while my practical self was
urging me to proceed up the valley in search of a bear.
Finally my practical self won, and I moved forward,
but always my inner self was whispering *Sheep!* and
leading my feet behind sheltering hills and away from
tell-tale air currents. So distinctly marked were my
feelings that I became amused and humoured my
inner self, until, on reaching the critical point of the
stalk,—which was a shallow snow-filled trench that led
upward across the mountainside,—I gave my feet free
rein and surrendered to the overwhelming interest of a
difficult approach. I should mention here that even if the
spots were sheep, the chances were an hundred to one
that they would prove to be ewes and lambs—which
I would not have molested; but if the animals were
rams—I would not have changed places with any man
in the Western Hemisphere!

"It so happened that the stalk was blind, as I was

forced to keep absolutely hidden during the entire approach, there being no cover on the mountainside. This fact kept me in total ignorance of what kind of beasts I was stalking until I had reached a point within two hundred yards of the point where the animals were lying. On reaching a small rock I took off my cap and raised my eyes slowly. One sheep was in sight—a young ram—and with the idea of at least seeing the rest, and possibly securing a photograph of the band, I dropped back into my little snow trench and began the difficult part of the stalk. It was an unorthodox approach, for I was stalking the sheep from below, but an unfavourable wind and great, smooth mountainsides above cut off all chances in that direction. Lying flat in the snow I wound my way upward. At times, by merely raising my eyes, I could see the young ram, and several times he stared fixedly in my direction, while I lay with my chin in the snow. After about three quarters of an hour creeping I reached a small boulder that proved to be my last cover. Lifting my head carefully I peered over, and then,—my heart pounded audibly in my throat,—for the tops of great curling horns showed above a little knoll, and I knew that I was within rifle shot of a band of rams.

"I sometimes think of the life in civilisation in comparison with the life in the open, for a man can live ten years of the ordinary existence in a large city without once experiencing the intense, overwhelming emotions that ten minutes of life in the wilderness often hold for him.

"After I had recovered my self-possession, I studied the band for the two largest heads, for we could not use more than the meat of two animals. There were six rams in the band; four old, battle-scarred veterans and two six-year-olds. They were lying in a difficult position for a shot, as a little bench cut off the view of the lower parts of their bodies, so that I only had a narrow strip to shoot at. My camera was about twenty feet behind me in the snow-trench.

"Having decided that I could not get closer to the sheep I pushed one foot forward, took a long sight from my knee, fired—and missed!

"With a great bound the band leaped to their feet and dashed up the mountainside. I shot again and missed, but this time I saw my bullet strike high, so holding lower I shot again and the largest ram fell. Turning at once to the rest of the band I singled out the sheep that seemed to carry the largest head, and had the satisfaction of seeing him drop to my first shot. With two large rams to my credit my thoughts flew to my camera, and I dashed back to the snow-gully and returned in time to make three exposures as the sheep crossed over the mountain.

"As I passed the first ram I photographed him as he lay and then proceeded to my second trophy, and after arranging him so that he would show to the best advantage, I exposed my last film. While I was putting my camera away I heard stones rolling on the mountainside above me, and looking up I saw one of the young rams coming back to the scene of the shooting. The first ram I had shot was lying below me and about seventy-five yards away, and the young ram galloped past me and stood by the ram's carcass. As I advanced he stood on the alert watching me. His graceful figure stood out clearly against the snows that draped the distant mountains, and for some time we stood quietly watching each other. He was not more than fifteen yards away, and I could see every movement of

OUR ROUTE UP THE CENTRAL NORTH-EAST RIDGE SHOWING THE
TRAIL. THE MAKING OF THIS TRAIL WAS HEART-BREAKING WORK
AND EVERY STORM THAT SWEPT THE PEAK NECESSITATED
OUR RE-BREAKING AND CHOPPING THE STEPS. WHILE
THE RIDGE APPEARS TO DIP IN PLACES, THE EFFECT
IS DUE TO THE ANGLE AT WHICH THE CAMERA
WAS HELD. THERE ARE ONLY TWO LEVEL
PLACES ON THE ENTIRE RIDGE.

Photo by Belmore Browne

his lithe body and the slow rise and fall of his white sides as he regained his breath.

"We stood for a long time and gazed so intently at each other that it became embarrassing, and I was almost relieved when the ram moved and broke the tension. He moved slowly away and seemed to show no fear until I walked up to his fallen companion, and then he seemed to understand, for he turned and passed rapidly over the mountain.

"The heads were the typical shape of the species, as both had a wide spread. They were not large in comparison with other heads I have secured, but were of good size for the sheep of the Mount McKinley region. The largest head measured: outside curve 34½ inches; circumference of base 14½ inches. The second head was slightly smaller. In the cool of the evening La Voy and I went back for the meat, with a sled and dog team. We pulled over the moss and heather while the sun sank through a crimson sky into the dim blue lowlands. Three caribou, one a great bull with massive velvet horns, swung over the mountain crest, while our dogs bayed furiously and strained at their tug-lines, and their baying echoed back and forth among the mountains until the silence slowly closed in again.

"The northern nights were beautiful beyond words. The sun sank only a short distance below the horizon, leaving a blue twilight that threw a veil of mystery over the valleys and mountains; the cool smell of the snows crept down from the grim ice-barriers of the main range, and the lowlands rolled away to the Yukon like a great blue sea."

Such was our life at the base of North America's highest mountain.

While the days went by we had kept one eye, as

it were, on the big mountain, but the time passed so rapidly that the hours had stretched into weeks before we realised it and the day soon arrived that we had decided on as the date for our final attack on the big mountain. Our departure was delayed, however. La Voy, while stalking a cow caribou and calf with his Graflex camera, fell on a sharp rock and cut his knee open to the bone. The cut was deep and the jagged rock had done such damage that I kept the cut open as long as possible and allowed it to heal by granulation. The delay, however, proved a benefit, for a villainous spell of weather overtook us and we were glad to be in a warm and comfortable camp. While La Voy's wound healed successfully it gave him much discomfort and his work on Mount McKinley under this handicap redounds greatly to his credit.

Just before our final advance on the big mountain an event occurred that gave us cause for the greatest anxiety. I had been watching a cow and calf caribou on the rolling hills of the east fork of the Clearwater.

On my way home I stopped on a high mountain shoulder to look about me. From my high point of vantage I could look into the big basin at the head of the McKinley glacier and see the upper snow-fields where we had left our sled and its valuable load. I was standing idly studying the great mountain's contours when a white cloud drew my eyes to the stupendous ice walls that rimmed the basin. As I looked the cloud grew larger and larger until it stretched out in a straight line across the cliffs and I knew that I was watching an immense avalanche. When the great mass plunged into the basin a huge cloud of snow shot high in the air until the mountainsides 5000 feet above were hidden by the white pall. It was a larger avalanche

even than the great sliding mass of snow that we had
seen near the South-West Ridge of the mountain in 1910.
Overcome with anxiety for our sled I waited breathlessly until the great cloud had disappeared, and in the
interim I could hear the deep thundering of the fall
rumbling back and forth among the mountains. When
the view was clear I eagerly turned my binoculars towards the head of the glacier and to my inexpressible
joy I could see crevasses crossing the snow-fields. If
I could see the crevasses the chances were that our
sled was not covered up beyond recovery, but when I
reported the news to my companions they worried
about the fate of our provisions.

CHAPTER XXVI

THE CONQUEST OF MOUNT McKINLEY

IT was on the 5th day of June that we began our final attack on Mt. McKinley. We took Arthur Aten and our dog team with us as far as the base of the first serac. It was a long, hard march and Aten remained all night, sharing my wolf robe. We awoke in a cloudy world and soon we were enveloped in a heavy snow-storm. Aten, fearful that he might be held by the storm, leaped on his sled and faded away into the white mist.

We now turned our minds toward back-packing our supplies to the head of the glacier where our sled and equipment were cached. Although we were travelling as light as we could we had all we could manage under the difficult conditions that we found on the glacier. The snow-storm continued for three days and we lay in our tent eating our valuable food and abusing the weather.

We were dumbfounded by the turn the weather had

322

SECOND VIEW OF OUR "COL CAMP" LOOKING DOWN FROM 13,600 FEET.
SHOWING THE McKINLEY GLACIER. THE "COL CAMP"
IS INDICATED BY THE ARROW.
Photo by Merl La Voy.

LOOKING DOWN ON OUR "COL CAMP" FROM 12,000 FEET.
ON THE LEFT IS THE GLACIER WE ASCENDED; ON THE RIGHT IS THE GREAT
CHASM, FALLING AWAY FOR 2000 FEET TO THE EASTERN FORK OF
THE MULDROW GLACIER.
Photo by Merl La Voy.

taken. All the mountains below us that had been
practically free of snow when we arrived on the Clearwater River were now buried deep in snow. We knew
it could not be the usual state of affairs for these same
mountains were grass-covered. If every summer was a
repetition of this one no grass could grow.

Under June 8th there is an interesting entry in my
diary:

The glacier has been very noisy all day; it has groaned
and cracked, and at short intervals there have been deep,
powerful reports, sounding for all the world like the boom
of big guns at a distance. We have been talking about this
queer noise but are undecided as to its cause. It must be
due to the settling of the great ice caverns under the tremendous weight of new snow.

It was not until we reached civilisation long afterwards
that we found that the unusual booming sound had not
come from the glacial caverns, but that it was made
by Katmai in eruption three hundred miles away—
Katmai, the volcano whose eruption buried Kodiak
Island in ashes! Later we found these Katmai ashes in
our teapot after we had melted snow, but again we accepted the easiest explanation and decided that the grit
in our teacups was merely dust blown from the cliffs.

After the snow ceased falling we were held by good
weather, for tons of snow hung poised on the steep cliffs
and the route over the seracs under these avalanche-
polished slopes was out of the question.

In order to make use of our time, La Voy and I
snowshoed six miles to Glacier Pass and brought back
an extra allowance of alcohol, sugar, pemmican, and
hardtack. On our return we saw as fine an avalanche
as it has been my luck to witness. It fell from the upper

portions of the North-Eastern Ridge, for a distance of about three thousand feet, and when it struck the glacier it threw a snow cloud more than one thousand feet high. It was an awesome sight and we had to lower our tent quickly lest the terrific suction of air caused by the falling snow should do it damage.

We were in our tent at the time waiting for the avalanche to occur in order that we could cross the serac in safety. As the first deep rumbling reached our ears, we scrambled, cameras in hand, out of the tent door and luckily succeeded in getting some good photographs before the snow cloud buried us in its chill embrace. At one o'clock on this day (June 8th) our thermometer registered 46 degrees in the sun. This was the highest temperature recorded by us on Mount McKinley and it is interesting to note that the temperature in the shade at the same moment was only 26 degrees! The big avalanche was followed by countless others, until the very ice shook and the sound blended into the steady rumble of thunder.

After the snow had settled we commenced our arduous advance up the glacier. The new snow made travelling slow, and we were forced to break trail with light loads.

La Voy's "game knee" gave him trouble, and while climbing the second serac he fell through into a deep crevasse while following in my footsteps, and injured his knee again. But after a good rest he was able to advance once more.

At this time we were under a great nervous strain; the constant lookout for crevasses and avalanches had a depressing effect on us, but we were also in great fear that an avalanche might have buried our cache of mountain equipment. I will never forget the excitement we laboured under as we ploughed slowly up over the last serac. Suddenly a tiny speck of black showed in the snow ahead, and running wildly forward we came to our precious sled. The tip of the ice-axe with which we had anchored it was the only thing in sight, and on shovelling away the snow, we found that the sled had been turned on its side by the terrific wind caused by the avalanche that I had witnessed from the Caribou hills beyond our base camp. The discovery of our cache was a great stimulus to us. Besides the necessary food and equipment we recovered many longed-for luxuries such as mountain sheep and caribou skins to sleep on, reading matter, and a pocket chessboard.

Our cache was on the right-hand side of the final amphitheatre. Looking across the glacier we could see an easy route leading to the col of the North-Eastern Ridge. Where the ridge sagged, its summit was only five hundred feet above the floor of the glacier. We were held once more by a blizzard, but the rest was not unwelcome and when the weather cleared we lost no time in advancing to the top of the col. Here we shovelled deep into the steep snow slopes close to the summit of the ridge. As we dug deeper we made a wall of the blocks of hard snow, and when our labours were completed, we were protected from storms and wind. One of our chief pleasures was the splendour of the mountain views. The glacier travel had been dangerous, but the dangers had been hidden and we missed the stimulation of being able to look out over the surrounding mountains, for we had been down in a deep ice-rimmed pit, where we were wrapped in chill clouds most of the time. But now everything had changed. Twenty steps from our tent and we could look out from the very top of the great Central North-Eastern Ridge. The first time that we

reached the top of the col our breath was taken away
by the awesome grandeur of the view. The walls on
the southern side were as savage a lot of ice-clad
precipices as the mind could picture.

We could not see the depths, for a sea of cold grey
clouds rolled ceaselessly one thousand feet below us, and
as we stood in awe watching them a shaft of sunlight
stabbed the upper clouds and turned the grey sea to
fire. Service's lines,

> I have stood in some mighty-mouthed hollow,
> That was plum full of hush to the brim,

came into my mind, and later when the clouds drew
away we could look down almost straight to cold
glacier depths two thousand feet below us.

In addition to the supplies that we had carried up the
glacier, we had at our "col camp":

```
Hardtack....................18 pkgs.
Man pemmican..............11–6 lb. cans
Raisins......................23 lbs.
Sugar........................18 lbs.
Tea (Lipton)................  1 lb.
Tea (tabloid)...............  1 lb.
Alcohol.....................  9 gals.
Chocolate ..................  7 lbs.
```

When we moved our supplies from the glacier to the
col camp we had a steep climb of five hundred feet to
negotiate, and at this point La Voy found that on steep
slopes of soft snow he could not depend on his knee.
Now La Voy's strength was one of the most important
factors in our attempt on the great peak, and as his
courage was of the highest quality I knew that his knee
was in a serious condition. In all the glacier work I

LOOKING DOWN THE GREAT NORTH-EASTERN RIDGE FROM ABOUT
13,400 FEET.

Photo by Belmore Browne.

broke trail as a matter of course as my light weight and long schooling in this work made it advisable. But La Voy's help on the great ridge was invaluable and as I looked up over the towering, knife-edged ridge, my heart sank at the possibility of his knee being seriously injured. There was only one thing to be done and that was to make the work as easy as possible for him, so I carried most of the dunnage, although he chafed under the new régime and amply made up for his lack of activity by shovelling out the deep holes in which we set our tent. It was in carrying an eighty-pound load from the glacier to our col camp that I first noticed the effect of our altitude, although it only made itself manifest by a slight acceleration of my breathing.

Our col camp was at an altitude of 11,800 feet, according to Professor Parker's Hicks and my Green aneroid barometer.

On June 19th we made our first reconnaissance on the ridge. Our plan was to climb to the Big Basin between the two great peaks and the reader will see how little we appreciated the immensity of the task that confronted us. We took with us ample food for six days, and in addition, extra clothing, films, cameras, glasses, compasses, barometers, a prismatic compass and level, anemometer, etc. The following account of our day's adventure is taken from my diary:

June 19th. Back from a very hard trip. We climbed to 13,200 feet through the softest of snow over as sensational a ridge as I have ever been on. Some of the slopes that we *traversed* were 60° or more, for I measured one that overhung a 2000-foot drop off that measured 50° on the clinometer, and there were many that I could not measure because we were afraid to stay on them longer than necessary. I broke and chopped our trail for five hours, and in places I had to first stamp down platforms in the soft snow before I could reach a firm footing.

La Voy's knee stopped us at 13,200 feet. Now the question is can he travel to-morrow? If he can and it's a good day we will take our camp outfit and climb to the Big Basin, and return for the food that we left on the ridge at 13,200 feet.

The above entry shows the optimistic view that I held concerning our reaching the basin. It was not until later that we realised to the full the gigantic size of the great mountain, as the next entry in my diary makes clear.

June 22d. Ridge Camp, altitude 13,600 feet. Much has happened in the last three days. On the morning of the 20th we started out in the firm belief that we would reach the edge of the Big Basin and camp before nightfall. It took us three hours to reach the point where we had left our packs on the first day. It was an impressive spot. The ridge was so sharp that I had to chop off the crest to make room for our feet.

On the left the ridge dropped away at a dizzy angle for 5000 feet to the surface of the east fork of the Muldrow Glacier, on the right it fell away almost straight for 2000 feet; you felt as if you were flying. In this narrow ridge we had chopped deep holes to insure the safety of our packs. From the packs onward there were no steps at all, and although I had had to remake a large proportion of our steps during the three preceding hours I started on confidently and we began to creep up the great knife edge of snow. As the time went on I began to feel the effects of the terrific labour. La Voy despite his willingness could not help me out as the steps were in soft snow and his knee was hurting him. After I had broken trail steadily for an hour, a rock that I had been working towards actually seemed farther away than when I started. As time went on the

constant gazing upward along the white ridge into the
sun's eye began to tell on me and by the end of the fifth
hour I was snow-blind and completely done up. I saw no
place level enough to camp and I supposed that we would
find hard ice underlying the snow that would prevent our
shovelling out a tent-site. I now knew that it would take
hours to reach the basin, where we had figured in minutes, in
fact I was beginning to realise what the mountain *is*—it is
reared on such a gigantic scale that ice slopes that only
look a few hundred feet high may be several thousand!
At last I turned to my companions and told them that I was
snow-blind and played out, and that I feared that I could n't
chop long enough to reach a camping place. About 100 feet
above there was a slight sag in the snow slope below some
rocks that were in their turn below the final rise of the
ridge where it swoops up a thousand feet to join a rock
peak that forms the southern gateway to the Big Basin.

After a council of war the Professor said,"Let 's try to
shovel a site in that sag above us." La Voy, who was fresh,
went to work and to our unbounded joy he struck hard
snow instead of ice, and in the course of two hours' hard work
we had a shelter on the snow slope. We first picked the
snow out with our ice-axes and then shovelled it out, the
blocks rolling down 2000 feet from the little platform.
While La Voy was finishing up Professor Parker and I
descended for the packs we had left on the first day. The
distance was close to 500 feet and *it had taken me two hours
of heart-breaking toil to lead the way up!*

Went to bed suffering from my eyes, which La Voy
doctored with boracic acid and zinc sulphate, and sick at
heart, as I now knew that McKinley was too big for us
with our present food supply of six days' rations. Marvellous sunset as we looked over a sea of clouds that stretched
to the end of the earth.

The next entry tells of the final day when we were
forced to change our plans and return for more food.

June 21st. Ridge Camp. Alt. 13,600 ft. Good day so we started (again) to pack some supplies into the Big Basin. After pounding down steps for an hour *we reached hard snow!* Oh! what a relief it was mentally as well as physically, for soft snow is treacherous stuff and on many of the steep *traverses* that we have made we have been afraid to *speak* for fear the reverberation of our voices would start the snow sliding. La Voy came forward generously and for eight hours we chopped alternately, each taking half-hour turns.

Now one of the strange laws of climbing is that the harder the leader works the easier it is for those who follow, for they can climb upward over five or six laboriously cut steps and then sit down on their axes and rest for five or ten minutes while the leader is chopping others. I enjoyed the rests to the full for it was the first time since I left Glacier Pass that I have been able to enjoy the climbing views.

But the work was so difficult that after seven hours of continuous work with La Voy chopping half the time *we rose only 800 feet!* We were again forced to leave our packs on a knife-edged ridge at an altitude of 14,400 feet. We were close to the great peak that forms the south gateway and we could just begin to see into the Big Basin!

On our return to camp we talked the matter over, and we decided that there was only one thing to do—namely to return to our col camp and pack up ten days' rations. It was a hard blow to us as it meant hellish labour, but it had to be done.

All day we have been above a sea of clouds—that may mean that we are at last above the bad weather. No ill effects from altitude yet, am enjoying my smoke as usual. Min. tem. June 21st, 4° below zero. June 22d, 3° below zero.

These entries will give the reader an idea of the difficulty of our climbing, but in return we enjoyed mountain views of the utmost magnificence.

LOOKING DOWN FROM 13,500 FEET ON THE NORTH-EAST RIDGE TO THE
EASTERN BRANCH OF THE MULDROW GLACIER 6000 FEET BELOW. .

Photo by Belmore Browne.

VIEW FROM THE " 15,000-FOOT CAMP." THE NORTHERN NORTH-EAST RIDGE
CAN BE SEEN FALLING AWAY INTO THE CLOUD BANK THAT COVERS
THE LOWLANDS DURING THE SUMMER MONTHS.

Photo by Belmore Browne.

On the following day—June 22d—we were awakened
by the howling of the wind, and on emerging from our
tent we found clouds abqut us.   As all we had to do to
reach our col camp was to follow the steps on the knife-
edge ridge we started down for our extra supplies.   It
was strange to think as we descended through the grey
pall that within a few inches of our feet the ridge
dropped away between two thousand and four thousand
feet.   Many of our steps were filled in solidly with
drifted snow, but it was far easier to remake them on
our way downward than it would have been while
ascending with loads.   In addition to our supplies at
our ridge camp we packed up:

> 18 lbs. of pemmican
> 3 gals. of alcohol
> 9 boxes of hardtack
> 8 lbs. of sugar
> 3 lbs. of raisins
> ½ lb. of tea

We also brought our short "climbing" snowshoes as we
thought they might be useful in the Big Basin.   We
figured on twelve days' food from our ridge camp at
13,600 feet.   Coming over the narrow arêtes we were
struck by heavy "wullies" or wind squalls that blew the
snow in clouds off into space.   We could hardly see
each other at times, and we drove our ice-axes deep
into the snow, and moved cautiously; it was spectacular
climbing.

By this time we were awful objects to look at; La
Voy and I were always more or less snow-blind, from
trail-chopping, and our eyes were swollen to slits and
ran constantly; we were all almost black, unshaved,
with our lips and noses swollen, cracked, and bleeding,

our hands, too, were swollen, cracked, and blood-
stained. As La Voy said, we would have served
"to frighten children into the straight and narrow
path."

The following day was clear although the usual cloud
carpet covered the lowlands. Taking our packs we
again attacked the great ridge and nightfall found us
triumphant at our ridge camp—we had dropped our
loads under the "South Gateway Peak" at an elevation
of 15,000 feet.

On the following day we advanced our camp to the
shelter of the rocks, where I made the following entry
in my diary:

"15,000-foot Camp."

We have packed up heavy loads from our ridge camp
in a little more than three hours as the steps high up were
not badly drifted. It was frightfully hard work and glad
we are to be camped in the lee of some great granite slabs,
with the sun warming our tent. This is the wildest and
most desolate spot imaginable. We are on the very edge
of the Big Basin that divides the two summits of Mount
McKinley. Below us all is mist and clouds; it seems as if
the earth, thinking we needed her no more, had withdrawn
from our lives.

The Big Basin is glacier filled. There are three seracs,
and between run easy snow slopes that promise an uneventful route to the base of the South Peak. All we have to do
now is to traverse below the cliffs we are camped under, and
we will be in the Big Basin.

It seems strange to realise that we are camped higher
than Mount Tacoma or the Matterhorn! We left enough
alcohol and pemmican at ridge camp to last us on our
return. We are wearing our snow glasses inside the tent
now, and my eyes are so bad that I sleep with glasses on.

In our 15,000-foot camp we were stormbound. An immense fall of snow occurred, and as we lay in our fur robes our ears were filled with the grandest natural music that I have ever heard, for during one entire morning the great amphitheatres thousands of feet below us thundered and boomed under the constant shock of avalanches, and through this awesome bass ran the shrill theme of shrieking wind. McDowell has put the thunder of the surf breaking on jagged reefs into music, but no man yet has written the song of the avalanche and the mountain storm.

Now up to our 15,000-foot camp we had noticed the altitude in one important respect only—Professor Parker and La Voy had been unable to eat their full ration of pemmican. Occasionally they let a meal go by without tasting it, and they attributed their inability to eat it to the fact that the pemmican was not good. I, however, suffered no inconvenience and ate as much as I wanted until I reached our 15,000-foot camp. On June 26th after the storm had passed we established a camp at 15,800 feet which we called our "16,000-foot camp." In the afternoon of the same day we advanced all our equipment with the exception of our camp outfit. That night I ate my ration of pemmican as usual, but a few hours after I began to suffer from abdominal cramps. The night was one long period of torture, and when morning came I made a vow that I would eat pemmican sparingly in the future. While the physical pain was bad enough the mental worry caused by our inability to eat pemmican was equally serious. Pemmican was our staff of life; on it we depended for strength and heat to carry us through the toil and cold of our high climb. Without it we would be reduced to a diet of tea, sugar, raisins, and a small allowance of chocolate, which was not enough to keep us warm, let alone furnish fuel for the hardest toil.

We were worn down to bone and sinew as it was and needed a strong food to give us strength; while we were as hard as iron we lacked the *rebound* that a well-fed man has—in the language of the training table "we had gone stale." We had learned too that it requires the same kind of energy to withstand bitter cold as is required in the accomplishment of hard physical work. Luckily, the average human being is an optimist; after worrying over the problem for an hour or two we decided that it was *uncooked* pemmican that disagreed with us and we dismissed the question after promising ourselves a pemmican pudding at our 16,000-foot camp.

Our progress upward through the Big Basin was uneventful except for the tremendous excitement we were labouring under. The cold too was intense. The leaves of my diary were so cold that I could not write without gloves. At our 16,000-foot camp with an alcohol stove going full blast and the warmth of our three bodies the temperature inside of our tent at 7.30 P.M. on the 26th of June was 5° below zero, and three hours later it was 19° below zero!

It was at this time that we began to devote ourselves to the study of how to conserve our body heat.

I have in the earlier part of my story given the weights of our different sleeping-bags, and as I can speak more accurately of my own experiences I will state the method I followed in trying to get a night's sleep.

My sleeping-bag weighed seventeen pounds. It was large and made of the best blue or "black" wolf fur. When I was ready to sleep I first enclosed my feet in three pairs of the warmest, dry Scotch-wool socks.

THE "16,000-FOOT CAMP." THE NORTHERN END OF THE SUMMIT CAN BE
SEEN DIRECTLY OVER THE TENT.

Photo by Merl La Voy.

"16,615-FOOT CAMP." THE HIGHEST CAMP EVER MADE IN NORTH AMERICA.
IT WAS FROM THIS POINT THAT WE MADE OUR TWO
ATTACKS ON THE SUMMIT.

Photo by H. C. Parker.

In addition I wore two suits of heavy woollen underclothing. Then came heavy woollen trousers covered with canvas "overalls" which keep the wind from penetrating, and the snow from sticking to, the wool trousers. On my upper body I wore two of the heaviest woollen shirts made; they were of grey wool with a double back and large breast pockets that doubled the front thickness. Over these shirts I placed a fine woven Scotch-wool sweater, and around my waist I wrapped a long "muffler" of llama wool. The collars of my shirts were brought close by a large silk scarf, while the ends of wool socks covered my wrists. Over all I wore a canvas "parka," the universal Alaskan wind shield with a hood trimmed with wolverine fur. My head was covered with a muskrat fur cap which covered my neck and ears and tied under my chin. My hands were protected by heavy Scotch-wool gloves covered with heavy leather gloves, and my feet were enclosed, in addition to the socks, by heavy soft leather moccasins. On retiring we melted the water for our breakfast tea for ice melts much quicker than snow and in this way we were able to warm the tent without a great waste of fuel. Despite the above elaborate precautions I can say in all honesty that *I did not have a single night's normal sleep above 15,000 feet on account of the cold!*

Professor Parker dressed more warmly than either La Voy or myself. He wore at night a complete suit of double llama wool besides his mountain clothing, and yet he could not sleep for the cold, although Anthony Fiala, leader of the Ziegler Polar Expedition, slept comfortably in a duplicate of Professor Parker's bag, clad only in underclothes when the temperature was 70° below zero! This fact illustrates the comparative effect of cold between sea level and 15,000 feet close to the Arctic circle. This susceptibility to cold, and our inability to eat pemmican, was the only way in which La Voy and I suffered from the altitude, although Professor Parker was weak and slightly nauseated on our final climb to the edge of the summit.*

On the 27th of June we carried our packs in two relays to the top of the second serac between the two great peaks and camped just below the last serac that forms the highest point of the Big Basin. We arrived with our last loads after the sun had gone down, and I have never felt such savage cold as the ice-fields sent down to us. We were in a frigid hollow at an altitude (corrected reading) of 16,615 feet. On the north the great blue ice slopes led up at an almost unclimbable pitch between the granite buttresses of the Northern Peak. On the south frozen snow-fields swept gently to the rock-dotted sky-line of the Central North-East Ridge which led in an easy grade to the final or southern summit of the great mountain. La Voy went to work with our shovel while I picked away the hard snow with my ice-axe. Despite our labours our feet and hands were beginning to stiffen as we pitched the tent and started our stove, and we were seriously worried for fear Professor Parker would freeze. On the next day we devoted our time to resting and making the most careful preparations for the final climb. My diary entry for the day follows.

"17,000-foot Camp" (our barometers placed us close to that altitude but the final readings of our hypsometer compared with our base camp barometer readings placed this camp at an altitude of 16,615 feet). Bitterly cold. Professor Parker feels the altitude. If it is clear we will "hit" the summit to-morrow. We only have 3,500 feet to climb. 3 P.M. same day—June 28th. Splendid loafing day—all

---

* The food we were eating was a sufficient cause in itself for nausea and weakness.—AUTHOR.

well rested, and indications good for a fine climbing day
to-morrow, but it has been blowing a gale on the upper
snow-fields, although what few clouds have formed have
been away below us. We will also be warm to-night as we
will not get chilled making camp as we did yesterday.
Have put in the spare time getting everything ready for the
"big day." Last night was warm, only 8° below zero, so
we are not so frightened by the weather, unless a blizzard
strikes us, and then anything might happen. We feel
somewhat like soldiers on the eve of a battle, for to-morrow
promises to be a good day, and if it is it will be the final day
of three seasons of endeavour and several years of thought,
planning, and hoping. If we "get there" we will be happy
men. There is nothing to stop us except a storm. The
route is easy; direct from camp to some rocks that lead to
the summit of the ridge 1000 feet above us, thence along
the ridge for perhaps a mile to the final dome which will give
us perhaps 2000 feet of ice-creeper climbing, and then our
dream will be realised. Robert Louis Stevenson says that
only one thing in life can be attained—Death; but Robert
never climbed a high summit after years of failure! We will
rise at 4 A.M. and start at 6, and we hope to make the climb
at the rate of 500 feet an hour, or seven hours in all, and
return in two—a nine-hour day.

8 P.M. same day. Beautiful night, have just come in
from studying the peak and weather—can look out over
the north-east end of the range and see each peak and
valley—also blue washes that mean timber 15,000 feet
below us; wish we had some here!

From our camp we saw the northern side of the horse-
shoe-shaped summit. The main ridge that we were to
follow led up to the northern *heel* of the horseshoe.
There it rose to the almost level summit formed by the
circular summit ridge. About one hundred yards from
the very edge of the summit there was a slight rise, swell-

ing, or hummock on the level ridge and this little hill is
in all probability the highest point on the North
American continent.

In both our 16,000- and 16,615-foot camps we had
tried to eat cooked pemmican without success. We
were able to choke down a few mouthfuls of this food
but we were at last forced to realise that our stomachs
could not handle the amount of fat it contained. The
reader will, no doubt, wonder why we placed such
dependence on one food and my excuse is that we put it
to every proof except altitude in 1910. Fate ordained
however that in that year we would not reach an altitude of more than 10,300 feet—close to the exact
altitude where the pemmican began to disagree with us
in 1912! Had we ascended a little higher we would
have discovered this mistake in time to profit by it.

The morning of our final climb dawned clear as
crystal. As I came out into the stabbing cold to report
on the weather the whole expanse of country to the
north-eastward stretched like a deep blue sea to where
the rising sun was warming the distant horizon.

True to our schedule we left camp at 6 A.M. Not a
sound broke the silence of this desolate amphitheatre.
At first the snow was hard and required little chopping.
We moved very quietly and steadily, conserving our
strength for possible exertions to come. At regular
half-hour intervals La Voy and I exchanged places,
and the steady strokes of our axes went on with scarcely
an intermission.

Between changes both Professor Parker and I checked
off our rise in altitude and to our surprise we found that,
although we thought we were making fairly good time,
we were in reality climbing only 400 feet an hour.
Close to the top of the big ridge 1000 feet above our

A STUDY IN ALTITUDE (FIRST VIEW).

THE MULDROW GLACIER AND THE TOP OF THE CENTRAL NORTH-EASTERN RIDGE
AS SEEN FROM 16,000 FEET BETWEEN MOUNT McKINLEY'S TWO PEAKS.

Photo by Belmore Browne.

THE SAME VIEW OF THE MULDROW GLACIER FROM ABOUT 15,500 FEET
ALTITUDE ON THE CENTRAL NORTH-EAST RIDGE. IN THE LEFT FORE-
GROUND LIES THE "BIG BASIN." IN THE CENTRE STANDS THE
LOWER END OF THE CENTRAL NORTH-EAST RIDGE WHICH
SPLITS THE MULDROW GLACIER INTO TWO STREAMS.
WE ASCENDED THE LEFT-HAND BRANCH.

Photo by H. C. Parker.

camp we ran into soft snow and we fought against this unexpected handicap at frequent intervals during the day. When we reached 18,500 feet we stopped for an instant and congratulated each other joyfully for we had returned the altitude record of North America to America, by beating the Duke of the Abruzzi's record of 18,000 feet made on Mount St. Elias. Shortly afterward we reached the top of the big ridge. Sentiment, old associations, and a desire for a light second breakfast halted us in the lee of some granite boulders. We had long dreamed of this moment, because, for the first time, we were able to look down into our battle-ground of 1910, and see all the glaciers and peaks that we had hobnobbed with in the "old days." But the views looking north-eastward along the Alaskan Range were even more magnificent. We could see the great wilderness of peaks and glaciers spread out below us like a map. On the northern side of the range there was not one cloud; the icy mountains blended into the rolling foothills which in turn melted into the dim blue of the timbered lowlands, that rolled away to the north, growing bluer and bluer until they were lost at the edge of the world. On the humid south side, a sea of clouds was rolling against the main range like surf on a rocky shore. The clouds rose as we watched. At one point a cloud would break through between two guarding peaks; beyond, a second serpentine mass would creep northward along a glacier gap in the range; soon every pass was filled with cloud battalions that joined forces on the northern side, and swept downward like a triumphant army over the northern foothills. It was a striking and impressive illustration of the war the elements are constantly waging along the Alaskan Range.

On the southern side hang the humid cloud-banks of the Pacific Coast, the very farthest outpost of the cloud armies of the Japan current; on the north stands the dry, clear climate of the interior, while between, rising like giant earthworks between two hostile armies, stands the Alaskan Range.

We absorbed these beauties as we wound back and forth between the granite boulders on the top of the ridge, and as we advanced the clouds began to thicken on the southern side, but through the deep blue chasms between, the well-remembered contours of the peaks we had explored in 1910—Beard, Hubbard, and Huntington—seemed like the faces of old friends.

As we advanced up the ridge we noticed a shortness of breath and Professor Parker's face was noticeably white but we made fast time and did not suffer in any other way. At a little less than 19,000 feet, we passed the last rock on the ridge and secured our first clear view of the summit. It rose as innocently as a tilted snow-covered tennis-court and as we looked it over we grinned with relief—we *knew* the peak was ours!

Just above us the first swell of the summit rose several hundred feet and we found hard crust and some glare ice where our ice-creepers for the first time began to be of use. Up to our highest camp we had used rubber "shoe-packs" with leather tops, but on our last climb we wore soft tanned moccasins covered with "ice-creepers" of the Appalachian Mountain Club design.

From the time that we had topped the ridge the great northern summit of Mount McKinley had claimed our attention. It rose directly opposite to us and every detail of its ice and rock stood out in bold relief against the northern sky. Report has it that the Lloyd Mount McKinley party had reached this peak or one of its northern shoulders and there raised a pole above a pile of rocks.

On our journey up the McKinley Glacier far below we had begun to study this peak. As we advanced closer and closer each pinnacle of the Northern Ridge stood out in turn against the sky until on the last days close to the southern summit every rock and snow slope of that approach had come into the field of our powerful binoculars. We not only saw no sign of a flag-pole but it is our concerted opinion that the Northern Peak is more inaccessible than its higher southern sister.

During our ascent of the ridge and the first swell of the final summit the wind had increased, and the southern sky darkened until at the base of the final peak we were facing a snow-laden gale. As the storm had increased we had taken careful bearings, and as the snow slope was only moderately steep all we had to do was to "keep going uphill." The climbing was now about of the same steepness as that we encountered in scaling the ridge above our camp, and as the snow was driving in thicker clouds before the strengthening wind we cut good steps. The step chopping reduced our progress once more to the 400-foot an hour speed.

The slope we were attacking was a round dome that came to a point forming the top and beginning of the northern heel. Before the wind and snow blotted the upper snow-fields from view we had had a good view of the inside of the horseshoe which sloped down to wicked-looking seracs that overhung a snow-field far below. Our one thought therefore was to keep well to the north so that in case we got lost in a blizzard there would be less chance of our descending among the crevasses at the top of the drop off. To accomplish our desire we cut our steps in zigzags of about the same length.

When we started up the last slope above the first swell of the final dome we were at an altitude of 19,300 feet. At 19,300 feet La Voy had begun his turn of chopping and as the lower portion of the summit was less steep than the upper slopes we succeeded in rising 500 feet during our combined turns at leading.

As I again stepped ahead to take La Voy's place in the lead I realised for the first time that we were fighting a blizzard, for my companions loomed dimly through the clouds of ice-dust and the bitter wind stabbed through my "parka." Five minutes after I began chopping my hands began to freeze and until I returned to 18,000 feet I was engaged in a constant struggle to keep the frost from disabling my extremities. La Voy's gloves and mine became coated with ice in the chopping of steps.

The storm was so severe that I was actually afraid to get new, dry mittens out of my rucksack for I knew that my hands would be frozen in the process. The only thing to be done was to keep my fingers moving constantly inside of my leather-covered wool mittens.

When my second turn was three fourths finished Professor Parker's barometer registered 20,000 feet. It would have been possible for him to set back the dial and get a higher reading but beyond this point it would have been dangerous to read the instrument had he been able too. The fury of the storm and the lashing clouds of steel-like ice particles would have made it next to impossible to read the dial.

On reaching 19,000 feet my barometer had registered within 100 feet of Professor Parker's, but as we rose higher my instrument—probably due to false compensation—had dropped with great rapidity to 17,200 feet,

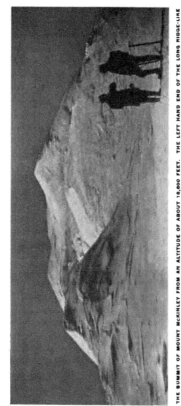

THE SUMMIT OF MOUNT McKINLEY FROM AN ALTITUDE OF ABOUT 18,400 FEET. THE LEFT HAND END OF THE LONG RIDGE-LIKE
SUMMIT IS LOWER ON ACCOUNT OF THE FORESHORTENING OF THE CAMERA. THE STORM THAT INCREASED
TO A BLIZZARD BEGAN TO BLOW JUST BEFORE THIS PHOTO WAS TAKEN.

From two photos by Belmore Browne.

or little higher than our camp between the two peaks!
From then until I returned to camp it was useless, but
on the following day it "recovered its composure" and
registered the same as Professor Parker's. Professor
Parker's barometer behaved with absolute regularity
throughout our whole trip, and as we had been able to
study the last slopes carefully and could approximate
accurately our speed in climbing, our calculations would
place the summit at 20,450 feet or 150 feet higher than
the United States Government triangulation. On
leaving, and returning to, our base camp, both our
barometers and a third that Aten had read twice daily
during our absence agreed closely; and furthermore
all three agreed closely with Brooks's and Reaburn's
contour lines.

After passing the 20,000-foot level the cold and the
force of the wind began to tell on me. I was forced
several times to stop and fight with desperate energy
the deadly cold that was creeping up my hands and feet.
My estimate at the time for the last quarter of my
period was 50 feet. As I stepped aside to let La Voy
pass me I saw from his face as he emerged from the
snow cloud that he realised the danger of our position,
but I knew too that the summit was near and determined to hold on to the last moment.

As Professor Parker passed me his lips were dark and
his face showed white from cold through his "parka"
hood, but he made no sign of distress and I will always
remember the dauntless spirit he showed in our most
trying hour. The last period of our climb on Mount
McKinley is like the memory of an evil dream. La Voy
was completely lost in the ice mist, and Professor
Parker's frosted form was an indistinct blur above me.
I worked savagely to keep my hands warm and as

La Voy's period came to its close we moved slower and more slowly. Finally, I pulled my watch from my neck inside my "parka" hood, and its hands, and a faint hail from above, told me that my turn had come. In La Voy's period we had ascended about 250 feet.

As I reached La Voy I had to chop about twenty feet of steps before coming to the end of the rope. Something indistinct showed through the scud as I felt the rope taughten and a few steps more brought me to a little crack or *bergschrund*. Up to this time we had been working in the lee of the north heel of the horseshoe ridge, but as I topped the small rise made by the crack I was struck by the full fury of the storm. The breath was driven from my body and I held to my axe with stooped shoulders to stand against the gale; I couldn't go ahead. As I brushed the frost from my glasses and squinted upward through the stinging snow I saw a sight that will haunt me to my dying day. *The slope above me was no longer steep!* That was all I could see. What it meant I will never know for certain—all I can say is that we were close to the top!

As the blood congealed in my fingers I went back to La Voy. He was getting the end of the gale's whiplash and when I yelled that we couldn't stand the wind he agreed that it was suicide to try. With one accord we fell to chopping a seat in the ice in an attempt to shelter ourselves from the storm, but after sitting in a huddled group for an instant we all arose—we were beginning to freeze!

I turned to Professor Parker and yelled, "The game's up; we've got to get down!"

And he answered, "Can't we go on? I'll chop if I can." The memory of those words will always send a wave of admiration through my mind, but I had to answer that it was not a question of chopping and La Voy pointed out our back steps—or the place where our steps ought to be, for a foot below us everything was wiped out by the hissing snow.

Coming down from the final dome was as heartless a piece of work as any of us had ever done. Had I been blind, and I was nearly so from the trail chopping and stinging snow, I could not have progressed more slowly. Every foothold I found with my axe alone, for there was no sign of a step left. It took me nearly two hours to lead down that easy slope of one thousand feet! If my reader is a mountaineer he can complete the picture!

Never in my life have I been so glad to reach a place as I was when I reached the top of the first swell below the summit.

Had the cold that was creeping stealthily upward from the tips of La Voy's and my hands and feet once taken hold we would have frozen in a few minutes, and the worst part of our fight on the summit was the fact that we were fighting a cruel danger that was *unseen!* In the cañon of the Yentna in 1906, where Barrill and I had been forced to take our lives in our hands ten times in less than an hour, it was a fair open fight against the rushing water, but in a fight against a blizzard you are struggling blindfolded against a thousand stabbing ice daggers.

Our troubles were not over, however, when we reached the base of the final dome, for here there were no steps and in descending through the hissing clouds of ice-dust I was led by the wind alone. Again I might have accomplished as much while blinded for my only guide was the icy blast striking my right shoulder. Had the wind shifted we would have perished, but after what seemed hours a dim shape loomed through the

storm—it was the highest rock on the great ridge and
our route was now assured. Finding the first rock
ended our first struggle on Mount McKinley's summit,
for in descending we kept in the protecting lee of the
great ridge. When the gale quieted enough to let us,
we talked! We cursed the storm that had driven us
back. La Voy said that we had done enough in getting
on top of the mountain, and that we had climbed the
peak because it was only a walk of a few minutes from
our last steps to the final dome. This was true, but
unfortunately there is a technicality in mountaineering
that draws a distinction between a mountain top and
the top of a mountain—we had not stood on *the top*—
that was the only difference! We reached camp at
7.35 P.M. after as cruel and heart-breaking a day as I
trust we will ever experience.

On the following day we could not climb. Almost
all our wearing apparel down to our underclothes was
filled with the frost particles that had been driven into
our clothing by the gale.

I have spent my life in the open and through the
handling of sailing craft have learned to approximate
the velocity of wind as accurately as the next man.
Professor Parker and La Voy too were both men who
had had much experience in the judging of wind.
The *most conservative* of our estimates of the climatic
conditions we fought against was a wind of fifty-five
miles an hour and a temperature of 15° below zero.
During the entire climb La Voy and I were free from
any ill effects from altitude with the exception of
moderate shortness of breath, and Professor Parker
suffered little more. La Voy and I both found that the
use of our arms in step cutting was far more exhausting
than leg work. I rolled and smoked a cigarette at

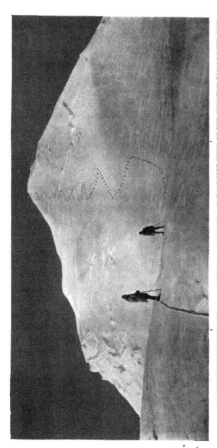

THE SUMMIT OF MOUNT McKINLEY, FROM AN ALTITUDE OF 19,000 FEET. THE HIGHEST POINT OF THE MOUNTAIN CAN BE SEEN JUST TO THE RIGHT AND APPARENTLY BELOW THE PEAK. WE WERE TWO HOURS AND A QUARTER REACHING OUR HIGHEST POINT, 20,300 FEET, SHOWN BY DOTTED LINE. THIS PHOTOGRAPH WAS TAKEN ON OUR SECOND ATTEMPT TO REACH THE SUMMIT. CLOUDS OF SNOW AND A FURIOUS WIND TURNED US BACK ON THIS ATTEMPT AFTER WE HAD REACHED 19,600 FEET. OUR STEPS CHOPPED ON THE FIRST DAY'S CLIMB COULD BE SEEN LEADING TO THE NEAREST SUMMIT WHEN THIS PHOTO WAS TAKEN. IN CLEAR WEATHER, PERHAPS FIVE MINUTES OF EASY WALKING WOULD HAVE TAKEN US TO THE HIGHEST POINT.

From these photos by Belmore Browne.

18,000 and 19,000 feet, and enjoyed the tobacco as I do in lower altitudes. Had the storm allowed me to, I would have smoked on top of the mountain. La Voy had never used tobacco in any form. Professor Parker is a light smoker and discontinued the use of tobacco while he was at high altitudes.

The drying out of our clothing was a difficult task as we had only one alcohol stove. To add to our difficulties La Voy and I both developed an attack of snow-blindness from our siege of step cutting and all day long the stabbing pains shot through our temples. Fate too ordained that the peak should be clear, although long "mares' tails" of snow stretching out to the north told us that the gale was still lashing the summit.

CHAPTER XXVII

THE END OF THE LONG TRAIL

THROUGHOUT the long day after our fight with the summit we talked food and weather conditions. We had now given up all thought of eating pemmican and were living, as in fact we had been living since leaving our 15,000-foot camp, on tea, sugar, hardtack, and raisins. Our chocolate was finished. We had cached our pemmican as we advanced according to the daily amount we were able to choke down, and we found on studying the matter that *we had lost ten days' rations in useless pemmican since leaving our 13,600-foot camp!* In our highest camp alone we had lost four days' rations! We were not only harassed by the thought of the food we had lost, but also by the memory of *the useless weight we had carried.* Moreover, we were forced to eat more of our hardtack and raisins in an attempt to gain the nourishment we had been deprived of by the loss of our pemmican.

This complication reduced us to four meagre day's rations, which meant that we could only make one more

348

attempt on the summit of Mount McKinley, and that attempt must be made on the following day.

The reader will realise with what breathless interest we studied the weather conditions. What had caused the storm on the summit? we asked each other. Was it a general storm sweeping in from the Susitna Valley, or was it a local *tourmente* caused by change of temperature? Similar questions filled our minds, and we decided to leave at 3 A.M. on our next attempt.

The following day, strengthened as far as our insipid food would allow, and with our eyes patched up by boracic acid, we started on our final attack.

The steps made on the previous day helped us and in four hours and a half or by 7.30 A.M. we had reached an altitude of 19,300 feet at the base of the final dome. From this point we could see our steps made on the first attempt leading up to the edge of the final dome, and from this point we also secured the photograph of the summit that appears in this book.

But our progress up the main ridge had been a race with a black cloud bank that was rolling up from the Susitna Valley, and as we started towards our final climb the clouds wrapped us in dense wind-driven sheets of snow. We stood the exposure for an hour; now chopping a few steps aimlessly upwards, now stamping backward and forward on a little ledge we found, and when we had fought the blizzard to the limit of our endurance we turned and without a word stumbled downward to our ridge. I remember only a feeling of weakness and dumb despair; we had burned up and lived off our own tissue until we did n't care much what happened! In a crevice on the highest rock of the main ridge we left our minimum thermometer; it, a few cans of frozen pemmican, and our faithful old

shovel, are the only traces of our struggle on the Big
Mountain.

We reached camp at 3 P.M. and after some hot tea we
felt a wild longing to leave the desolate spot. Packing
our necessities carefully we shouldered our light loads
and struck off down the glacier. I turned on the edge
of the glacier bench for a last look at our old camp.
Stuck deep in the snow our battered shovel showed
black above a foot-trampled blur, while above, the
roar of the wind came down from the dark clouds
that hid the summit.

The greatest difficulty that we had to overcome on
Mount McKinley was the transportation of our tents
and equipment. Moreover, we were constantly worried
by the thought that we might reach a point on the
mountain where it would be impossible to camp.
Without a shovel, we could never have reached the
dome of Mount McKinley.

The threatening aspect of the sky and the fear of being
caught in a blizzard without sufficient food lent wings
to our feet, and in about three hours, by the aid of our
old trail which still held in places, we reached our 15,000-
foot camp.

The drop to a lower altitude combined with a comparatively warm night allowed us to enjoy a delicious
night's rest. We had spent seven days above 15,000-
feet; six days above 16,000 feet, and four days above
16,615 feet. From the day that we left our 15,000
foot camp we had existed on tea, sugar, hardtack,
and raisins. I need hardly add that we were glad to
descend.

At our 15,000-foot camp we recovered our snowshoes
and at 8 A.M. on the morning of July 2d we started
down the Central North-East Ridge. My diary adds

OUR CAMP ON THE NORTHERN SIDE OF MOUNT McKINLEY AFTER THE
EARTHQUAKE OF JULY 6, 1912.

Photo by H. C. Parker.

SLEDDING UNDER DIFFICULTIES. WE USED A SLED WITH WOODEN RUNNERS
AS LONG AS WE WERE IN "MOSS COUNTRY." AFTER
THAT WE PACKED THE DOGS.

Photo by H. C. Parker.

that it was a morning of "unmitigated hellishness" as we were enveloped in clouds and wind-driven snow. At 13,400 feet I went snow-blind again and walked off a cornice while leading, but as the thin edge broke under me I drove my axe home in time to keep the strain off the rope. In four and one half hours of continuous work we reached the col camp at 11,800 feet. We were a thankful group of men as we rested luxuriantly in our partly drifted in hollow.

After resting and drinking some hot tea we ate a little pemmican and after a second rest we dropped down to our sled at the head of the glacier. At this point La Voy stated that he could pull one hundred pounds on the sled more easily than he could carry fifty pounds. I knew the glacier so intimately that I could lead over our back trail through anything but a "black" fog or a blizzard. We therefore loaded the bulk of our necessities on the sled and started down the glacier, La Voy bringing up the rear with the loaded sled. We came down easily as far as travelling went, but our month's absence had seen a great change in the glacier and large crevasses had appeared all over; these and a heavy fog kept me on a wire edge, until, fearing that I would miss a narrow pass through a bad serac, we camped. As it was 8.30 P.M. we "called it a day's work" and turned in for a sleep.

When we awoke the following morning we found ourselves in the exact centre of the pass I had hoped to find. Packing up quickly we crossed a second large expanse of snow, and so exact was our course that my axe rang on an empty pemmican tin that we had left on our former ascent of the glacier, and which had been buried by the snows. We came down over the big serac without trouble although numerous new crevasses gashed the steep slopes, but at the base, on the little bench where La Voy had fallen into the crevasse, I went snow-blind again and we had to camp. Boracic acid and zinc sulphate patched me up once more, but a dense fog kept us in our little tent. We conserved our strength by resting and at 7.30 P.M. the fog lifted and we started downward again.

By this time I was suffering nervously from the constant strain and responsibility of choosing the way, and I made a vow that the next stop we made would be beyond the reach of the accursed crevasses. We travelled slowly but steadily; one by one the well-remembered landmarks passed by. At last at the head of the lowest serac a dim yellow stain in the snow drew my attention. It was so faint that looking down nothing could be seen, but squinting ahead it lay in a dim yellow line. I waited for a well-known crevasse to verify my wild hope, and then I yelled the joyful news to my companions—we had found our old trail! In places it crossed crevasses that had opened since we used it but on the whole it was a Godsend and it led us safely to the base of the last ice-fall.

Nothing remained now but the journey down the "flat" to Glacier Pass and we did not hesitate. The glacier surface had melted down to ice which had over-flowed in places so that we broke through into the slush, but not a crevasse appeared. Several large streams rushing through the trenches they had worn in the solid ice gave us some trouble, but soon the bare mountainsides greeted our snow-tired eyes and at 3 A.M. we pulled our sled over the moraine and laid our tired bodies on soft warm earth. It was the first time in 30 days that we had lain on anything but snow or ice!

We finally summoned enough energy to eat a little

and pitch our tent and then we slept "like dead men" until the afternoon. When we awoke there was a warm breeze blowing up through the pass, and with it came the smell of grass and wild flowers. Never can I forget the flood of emotions that swept over me; Professor Parker and La Voy were equally affected by this first "smell of the lowland," and we were wet-eyed and chattered like children as we prepared our packs for the last stage of our journey.

All our thoughts were centred on Arthur Aten. We had told him that we would return in fourteen days and now our absence had stretched to twice that number. Vivid pictures of possible accidents flashed through my mind and we made our last preparations in feverish excitement. Two mountain sheep came to within seventy feet of our tent and watched us in surprise before moving away.

La Voy and I shouldered eighty-pound packs for our trip to camp and in our weakened condition we made "heavy weather" of it. The joy of feeling grass underfoot repaid us for all our troubles, however, and our concern for Aten drove us onward.

When we came out of the Pass into the valley of the Clearwater we encountered a band of fifty caribou and while we rested they trotted excitably about until by a concerted flank movement they caught our scent and floated like a great brown carpet across the mountainsides. So it went, in turns of long packs and short rests while the sinking sun flooded the western sky with gold. At last the old rock above our camp came into view and Professor Parker went ahead.

Then we saw a figure clear cut against the sky. Was it a man or a wild beast? was the thought that flashed through my mind, until a second smaller shape appeared

23

—a dog! And our joyful yells echoed down the valley.

Aten came to meet us, tears of happiness running down his cheeks, and we forgot our stiff-necked ancestry and threw our arms around each other in a wild embrace, while over us, under us, and all around us surged an avalanche of woolly dogs.

Aten's month in the wilderness was a hard ordeal. For many weary days, with a mind tortured by thoughts of possible accidents, he had spent all his spare time on the rock lookout station with his binoculars sweeping the head of the valley where we were to come down out of the snow. We were happy men when we lay on our soft caribou robes in our storm-battered old tent talking of the days of our separation. In my long experience in the North I have never seen men who showed more signs of hardship than we did. My waist line has decreased from 30 in. to 23½ in. during the month we spent on the ice, and Professor Parker and La Voy were equally emaciated.

Our greatest cause for satisfaction was that whatever we had done had been accomplished by our own unaided efforts.

While we had been trying in vain to scale the *impossible* southern cliffs our friends had been urging us to hire Swiss guides. Not knowing the country as we did, they did not realise that with the exception of the few Swiss guides that had climbed in the Himalayas we could not have found men who knew the game as well as we did, and that guides would refuse to do the work of porters that we were called upon to do. Furthermore, in all the wilderness exploration, the handling of boats, rafts, horses, dogs, and securing meat, they would have been "cheechakos," and an added care.

CLARK'S AND FINK'S PLACER MINE ON MOOSE CREEK.

But aside from this, Professor Parker, La Voy, and I were moved by a desire to establish as Americans the altitude record of North America; there would have been little credit or satisfaction in paying a man from a foreign country to lead us to our goal. Although on account of climatic conditions I am unable to call this book, *The First Ascent of Mount McKinley*, we are equally proud of our conquest of the great peak, for from the point where our ice steps stopped, the climbing ceased; from there onward it was a short walk to the goal we gave so much to reach. If Mount McKinley is ever climbed to the final dome the men who climb it will follow the very trail we pioneered, until, weather permitting, they walk the short distance upward along the gently sloping ridge to the little snow knoll that forms the highest point on the continent. Were it not for this fact we would not have rested from the task we tried so long to accomplish.

In the many strenuous days that we spent on Mount McKinley's ice and snow, we often longed for the peace and comfort of our base camp on the Clearwater. And yet it was in our base camp two days after our return that we were subjected to the strangest and most exciting experience of our entire trip.

It was the evening of July 6th. Professor Parker was resting inside the big tent. La Voy, Aten, and I had been drying and airing our mountain tent and duffle and doing odd jobs around camp. The sky was a sickly green colour, and the air seemed heavy and lifeless. After finishing our work we rested in the heather and talked of our plans for our coming journey to the Yukon.

The sky reminded me of sinister skies that I had seen on the eastern seacoast before heavy storms, and I

turned to Aten and said that were I on a boat I would
overhaul the ground tackle and see that everything was
snug because it looked like "dirty weather." The
words were scarcely out of my mouth before a deep
rumbling came from the Alaskan Range. I can only
compare the sound to thunder, but it had a deep hollow
quality that was unlike thunder, a sinister suggestion
of overwhelming power that was terrifying. I remember that as I looked, the Alaskan Range melted into
mist and that the mountains were bellowing, and that
Aten was yelling something that I could not understand
and that the valley above us turned white—and then
the earth began to heave and roll, and I forgot everything but the desire to stay upright. In front of me
was a boulder weighing about two hundred pounds.
We had pulled it there with a sled and dog team to
anchor our tent; it had sunk into the moss from its own
weight, and as I watched, the boulder turned, broke
loose from the earth, and moved several feet.

Then came the crash of our falling caches, followed
by another muffled crash as the front of our hill slid
into the creek, and a lake near by boiled as if it was hot.

The mossy surfaces of the hills were opening all about
us, and as the surface opened the cracks filled with
liquid mud, and then suddenly everything was still.
We stood up dazed and looked about. The Alaskan
Range was still wrapped in the haze of avalanche dust,
and the country far and near was scarred, and stripped
of vegetation where the earth had slid. Our dogs had
fled at the beginning of the quake and we could hear
them whimpering and running about through the
willows.

Aten, with his pocket full of tobacco, was asking me
impatiently for mine—and then we began to laugh. We

ran to the tent to see how Professor Parker had fared,
and then we howled again, for as we pulled the flaps
aside it seemed as if everything that was movable,
including the stove, had fallen in a heap. The stove
had overturned and a great flat rock which we used as a
base for the stove had moved towards the tent door.

While we were restoring order out of chaos, Aten,
who was standing by the tent door, exclaimed: "Good
God! Look at Brooks!" As we dashed out of the
tent an awe-inspiring sight met our eyes. Just east of
Mount McKinley stood a magnificent 12,000-foot peak.
It was somewhat like the Matterhorn in shape, and
formed the culminating pinnacle in a range some six
miles in length that formed the eastern wall of the
main eastern fork of the Muldrow Glacier. As this
mountain was the finest peak east of Mount McKinley
we were anxious to give it a worthy name and we
decided to name it after Alfred Brooks, who had led the
first survey party through this part of Alaska. While
we were uncertain as to whether or not Brooks's name
had already been attached to some other Alaskan
mountain, we always spoke of the great peak as Mount
Brooks. Now, as we reached the open and turned our
eyes towards the mountain, we saw that the whole
extent of the mountain wall that formed its western
flank was avalanching. I have never seen a sight of
such overpowering grandeur. The avalanche seemed
to stretch along the range for a distance of several miles,
like a huge wave, and like a huge wave it seemed to
poise for an instant before it plunged downward onto
the ice-fields thousands of feet below. The mountain
was about ten miles away and we waited breathlessly
until the terrific thunder of the falling mass began to
boom and rumble among the mountains.

Following the inspiring salvos of nature's artillery came the aftermath we had learned to look for. Beyond the range that rimmed our valley a great white cloud began to rise. As it came into view and began to obscure the Brooks range we could almost check off its growth as it billowed upward with startling rapidity, two—three—four thousand feet until it hung like a huge opaque wall against the main range, and then it fell—the range that rimmed our valley was blotted out and the great wave of avalanche débris came rushing down our valley. We were already at work, strengthening our tent in frantic haste.

We knew that the cloud was advancing at a rate close to sixty miles an hour and that we did not have much time to spare. But with boulders to hold the bottom and tautened guy-ropes, we made the tent as solid as possible and got inside before the cloud struck us. The tent held fast, but after the "wullies" passed, the ground was spangled with ice-dust that only a few minutes before had formed the icy covering of a peak ten miles away!

Before we rolled up in our sleeping-bags, we took a last look about us. In every direction the earth and mountains were seamed and scarred and a great dun-coloured cloud of ice- and rock-dust hid the Alaskan Range. The streams, too, were flooding their banks, and ran chocolate-coloured from the earth-slides that had dammed them. As we compared our adventures and sensations, we thought of the band of fifty caribou that we had seen in the head of the valley—what a sight they must have presented when the earthquake struck them! Fifty wild beasts plunging, falling, and wild-eyed with terror—I would give much to have been on a hillside nearby!

THE AUTHOR FORDING THE McKINLEY FORK OF THE KANTISHNA WITH A
ONE-HUNDRED-POUND PACK AND DOGS IN TOW.

Photo by Merl La Voy.

READY FOR THE 250-MILE TRIP TO THE YUKON.

THE "POLING-BOAT" THAT WE FOUND AND REPAIRED ON MOOSE CREEK.

Photo by Merl La Voy.

The earthquakes continued at regular intervals for
about thirty-six hours. None of them could compare
in strength with the first shock, but many of them were
severe enough to wreck a modern city. Strangely
enough most of the shocks were preceded by a deep
detonation. The sound resembled the noise made by
exploding steam, and it came always from the same
place—Mount McKinley. Experts on seismic dis-
turbances have told me that the sound does not precede
the disturbance, but in our case the reverse was true.
We would be sitting in our tent, when suddenly the
deep, explosive noise would reach our ears. One of us
would say, "Here comes another," and if the explosion
was of sufficient power we would take the precaution
of seeing that our teapot was in a safe place. And
then, after a few seconds had elapsed, the quake would
reach us. After going through such an experience as
the big quake, one realises, for the first time, the gigantic
power of the forces of nature, and understands with
what ease great mountain ranges have been formed.

My strongest impression immediately after the quake
was one of surprise at the elasticity of the earth. We
speak of being on "solid ground," but while the earthquake was occurring one felt as if the earth's crust was
a quivering mass of jelly.

With Mount McKinley's farewell salute still ringing
in our ears, we turned our faces northward, towards
the Yukon. We still had 250 miles of wilderness before
us and our days were still full of the joyous incidents of
the wild life.

Shouldering as much as we could carry, we put what
was left on our faithful dogs, and wandered downward
across the foothills looking for a likely stream to carry
us to "the outside." We camped with miners on the

banks of rushing streams where the gold lay yellow in
the sluice-boxes; we drifted down silent rivers where
leaping greyling flashed in the air; we camped on birch-
covered flats, where moose, wet from the river, stampeded among our crazed dogs; and we floated past
sun-drenched banks where Canada geese splashed,
honking, from our path.

I would like to tell of the sun-bronzed "sour-doughs"
who took us in, and lavished on us the riches of the
land, Clark, Fink, Hauselman, and Dalton of Eureka
Creek; of Mother McKenzie who built the log palace
on Glacier River, and of the broad-backed Tanana that
swept us to our journey's end. But I am loath to leave
my old companions and our tent in "the happy hunting-
ground." My patient reader has followed us over a
long trail and it is better that we part there, high up
among the caribou hills of the Alaskan Range, where
to the southward, cloud-like against the blue, stands the
mighty peak named by the Kantishnas in their wisdom
—Tennally—The Big Mountain.

APPENDIX

ALTITUDE AND TEMPERATURE READINGS ON AND NEAR MOUNT McKINLEY

BY

Professor Herschel C. Parker

July 24, 1910

(Close to highest point reached on South-West Ridge of Mount McKinley)

Boiling-point = 194.00° (about 9 A.M.).
Air temperature = 29°.
Aneroid barometer = 20.00 in.
Boiling-point corresponds to barometric pressure of 20.69 in.
Correction on aneroid = 20.69 − 20.00 = 0.69 in. (+).
Reading of aneroid at highest point (9.40 A.M.) = 19.50 in.
Corrected reading = 20.19 inches.

Base Camp

Altitude approximately 450 ft.
Corrected reading of barograph = 29.26 in.
Temperature = 49°.

Calculation

29.26 in. = 26,957 ft.
20.19 in. = 17,263 ft.
_____
9,694 ft.

Mean temp. of air = $\frac{49° + 29°}{2}$ = 39°.

Correction factor for temp. = 1.0155.

9,694 ft. × 1.0155	=	9,844 ft.
Correction for latitude	=	−25 ft.
" " altitude	=	+30 ft.
		9,849 ft.
Base camp		450 ft.
Highest altitude	=	10,299 ft.

JULY 16, 1910 (5 A.M.)

(Summit of Explorers' Peak)

Boiling-point = 196.4°.
Air temperature = 26°.
Aneroid barometer = 20.95 in.
Boiling-point of 196.4° corresponds to barometric pressure
  of 21.75 in.
Correction on aneroid barometer = 21.75 − 20.95 = 0.80 in.
  (+).

Base Camp

Corrected reading of barograph = 29.22 in.
Temperature = 56°.
Altitude approximately = 450 ft.

Calculation

29.22 in. = 26,921 ft.
21.75 in. = 19,208 ft.
——————
7,713 ft.

Mean temp. of air = $\dfrac{26° + 56°}{2}$ = 41°

Correction factor for temp. = 1.020.

7,713 feet × 1.020 =   7,867 ft.
Correction for latitude =   −25 ft.
"   "   altitude =   +23 ft.
——————
7,865 ft.
Base camp   450 ft.
——————
Altitude of Explorers' Peak =   8,315 ft.

JUNE 28, 1912

(Highest camp on Mount McKinley, 3.30 P.M.)

Boiling-point $\begin{cases} \text{Ther. \# 8163} = 182.00° \\ \text{Ther. \# 8165} = 182.04° \end{cases}$

Air temperature $\begin{cases} \text{Minimum ther.} = 8° \\ \text{Ther. \# 3372} = 9° \end{cases}$

Hicks aneroid barometer = 16.18 in.

Base Camp

Altitude by contours = 2500 ft.

	Morning	Noon	Evening
Aneroid reading	27.22 in.	27.20 in.	27.18 in.
Temperature	62°	66°	67°

Calculation

Boiling-point of 182° corresponds to barometric pressure of 15.97 in.
(From Galton's tables by "exterpolation.")
Correction on aneroid barometer = 16.18 − 15.97 = 0.21 in. (−).

27.20 in. = 25,050 ft. (Loomis tables.)
15.97 in. = 11,137 ft.
 _____
13,913 ft.

27.20 in. = reading base camp.
15.97 in. = " at highest camp.

Mean temperature of air $= \dfrac{66° + 9°}{2} = 37.5°$

Correction factor for temperature = 1.012.

13,913 ft. × 1.012	=	14,080 ft.
Correction for latitude 63°	=	−25 ft.
" " altitude	=	+54 ft.
" " altitude base station	=	+6 ft.
Altitude above base station	=	14,115 ft.
" of " "	=	2,500 ft.
" above sea-level	=	16,615 ft.

NOTE ON THE METHOD OF DETERMINING ALTITUDES

When difficult conditions of transportation have to be considered and long and arduous work of exploration must be done before even the base of a mountain is reached, such conditions as we encountered on our various expeditions to Mount McKinley, the subject of reducing the scientific outfit to its simplest terms is of the greatest importance. The method of determining the mountain altitudes that are attained must, of course, be a barometric one, that is it must depend on the measurement of atmospheric pressures and also temperatures.

For the measurement of pressures, we have the choice of several methods; 1st, the standard mercurial barometer; 2d. some modified form of the mercurial barometer; 3d, the aneroid barometer; 4th, the hypsometer or boiling-point apparatus 5th, a combination of the aneroid barometer and hypsometer.

The standard mercurial barometer is quite out of the question for any really difficult work in mountaineering. Its considerable length makes it inconvenient to transport, especially as it must be carried in a vertical position, and any severe shock may crack the glass due to the weight of the mercury, or the vacuum may deteriorate from other causes and render the readings worthless.

Several modifications of the standard barometer may be employed which are much more portable in form, but all appear to be more or less unreliable in practice. Where only considerable elevations are to be measured, for instance those over 15,000 feet, a mercurial barometer of only 15 inches in length can be used, although it requires almost equal care in transportation. We carried a mercurial barometer of about 20 inches in length for a portion of the distance on the 1910 expedition, but some of the mercury leaked from the cistern, probably owing to a severe shock in transit, and it is doubtful if the readings could have been relied upon afterward. A so-called pocket barometer in which rubber tubing is employed has also been used for approximate readings, but here again is the doubt of having a perfect vacuum and the difficulty in adjusting the apparatus to a truly vertical position.

A short form of barometer known as the Mariotte makes use of the method of compressing a given amount of air to a constant volume and measuring the corresponding pressure by means of a mercury column. The writer has made many experiments with this instrument in the laboratory but even under the best conditions found it difficult to obtain concordant sets of readings. Probably a considerable error is introduced by the heating of the air due to too rapid compression.

The aneroid barometer is most convenient for rapid approximate work but the readings can never be relied upon unless checked by some other method. The error under certain conditions, such as keeping the instrument for some time at a considerable altitude, may be very great indeed, amounting even to 500 feet or 1000 feet, or sometimes more at elevations above 10,000 feet. This error is usually progressive and renders the apparent altitude too great. A barometer known as the Watkin Mountain Aneroid is an improved form in which the delicate spring mechanism controlling the reading is thrown out of gear from the vacuum box when not in use. Of course this eliminates the error due to the viscosity of the spring and the readings are much more dependable. A considerable error in some instruments seems to be due, however, to an imperfect compensation for temperature, and in others both the altitude and pressure scales appear to be inaccurately calibrated.

The hypsometer or boiling-point apparatus in the hands of an expert or when used with proper care is absolutely reliable and satisfactory in every way. The instrument is very portable and almost unbreakable, except the thermometers, of which several extra ones should always be taken, carefully protected in brass cases. The temperature readings may be made with a possible accuracy that corresponds to a difference in altitude of from 10 feet to 20 feet. This is about the same accuracy as that obtained with a mercurial barometer making the readings to .01 inch. Of course, it requires some time to set up the apparatus and it must be protected from strong winds so that it is often better to make the readings inside a mountain tent. This is not always convenient or possible on the summit of a mountain so that a modification of the method has often to be adopted in practice.

The above difficulty is overcome in the following manner: the hypsometer is carefully read in the highest mountain camp or some sheltered spot near the summit; the aneroid barometer is also read at the same time and the correction noted; the difference in altitude between this point and the summit of the mountain is then taken by means of the aneroid and the proper correction made for the error of the barometer.

It is well-known that while the aneroid barometer is subject to large errors or great differences in altitude and when a long time has elapsed between the readings, it may be relied upon for considerable accuracy when the readings are taken for only small differences in altitude and the time between the readings is comparatively brief.

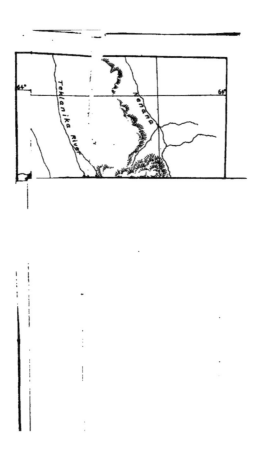

INDEX

THE 1906 EXPEDITION

THE 1910 EXPEDITION

THE 1912 EXPEDITION

A

Milton Keynes UK
Ingram Content Group UK Ltd.
UKHW021423040324
438892UK00006B/104